American experimental music, 1890–1940

American experimental music, 1890–1940

DAVID NICHOLLS

Department of Music
University of Keele

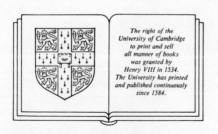

The right of the
University of Cambridge
to print and sell
all manner of books
was granted by
Henry VIII in 1534.
The University has printed
and published continuously
since 1584.

Cambridge University Press
Cambridge
New York   Port Chester   Melbourne   Sydney

Published by the Press Syndicate of the University of Cambridge
The Pitt Building, Trumpington Street, Cambridge CB2 1RP
40 West 20th Street, New York, NY 10011-4211, USA
10 Stamford Road, Oakleigh, Melbourne 3166, Australia

© Cambridge University Press 1990

First published 1990
First paperback edition 1991

Printed in Great Britain at the University Press, Cambridge

British Library cataloguing in publication data

Nicholls, David
American experimental music, 1890–1940
1. American experimental music, 1890–1940
I. Title
780′.973

Library of Congress cataloguing in publication data

Nicholls, David.
American experimental music, 1890–1940 / David Nicholls.
    p.   cm.
Bibliography.
Includes index.
ISBN 0–521–34578–2
1. Music – United States – 20th century – History and criticism.
2. Music – United States – 19th century – History and criticism.
3. Composition (Music) I. Title.
ML200.5.N55 1989
781.773 – dc19   89–563 CIP

ISBN 0 521 34578 2 hardback
ISBN 0 521 42464 X paperback

To Tamar

Contents

Preface

This book is a much-compressed revision of a Ph.D. thesis submitted to the University of Cambridge in 1985; that thesis, in turn, was a much-compressed, written out, version of the very many analyses of American experimental pieces which I had been working on since 1979. The intention now, as then, is primarily to explore through analysis the music and ideas of a number of twentieth-century American composers and, particularly, to try to explain the new compositional techniques invented and employed by them.

The main losses in this version of the material are in number of works considered and number of musical examples given. Ideally, the reader should proceed through the book with the relevant scores and records to hand, as words are a poor substitute for the aural and visual impact of the actual music. But a minimum of relevant examples has been retained here, and so it should still be entirely possible to read the book without reference to other materials.

The main gain in this version has been the opportunity to concentrate on a smaller number of works and, conversely, to broaden the content to include some biographical detail, plus a more general discussion (in chapters 1 and 6) of the small-scale and large-scale cultural contexts within which the principal figures discussed here existed. However, it is quite plausible that any of the main analytical chapters (2 through 5) might be read in isolation.

A basic knowledge of the American experimental tradition has been assumed on the part of the reader, though such a knowledge is not in any way a prerequisite to the understanding of the book. Further biographical (and other) detail should in the first instance be sought from either the *New Grove Dictionary of Music and Musicians* (here called *The New Grove*) or its American counterpart, the *New Grove Dictionary of American Music* (here called *Amerigrove*); subsequently, readers should refer to those sources identified in the notes and in the bibliography. Details of scores and records of the music under discussion are given in the appendix, where these are available.

A number of conventions have been employed in the text and musical examples:

1 All references to literary sources are identified by author and title, plus page number where appropriate. Sources can then be identified in full from the bibliography.
2 Codes (such as (W11), (505), etc.) following the titles of works by Ives and Cowell refer to extant work-catalogues:
      Cowell – William Lichtenwanger's *The Music of Henry Cowell*;
      Ives   – John Kirkpatrick's catalogue in *The New Grove* (vol. 9, pp. 421–429) and *Amerigrove* (vol. 2, pp. 509–519).

3 Where specific pitches are referred to, the following system applies: c′ = middle C; each octave begins on C and rises to B. Thus C͟→B͟; C→B; c→b; c′→b′; c″→b″; etc.

4 Where tonalities are referred to, major keys take upper-case type (e.g. C major) and minor keys take lower-case type (e.g. a minor).

5 Intervals are often described in the text, figures and examples according to the following formula:

m2 = semitone; M2 = tone; m3 = minor third; M3 = major third; 4 = fourth; Π = tritone; 5 = fifth; m6 = minor sixth; M6 = major sixth; m7 = minor seventh; M7 = major seventh; 8 = octave; m9 = minor ninth; M9 = major ninth.

An arrow (↑ or ↓) following an interval shows whether it rises or falls (e.g. g′–a′–ab′, intervallically, is M2↑–m2↓).

Furthermore, in a few instances, groups of intervals are classed as follows:

C = major consonance (unison, 8, 5, 4)
c = minor consonance (m3, M3, m6, M6)
d = minor dissonance (M2, m7, M9)
D = major dissonance (m2, Π, M7, m9).

6 In some musical examples, an asterisk following the identifying rubric indicates that accidentals apply only to those pitches they immediately precede.

The initial funding for the research on which this book is based, both in the United Kingdom and in America, was provided by the Department of Education and Science (Major State Studentship) and St John's College, Cambridge (Pendlebury Scholarship). It has subsequently been supported by the Faculty of Music of the University of Cambridge (William Barclay Squire Fund) and Selwyn College, Cambridge (Keasbey Research Fellowship in American Studies). To these various benefactors I am extremely grateful.

A number of individuals, libraries, and other bodies have helped in various ways at various times. Thanks are particularly due to: Richard Andrewes, William Brooks, John Cage, Nicola Constable, Michael Copley, Peter Dickinson, Alexander Goehr, Robin Holloway, Andrew Jones, John Kirkpatrick, Oliver Knussen, William Lichtenwanger, William Parsons, Vivian Perlis, Jay Rozen, Michael Seeger and Peggy Seeger; to the Pendlebury Library and University Library, Cambridge, Keele University Library, the BBC Music Library, the Performing Arts Research Center of New York Public Library, Los Angeles Public Library, the Library of Congress, Washington, DC and the Library of the School of Music, Yale University; and to Peters Edition Ltd (London) and Henmar Press Inc. (New York), Universal Edition (London), Boosey and Hawkes Ltd and G. Schirmer Ltd.

My Ph.D. dissertation was supervised by Hugh Wood, and the production of this book by Penny Souster and – as copy-editor – Ginny Catmur; to all three I am indebted.

Finally, none of this work would have been possible without the support, encouragement and love of my wife, Tamar; it is to her that this book is dedicated.

Acknowledgements

Acknowledgement is made for permission to quote from the following copyright sources:

Associated Music Publishers	Cowell	*Antinomy, Ensemble, Rhythmicana, String Quartet No. 1, The Tides of Manaunaun*
	Ives	*Psalm 67*
The Estate of Charles Seeger	Seeger	'On Dissonant Counterpoint'
The Estate of Ruth Crawford Seeger	Crawford	*Three Chants*
Edwin F. Kalmus	Ives	*Set for Theatre or Chamber Orchestra*
Marion Boyars Publishers Ltd	Cage	*For the Birds*
Marion Boyars Publishers Ltd/W.W. Norton & Company, Inc.	Ives	*Memos* (ed. Kirkpatrick)
Mobart Music Publications, Inc.	Ives	*Central Park in the Dark*
Peer International Corporation	Ives	*From the Steeples and the Mountains, In Re Con Moto Et Al, Largo Risoluto No. 1, Largo Risoluto No. 2, Scherzo: Holding Your Own, Scherzo: Over the Pavements, Tone Roads No. 1, Tone Roads No. 3, Trio, The Unanswered Question*
Peters Edition Ltd	Cage	*Bacchanale, Composition for Three Voices, First Construction (in Metal), Five Songs, Metamorphosis, Music for Wind Instruments, Quartet, Second Construction, Solo. . .and Six Inventions, Sonata for Clarinet, Sonata for Two Voices, Trio, Two Pieces for Piano*
	Cage/ Harrison	*Double Music*
	Cowell	*A Composition, Quartet Euphometric, Quartet Romantic, United Quartet*

Tetra/Continuo Music Group, Inc.	Crawford	*Diaphonic Suite No. 1, Diaphonic Suite No. 2, Diaphonic Suite No. 3*
Theodore Presser Company	Crawford	*String Quartet, Three Songs*
	Ives	*Fugue in Four Keys, Overture, 1776, Psalm 24, Psalm 25, Psalm 54, Psalm 90, Psalm 100, Psalm 135, Psalm 150, Three Harvest Home Chorales, Three-Page Sonata*
	Ruggles	*Angels, Evocations, Portals, Sun-treader*
	Seeger	*Psalm 137, The Letter*

1 Introduction: The new and the experimental

> Many American composers, I believe, have been interested in working things out for themselves to a great extent. . .
> Charles Ives, *Memos*

Until the last decade of the nineteenth century, music written by American composers was almost invariably modelled on the theory and practice of European convention. Indeed, concert programmes consisting of either European or European-influenced music dominated American musical life well into the twentieth century, and many American composers continued to consider themselves not fully trained until they had studied in Europe. Thus the norm before about 1914 was to study at a German conservatory, and in the 1920s and 1930s to be taught by Boulanger in France.

Around the turn of the century, however, a national musical consciousness began to emerge in America. Subsequently, as composers increasingly turned away from Europe, this took many forms. Of these, by far the most consistent and stimulating has been that of experimentalism: consequently, Europeans nowadays often look to America as a major source of new musical ideas.[1]

The list of composers who brought about this change is large: Charles Ives, Carl Ruggles, Edgard Varèse, Charles Seeger, Dane Rudhyar, Henry Cowell, George Antheil, Ruth Crawford, Harry Partch, John Cage, Conlon Nancarrow, Henry Brant and Lou Harrison to name only thirteen out of many working in the period up to the Second World War. This book will concentrate on six of these, whose music and ideas embody the main thrust of American experimentalism during its first half century: Ives, Seeger, Ruggles, Crawford, Cowell and Cage.

There are several historical factors which set this group apart. Five of the six composers (Ives being the exception) were associated through more or less formal teaching. As Chairman of the Department of Music at the University of California, Berkeley, between 1912 and 1919, Charles Seeger was Cowell's first and only mentor in composition. By February 1920, Cowell had met Ruggles and, perhaps a little later, introduced him to Seeger; certainly, Ruggles spent the summer of 1921 at the Seegers' place in Patterson, New York, and by October 1929 Seeger was 'a father to him'.[2] During 1929–30, while lecturing in New York, Seeger (at Cowell's instigation) also taught Ruth Crawford; and it was Cowell himself who, principally in New York in 1934–35, introduced the young John Cage to many new ideas and compositional techniques. (There is a further connection here, in that Cage's first composition teacher – Richard Buhlig – had in earlier years been a friend and piano teacher of Cowell.)[3]

Cowell, Crawford and Seeger are also linked through their involvement, in the early 1930s, in the New York-based left-wing Composers' Collective. Cowell, in 1931, had been one of the Collective's founders; Seeger and Crawford joined soon afterwards. Partly as a result of their involvement in the Collective, both Seeger and Crawford became increasingly affected by the apparent contradiction between their political beliefs and their artistic position. (This can be sensed in Crawford's setting of H.T. Tsiang's overtly political texts in her *Two Ricercari* of 1932–33.) For this reason – as well as because of the births between 1933 and 1944 of four children (she and Seeger had married in October 1932) – Crawford after 1933 turned away from composition, and towards the transcription, arrangement and publishing of folk songs, also using these materials in children's education.[4] Cowell, too, followed the general populist trend of this period in his use of ethnic materials in his music from the mid-1930s onwards.

Ives' compositional training and extra-musical career (see chapter 2) were quite different. Furthermore, his life as an active composer was finished before those of Crawford and Cage had even begun. But because musicians and audiences were unready for his music during the years of its composition, the initial period of his public recognition (during the 1920s and 1930s) coincides with that of Ruggles, Cowell, Crawford and Cage. Additionally, it was Ives' experimentalism (in terms of both newness of technique and inclusivity of vision) rather than his more conventional works which first attracted the attention of Cowell, Nicolas Slonimsky and others – in effect, he was discovered in reverse.[5]

The fortune Ives had made in insurance supported both his own publications (in the early 1920s, of the *Concord Sonata* and its associated *Essays*, and of the *114 Songs*) and a variety of Cowell's activities.[6] Prominent among these were the quarterly magazine *New Music* (founded in 1927) and its related orchestra series and recordings – all of which featured the work of Ives, Ruggles, Crawford and Cowell during the 1930s – and the Pan-American Association of Composers (PAAC). This, though supposedly the brainchild of Varèse, was actually managed for most of its short life (1928–34) by Cowell. Its concerts featured a number of works by Ives, Ruggles, Crawford and Cowell himself; that given in Paris on 6 June 1931 was typical in its inclusion of Cowell's *Synchrony*, Ives' *Three Places in New England* and Ruggles' *Men and Mountains*.

The PAAC, *New Music* and Cowell's 1933 book *American Composers on American Music* all sought to promote the cause of America's more avant-garde composers. For they, unlike the acceptable Europeanised modernists (for instance Aaron Copland, Walter Piston, Roger Sessions, Virgil Thomson and perhaps Roy Harris) lacked the patronage of major soloists, conductors, orchestras and publishers. This, in part, was a consequence of the fundamental split which had occurred in 1923 in the International Composers' Guild, between Varèse's supporters – among whom were included Ruggles and to a lesser extent Cowell – and those who left to form the League of Composers. Thus the radicals' grouping together was essentially a conscious act, rather than being merely a convenience of retrospection. The main body of PAAC/*New Music* activists included at various times Varèse, Ruggles, Wallingford Riegger, Adolph Weiss,

John J. Becker, Nicolas Slonimsky and – behind the scenes – the wealthy patroness Blanche Walton. But the main driving force was Cowell, and the indispensable chief stoker Ives.

This grouping was in fact recognised at the time both by the composers themselves and by others. As early as 1928, Pitts Sanborn of the *New York Telegram* named Ruggles, Varèse and Cowell as the radicals of the moment, while in 1931 the critic of the *Boston Post* referred to Ives, Ruggles and Cowell as 'the lunatic fringe of modern music'.[7] Finally, Cowell described himself as an 'indigenous American' composer in his quasi-introductory chapter to *American Composers on American Music*; and among those he similarly tagged were Ives, Ruggles, Seeger and Crawford.[8]

Thus there is some justification for discussing here certain composers at the expense of others. The vast and highly eclectic outputs of Ives and Cowell contain much music of an overtly new and experimental nature; and their compositional techniques were far ahead of their time. Charles Seeger's teaching was responsible for the compositional maturing of both Cowell and Crawford, while the developing body of thought which lay behind his theoretical essay 'On Dissonant Counterpoint' (1930) provided the intellectual base for many of the more advanced compositional experiments of his two most successful students. Indeed, Ruth Crawford's music is in many ways the practical complement to Seeger's treatise. Ruggles, too, was much taken with Seeger's ideas, as is shown primarily in the pitch content of his pieces from the 1920s onwards. But in other respects, Ruggles' music owes as much to late Romanticism as to modernism, and lies essentially to one side of the main thrust of American experimentalism. For this reason it will not be included in the discussion in chapter 6.

Varèse's compositional technique has already been subjected to particularly rigorous analysis which needs no duplication here.[9] Furthermore, it can be argued that while he played a very active part in America's avant-garde musical life during most of the 1920s and 1930s, Varèse – like a number of other immigrants – never really became an American composer. (Nor, for that matter, did his works – as opposed to his ideas and example – exert much influence on his new compatriots.) For the very individual (and fundamentally French) musical languages of both Varèse and Dane Rudhyar are basically unrelated to the development of 'a style distinctly rooted in the feelings and traditions'[10] of the United States.

Of younger composers, Lou Harrison is mentioned briefly in chapters 3 and 5. The music of George Antheil is at best sub-Stravinskyan, while the most important work of Harry Partch, Henry Brant and Conlon Nancarrow has been produced since the Second World War. But John Cage's music from this period is available and relatively mature: it continues many of Cowell's experiments, and contains the seeds of important subsequent developments. Indeed, Cage's post-war position as an international guru of experimental activity is very much based on his pre-war experiences.

Perhaps the final words of introduction should come from Henry Cowell, who in his 1933 symposium *American Composers on American Music* subtly distinguished between the various types of composer then working in America:

All the foregoing categories include men of great value, and valuable music can be written in any of the ways they represent. It is particularly not my desire to criticise adversely composers who follow European standards.[11]

Two years earlier, however, he had been less generous in his distinction:

The real division among the modern American composers now, a sharp one, is between those who regard music as something for the purpose of amusement, and those who regard it as a medium for expressing greater depths of feeling. The former group, that work closely together, is composed of men who have studied for the most part in Paris, and have become distinctly influenced by certain modern French philosophical trends. The latter group are for the most part made up of men who have studied in America, and who, although often cruder in technique than the others, are building up a style distinctly rooted in the feelings and traditions of the country.[12]

2 In Re Con Moto Et Al

Experimentalism in the works of Charles Ives (1874–1954)

> All the wrong notes are right. . .I want it that way.
> Charles Ives, Note on the manuscript of *The Fourth of July*

The life and works of Charles Ives are riddled by paradox.[1] Though often referred to as America's greatest composer, his working life was spent in the world of insurance. His musical training consisted of a thorough grounding in traditional harmony and counterpoint, learned from his father – George Ives (1845–94) – and, at Yale between 1894 and 1898, from Horatio Parker (1863–1919). But Ives also inherited his father's 'natural interest in sounds of every kind, everywhere, known or unknown, measured "as such" or not'.[2] And while he is renowned for his early invention of many advanced compositional techniques he was, as John Kirkpatrick has pointed out, 'primarily a melodist'[3] – as much a composer of sentimental ballads as of avant-garde instrumental works. Stylistic diversity is not in itself unusual – Beethoven, after all, had written canons, dance movements and folksong arrangements as well as symphonies, sonatas and string quartets. But the degree of inclusivity (and, indeed, *rapprochement* between seemingly exclusive styles) found in Ives' music, both from work to work and eventually within individual works, is quite unprecedented. This is illustrated, in the former case, by the seemingly alien settings of *Spring Song* (Z78) (14 Aug. 1907) and *Soliloquy* (Z79), written soon afterwards. The former is charming, tonal and pleasing to the ear (though it ends in the subdominant rather than the tonic); the latter features wild chromatic declamation and underlying, distinctly non-tonal, interval chords. Inclusivity *within* a work is illustrated by the ordered pandemonium of *Hawthorne* (X19,ii) (1911) and the second movement of the Fourth Symphony (V39,ii) (1911–16), in each of which a wide selection of contrasting materials is juxtaposed and superimposed.

Ives' eclecticism can best be explained through his growing perception, in his formative years, of what music could or should be.[4] George Ives' open-mindedness – which saw Bach and Stephen Foster as equals – was the background against which his son was exposed first to the 'useful' music-making of Danbury (whether sacred or secular) and later to the 'abstract idealism' of Parker. Once Ives had given up (public) music in 1902, following the failure of *The Celestial Country* (Y23) (1898–99), he was free to evolve from these various influences towards the eventual quasi-Transcendentalist view of art expressed in the *Essays before a Sonata*. In this, and in many other aspects of his creative development, Ives was unflinchingly supported by his wife, Harmony (1879–

1969). Indeed, it is no coincidence that Ives' greatest period of experimentalism, dating from 1905–06, follows on directly from the beginning of his romance with her (they were married in 1908).[5]

Ives' experimentalism is of two basic kinds:

1 the production of overtly experimental works in which, generally speaking, he tries out new compositional techniques;
2 the production of music in an unprecedentedly wide variety of supposedly exclusive musical styles and, more importantly, the integration of these styles into a pluralistic whole.

In the latter category, amongst other things, we find Ives continuing and developing many of the traditions of nineteenth-century American art and popular music. This is shown in various ways by songs like *The Circus Band* (Z20) (?1894), *Kären* (Z30) (?1895), *At the River* (Z101) (?1916) and *The Greatest Man* (Z140) (?Jun. 1921), and such instrumental works as the First and Second Symphonies (V8/V11) (1895–98/1900–02) and the First String Quartet (W1) (May 1896). More complex are the mature 'pluralistic' works – including the Second String Quartet (W19) (1907–13), Fourth Symphony (V39) (1909–16) and Second Piano Sonata (X19) (1910–15) – which, in their individual movements and as a whole, tend towards the collage-form which is a logical development of stylistic diversity. This, together with the sheer size of many of these pieces, demands (and deserves) much more detailed examination than can realistically be afforded here. However, a relatively brief study of a relatively simple collage work – 'In the Inn' (1906–11) from the *Set for Theatre or Chamber Orchestra* (V22) – will be included.

Apart from the availability of the music, though,[6] there is little limitation on the discussion of those purely experimental works of the former category, and consequently it is upon these that this chapter will concentrate. For in his experimental pieces Ives often tried out – in a pure, private way – techniques which could later be less inflexibly absorbed into other, more public, works. It is hoped that the examination of these techniques, together with the necessarily brief consideration of stylistic diversity and collage, will therefore go some way towards explaining the very complex inner workings of Ives' greatest music.

As was indicated previously, the earliest stimulus to Ives' experimental imagination came from his father who, although he did little composing, made many explorations into unknown musical territories including bitonality, quarter-tones, and spatial separation of instrumental groups.[7] Among the first of Ives' works to reflect this liberal musical education are the series of Psalm settings which probably date from the summer of 1894.

In the outer sections of *Psalm 150* (Y13) Ives approaches bi- or polytonality, as the basic tonal triads of the harmony are chromatically 'decorated' by the superimposition of other proximate tonal triads (see example 2.1). However, as with the majority of Ives' experiments, this probably grew from a desire to fix in his music something heard or experienced in real life. In this case a likely explanation is found in

Example 2.1. Ives: *Psalm 150* (Y13); bars 1–5
© 1966 & 72 Merion Music, Inc. Used by permission of the publisher.

the way, at an outdoor meeting. . .the fervor of the feeling would at times. . .throw the key higher, sometimes a whole tone up – though Father used to say it [was] more often about a quarter tone up.[8]

Thus, in *Psalm 150*, the 'excitement' of the singers causes the chromatic side-slipping to adjacent tonalities, as well as the compacting of tonic and dominant, the anticipation of new tonalities, and the occasional intrusion of other 'wrong' pitches, often as chromatic passing notes.

Psalm 150 also includes, as its middle section, an example of a fugue written 'the wrong way'[9] – in this case with each successive entry of the subject being a tone higher than that of the previous voice. This can be viewed as part of a larger scheme of conscious polytonal experimentation, probably devolving from the 'boy's fooling' of 'left-hand accompaniment in one key and tune in right hand in another'.[10] As Ives later wrote,

if the first statement of the theme is in a certain key, and the second statement is in a key a 5th higher, why can't (musically speaking) the third entrance sometimes go another 5th higher, and the fourth statement another 5th higher?[11]

Indeed, two such fugues exist – *Song for Harvest Season* (Z17) (1893) and *Fugue in Four Keys on 'The Shining Shore'* (V9) (1897). In the first of these, the four parts are written in C, F, Bb and Eb respectively (i.e. each successive entry is a *fourth* higher than its predecessor); in the second, successive entries are in C, G, D and A. The polytonal openings of both pieces are much concealed by the

pitches of their subjects. For instance, that of the *Fugue in Four Keys on 'The
Shining Shore'* outlines the dominant and tonic of each new key, interlocking
neatly with the harmonic implications of the existing line(s) (see example 2.2).

Example 2.2. Ives: *Fugue in Four Keys on 'The Shining Shore'* (V9); bars 1–16
© 1975 Merion Music, Inc. Used by permission of the publisher.

Up to bar 15, indeed, the harmony consists not so much of four superimposed
keys as of a single, extended decoration of C major, spiced with added seconds,
sharpened fourths, sixths and sevenths. With the arrival of the A major subject
the tonality becomes more confused, but the feeling is still one of strengthening
through added notes rather than weakening through tonal ambiguity.

However, there are some important differences between this work and the
Song for Harvest Season. For while the earlier piece is a short song with quasi-
fugal pretensions, 'The Shining Shore' is an extended essay in true fugal style.
Thus the exposition (bars 1–24) is overlapped and succeeded by a series of
real and false middle entries, often involving syncopation and partly in stretto
(bars 22–41), which in turn are followed by a canonic episode (bars 42–46).
Having effectively cadenced into A major, the music subsequently descends
polytonally to the dominant seventh of F. What is interesting about this thirteen-
bar passage (bars 47–59) is that Ives – seeking to control the tonal confusion he
has created – places the polytonal descent over a pedal C in the 'cellos and

basses. Indeed, this pedal-note – with the later addition of the G a fifth higher –
underpins all of the remaining music. Thus Ives makes one part *primus inter
pares*, at the same time giving the wide-ranging harmony a firm tonal root and
fixed point of reference. Many later – and distinctly less tonal – works are similarly founded on fixed pedal points.

The serene closing section (bars 60–77) approaches the 'four keys' of the title
in a slightly different way: over the pedal C–G already mentioned, two quite
separate layers are created. The more obvious of these consists of the melodies
played by the trumpet (in A) and the flute (in G). Below this, the upper strings –
moving in regular crotchets, but phrased as if in $\frac{4}{4}$ rather than the given $\frac{3}{4}$ – shift
polytonally from triad to triad. Initially, their orbit consists only of C, D and E,
but later widens to include f♯, B and c♯. Finally, they come to rest on A
(approached via the 'plagal' d) only to be succeeded by a solo quartet of violins
playing a second plagal cadence, this time in D. Thus in the final two bars Ives
re-presents harmonically rather than melodically the original 'four keys' of the
work's title.

In the works discussed above bi- or polytonal harmony is employed only
indirectly – as decoration, or as the result of polytonal polyphony. In other
pieces, however, Ives uses such harmony directly: isolated examples are found
in the interludes of *Variations on America* (X3) (?1891) and in the *Prelude on
Adeste fideles* (X12) (?Dec. 1897). But the earliest substantial usage appears in
Psalm 67 (Y14), which again probably dates from the summer of 1894. The basic
formal shape of this piece is a kind of arch with coda – <u>A</u>i–<u>A</u>ii–<u>B</u>–<u>C</u>–<u>B</u>–<u>A</u>iii–
<u>Coda</u>; but while these divisions reflect the structure of the text, the music
which fills each section is more idiomatically conceived. The <u>A</u> variants are all
based on a simple bitonal principle: the female voices sing a major triad, which
the male voices support with its dominant minor, in either root position or
second inversion.[12] There are only a few exceptions to this general rule: note in
example 2.3 the chromatic alteration in bar 2, the use of *first* inversion dominant
minor chords in bars 3 and 4, the added note in bar 6 (fourth quaver) and the

Example 2.3. Ives: *Psalm 67* (Y14); bars 1–7

reversal of rôles (men taking major triad, women its dominant minor) in bars 5–6. This last kind of 'reversed' writing also appears in the B sections, as does a hint of the freer, polyphonic writing which dominates section C.

The principal cadences of the piece are very carefully handled: the transition from Ai to Aii via the bitonal secondary dominant of g has already been seen in example 2.3. The transition from Aii to B (bars 11–12) is effected via a bitonal imperfect cadence, while the close of B (bar 15) features a compromise chord. Ives reverses rôles, the men having C major (second inversion) and the women g minor, but then treats the soprano d″ as a suspension which resolves onto c″. This forms a chord of C7 – the dominant seventh of the F major of section C. However, we should note that even here Ives treats tonality with great ambiguity: the initial rising F major arpeggio is immediately followed by a 'modal' downward descent. Thus the opening canon of C shifts between various tonal implications. It is worth noting in this context that even during the work's opening passage additional ambiguity was created by the appearance of the 'modal' E♭/b♭ complex in the otherwise C/g-dominated music (see example 2.3, bars 3–4).

Harmonic bitonality is restored during bar 21, the transition to the repeated B section again being effected via a bitonal imperfect cadence. B's compromise chord of C7 now leads directly to the C/g complex which opens Aiii (at bar 27), while the chanted Coda (bars 33–35) consists of a bitonal plagal cadence, approached from the bitonal secondary dominant of g.

The norm in Ives' music is that once a new technique has been successfully tried out in a piece – as bitonality was in *Psalm 67* – then it becomes simply another available colour in his ever-widening palette of compositional resources. Consequently, from this time onwards bitonality seldom dominates any work, but rather is used relatively sparingly at appropriate moments. There are many examples of bitonal passages in later Ives pieces, among which might be mentioned those in *December* (Y32/Z93) (1912–13/?1913), *An Election* (Y39/Z133) (Nov. 1920/1921), and *Premonitions* (V40,iii/Z132) (Jan. 1918/1921), as well as that which opens the song *Requiem* (Z86) (Nov. 1911).

During the summer of 1894, Ives also experimented with other new compositional devices. *Psalm 54* (Y15), like *Psalm 150*, is shaped as a kind of ternary structure, with a double canon making up most of its middle section (bars 14–43). Its outer sections are concerned primarily with the exploration of whole-tone melody and harmony. The music is arranged in two distinct layers: at the base we find the men singing plodding minim whole-tone (i.e. augmented) triads. These first move down six whole tones (c′ to c) before rising a semitone and moving up five whole tones (c♯ to b).

In the opening section this process is then repeated before the final quasi-cadential C major triad of bar 13. Over this the female voices provide a rhythmic counterpoint, moving basically in whole and divided minim triplets; their music is initially whole-tone (bars 1–2, varied as 7–8) but then becomes increasingly chromatic. All of the above points are illustrated by verse 2 (bars 7–13; example 2.4). The return to this music after the middle section is fairly literal,

Example 2.4. Ives: *Psalm 54* (Y15); bars 7–13
© 1973 Merion Music, Inc. Used by permission of the publisher.

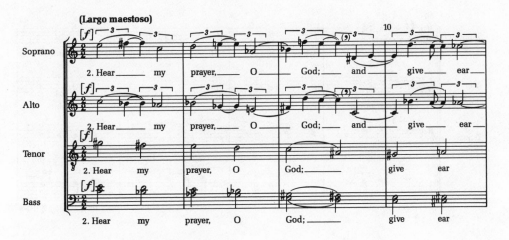

though with one fundamental change: the two layers of the opening section are
now inverted, so that the women have the plodding whole-tone triads and the
men the freer, chromatic triplets. Also, a new plagal cadence is added at the end
(see example 2.5).

The formation of independent musical layers seen here, and the freedom with
which Ives rearranges their relationships to each other, has important conse-
·quences in his later music.

Even more remarkable is *Psalm 24* (Y16); here, the musical form is related to
the verse-structure of the text, with each verse being assigned a specific interval
(or intervals) from which the majority of its melodic and harmonic content is
derived (figure 2.1). Furthermore, these basic intervals are arranged in an
expanding, then more freely contracting, sequence. Thus in verse 1 the soprano
and bass lines 'pan out' from c′, moving chromatically throughout (see example 2.6).

Example 2.5. Ives: *Psalm 54* (Y15); bars 50–57
© 1973 Merion Music, Inc. Used by permission of the publisher.

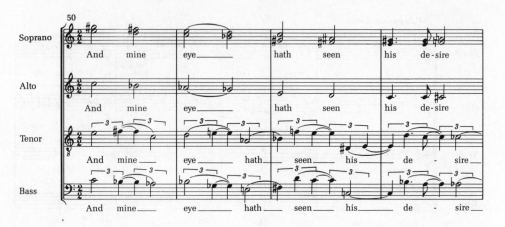

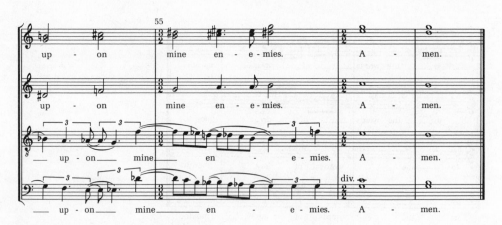

Figure 2.1. Structure of Ives' *Psalm 24* (Y16)

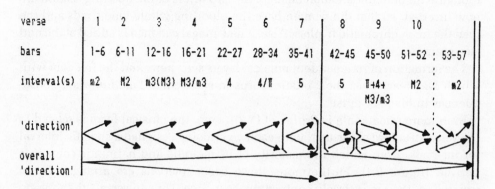

Example 2.6. Ives: *Psalm 24* (Y16); bars 1–6
© 1955 Merion Music, Inc. Used by permission of the publisher.

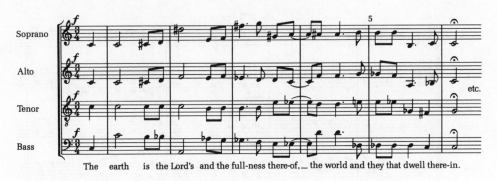

The earth is the Lord's and the full-ness there-of,— the world and they that dwell there-in.

Ives does not follow his plan slavishly: rather, he uses his pre-arranged source material freely and appropriately. The panning of the outer voices is disguised by octave displacements which highlight significant words ('Lord's', 'fullness'). Both the movement of the inner parts and the four-part harmony thus defined are handled with care and freedom; and the rhythmic content is at all times relevant to and derived from the text. These points are even more clearly illustrated in later verses. For instance, verse 2 includes the occasional use of pitches which lie outside its basic whole-tone scale (e.g. the alto g' of bar 10); and rather than completing the full 'cycle' back to c, Ives chooses to end with a descriptive chord at 'floods' (bar 11).

In verse 3 the initial basic interval is a minor third. But a number of the progressions are interrupted by other pitches, and at the end of the verse major thirds and diatonic harmony appear to characterise the 'holy place' of the text (bars 15–16). In verses 5 and 7 the potential monotony of quartal and quintal melody and harmony is avoided by the use of occasional chromatic sideslips, while the alternating tritones and fourths of verse 6 are completely thrown by the 'gospel' setting of 'O Jacob' in bars 33–34.

The freest writing is reserved for the quasi-retrogression of verses 8–10. Here we find not only a much quicker progression between intervals, but also some of the richest harmonic writing in the whole piece (see example 2.7). The outer parts here are much more freely directed than in verses 1–7; this tendency reaches its natural conclusion in the return (in the soprano) to outward chromatic panning in the final bars.

The kind of interval structuring employed in *Psalm 24* recurs in various guises in numerous later works, including the *Processional (Let there be Light)* (Y29) (1901), *Central Park in the Dark* (V23,ii) (Jul.–Dec. 1906), *Over the Pavements* (V20) (1906–13), *Soliloquy* (Z79) (1907), *Tone Roads No. 3* (V38,iii) (1915) and *On the Antipodes* (Z145) (1915–23).

In the remaining works of the period up to 1901, the main thrust of Ives' experimentation continues to be concentrated into the pitch content of vocal works. The music which opens the bi-choral *Psalm 100* (Y24) (1898–?99) is very

Example 2.7. Ives: *Psalm 24* (Y16); bars 45–52
© 1955 Merion Music, Inc. Used by permission of the publisher.

similar to that of *Psalm 150*, in its chromatic side-slipping to adjacent tonalities. In verse 2 (bars 5–8) the interval between basic and decorating triads expands to include the fourth (compacting of tonic and subdominant), fifth (compacting of tonic and dominant), tritone and minor sixth. This kind of texture also dominates the final section (bars 27–33, part of verse 5), though here the decorating triads are reinforced by bells.

The two middle sections develop this basic texture. Section B̲ (verse 3, bars 9–15) finds choir 1 and the bells performing a very quiet and simple triadic pattern focussed on c′ (see example 2.8). Choir 2's music – marked *forte* – consists of a chromatically descending harmonic sequence in which first inversion triads are alternated with their dominant sevenths (e.g. C–G7–B–F♯7–B♭–F7). The sequence is further strengthened by the omission of the third from each dominant seventh chord – the missing pitch becomes the key-note for each subsequent first inversion triad. Choir 2 completes a full cycle of all twelve major keys before coming to rest in C major.

This separation of the two musical layers by both pitch content and relative dynamic level is taken a stage further in section C̲. Here choir 2 has a loud

Example 2.8. Ives: *Psalm 100* (Y24); bars 9–11
© 1966 Merion Music, Inc. Used by permission of the publisher.

diatonic chordal sequence (bars 16–19, varied as 20–22) based in F major, followed by a repeated quasi-cadential pattern (bars 22–24; 24–26). Against this choir 1 ('Boys or Solo Quartet, or Violin, or Organ') performs quiet, off-beat, chords 'as an echo'. This kind of effect is related to the bitonal 'boy's fooling' mentioned earlier. But here, and in many later instances, Ives is working with ideas way beyond the scope of simple polytonality. The 'echo chords' can be viewed in two alternative (and not necessarily exclusive) ways. The first of these is of the echo chords being acoustically related to the loud triads, as if reinforcing remote upper partials of their harmonic spectra. (Some years later Henry Cowell's system of polyharmony was based on just such a principle – see chapter 4.) However, this explanation alone is somewhat unsatisfactory. What is more likely is that Ives was trying to recreate – albeit on a small scale – yet another experience from his early life:

The writer remembers hearing, as a boy, the music of a band in which the players were arranged in two or three groups around the town square. The main group in the bandstand at the center usually played the main themes, while the others, from the neighboring roofs and verandas, played the variations, refrains, etc. . . .The writer remembers, as a deep impression, the echo parts from the roofs played by a chorus of violins and voices.[13]

This memory – presumably of one of George Ives' experiments – prompted many passages in his son's music, of which the present portion of *Psalm 100* would seem to be the earliest. The spatial implications of this story – of musical foreground and background both real and imagined – are more fully worked out in such pieces as *The Unanswered Question* (V23,i), *Central Park in the Dark* (V23,ii), *Hawthorne* (X19,ii) and the Fourth Symphony (V39) (first, second and fourth movements). But even in *Psalm 100*, choir 1 sounds as if it is singing in the next room. . .or the next valley.

If much of *Psalm 100* can be seen as a development of ideas first encountered in *Psalm 150*, then those used in *Psalm 25* (Y26) (1899–1901?) are logically developed from the middle section of *Psalm 54*. The texture of this large-scale work is mainly canonic: the imitation is generally exact, and the lines (and consequently the harmony) very chromatic. On three occasions, however, there are free polyphonic intrusions into the structure. In the first of these (bars 94–98) the polyphony is mainly in five parts and harmonically conceived. The second (bars 126–129) contains mainly unison melodic writing, but in its final bar includes the first suggestion of another trait which becomes important in Ives' later music: that of 'massed voices'. Although the writing here never extends beyond six parts, in the final intrusion (bars 145–152) there is a progression from one part (the initial bass solo) to a massive seventeen-part final chord (example 2.9).

Example 2.9. Ives: *Psalm 25* (Y26); bars 145–151
© 1979 Merion Inc. Used by permission of the publisher.

† Manuals double choral harmony.

From these homorhythms it is a relatively small step to the polyrhythmic massed voices of *Lincoln* (Y31) of 1912. Hitchcock has suggested that in this kind of writing

Ives may have had in mind a Lincolnian 'people's chorus', a mass of voices speaking out as one. . .[the] heterophonic clusters [having] the effect of collective, not individual, statement.[14]

Equally likely is Ives' remembrance of musical incidents from his childhood:

at the outdoor Camp Meeting services in Redding, all the farmers, their families and field hands, for miles around, would come afoot or in their farm wagons. . .the great waves of sound used to come through the trees. . .sung by thousands of 'let out' souls. . . Father. . .would always encourage the people to sing their own way. Most of them knew the words and music (theirs) by heart, and sang it that way. If they threw the poet or the composer around a bit, so much the better for the poetry and the music.[15]

Examples of massed voice effects, both homo- and polyrhythmic, are found in *Lincoln* at bars 35–38 and 43; and elsewhere, in *An Election* (Y39) (Nov. 1920), *Psalm 90* (Y40) (1894, rev. 1924) – which is discussed later – and in verse 7 (bars 47–52) of *Psalm 135 (Anthem Processional)* (Y27) (1900?).

This last work is framed by two large sections (bars 1–40; 73–102) in which a constant quasi-$\frac{4}{4}$ drum pattern underpins three related kinds of mainly $\frac{5}{8}$ music for voices, brass and organ. The middle portion of *Psalm 135*, though, falls into three unequal parts: the first and second of these (verses 6 and 7, bars 41–46 and 47–52) are linked through their sharing a regular minim bass drum pulse. But while verse 7 consists of the massed voice writing mentioned earlier, verse 6 is fairly consistently limited to four harmonically related parts. However, both verses share a common harmonic language, created through the addition to common triads of other pitches. In verse 6 this resembles the technique of dissonating triads developed later by Charles Seeger (see chapter 3), while in verse 7 a number of approaches are used:

1 as in verse 6, a triad has a dissonantly related pitch added to it, often in the bass;
2 as above, but with the bass pitch further dissonated by the addition of a pitch a tritone below;
3 simple bi- or polytonality.

The third portion of the middle section (verses 13–14) is written over a pedal D, and falls into two halves (bars 53–62 and 62–72). Although the polyphonic choral writing seems very chromatic, it is kept in check not only by the pedal-note on organ and timpani, but also by the use of a series of harmonic reference points. (Their use is conscious, and marked in the manuscript.) In bars 53–62 these are all minor triads, related through a descending, then ascending, whole-tone scale (example 2.10). Note here the articulation of this series of harmonies through the 'cadential' brass writing, every new key-note being approached melodically from its dominant.

Example 2.10. Ives: *Psalm 135* (Y27); bars 53–62
© 1981 Merion Music, Inc. Used by permission of the publisher.

In bars 62–72 the process is repeated, but this time the triads are all major, rather than minor, the only exceptions being the pivotal and concluding d minor triads, in bars 67 and 72 respectively. Thus in the space of twenty bars the music encompasses ('modulates through' is too strong a term) all 24 available keys. The chromaticism of this passage, like that of verse 3 of *Psalm 100*, points the way forward to the kind of writing that 'has a nice name nowadays – "atonality"'[16] as well as exhibiting to the full Ives' powers of technique and invention.

Equally confused, from a tonal point of view, is the second of the *Three Harvest Home Chorales* (Y28) – 'Lord of the Harvest' (?1901) – which is built from a series of accumulating strata (see figure 2.2). All of the strata are present in

Figure 2.2. Structure of Ives' 'Lord of the Harvest' (Y28,ii)

section	Intro	Verse 1	Interⁿ.1	Verse 2	Verse 3	Interⁿ.2	Verse 4 (concl.)
bars	1-12	13-24	25	26-38	39-50	51-53	54 - 60
layers	U	U T		Ui T B	U T B F		Ui T B F
	pedal C♯ ───→
tempo	Adagio maestoso	Andante risoluto		Moderato con moto	Allegro maestoso	meno mosso	più mosso molto risoluto
dynamic	p	mf	f	f	ff	f	ff

verse 3 (example 2.11). The most fundamental stratum is the low C♯ pedal-note
which sounds throughout the piece. Placed over this in the Introduction is a
twelve-bar cyclic series of triadic chords (U) which descend, then ascend,
by whole-tones and move in regular minims. Despite its similarity to other
whole-tone chord-series in early Ives works (for instance those in *Psalm 54* and
Psalm 135) a unique feature of this series is its creation of new harmonic relationships in the quasi-retrogression of its eighth to twelfth bars. For while
each bar appears in its correct retrograded position, the major–minor ordering

Example 2.11. Ives: *Three Harvest Home Chorales* (Y28),ii; bars 39–50 [*Note:* Some details, including tempo and dynamics, may vary in other versions.]
© 1949 Merion Music, Inc. Used by permission of the publisher.

Example 2.11. (cont.)

† Includes some rhythmic renotation.

within each bar remains unchanged. Thus the tonal progression of the second to fourth bars

B b | A a | G g

reappears in the tenth to twelfth bars as

G g | A a | B b

In the first verse of the chorale, a tenor line (T) moving in triplet minims is added; its pitches are often related to those of U, though its melodic line is not. The next addition is of a bass line (B) which moves in triplets against those of T (i.e. the three layers move in rhythmic ratios of U4:T6:B9). Once again the pitches are related to those of U, though the melodic line is not. But as in medieval writing, while the two added lines (T, B) both relate to the 'tenor' U, they do not relate to each other.

The final layer is that of the combined soprano and alto parts (F): these move homorhythmically, at first in decorated semibreves, then in minims and crotchets. Their pitches are initially a fifth apart but are later somewhat freer, though they at all times relate to those of U.

However, the overall shape of the chorale is not as simple as might have been suggested by the above description. In verses 2 and 4 the harmonic pattern U is altered: bars 54–60 consist of a variant of U, over which truncated versions of T, B and F are presented. In verse 2 the harmonies of bars 26–28 are very similar to those of bars 54–56, though the overlying T and B lines are essentially unchanged. Of the two interruptions, the first consists simply of a tenor chant on c♯' over the harmony of bars 26/54. The second opens with an octave chant on C♯s (bar 51) but this is followed by two bars of homorhythm (chords of c♯ and f♯). The accompanying music consists of three added-sixth chords over the pedal-note C♯. The total effect is of polytonality.

One final point worth noting here is that the dynamics and tempi of 'Lord of the Harvest' are integrated into its overall accumulating structure. The music progresses from one layer (U), played quietly and slowly, to four layers, played loudly and quickly; and while this progression is twice broken by the chanted interruptions, and further articulated by the variations of verses 2 and 4, the whole work is held together by the fundamental C♯ pedal-note of the accompaniment.

Much of the discussion so far has been concerned with Ives' experimentation in the realms of pitch. As was mentioned earlier, the norm in Ives' work seems to be that once a technique has been successfully tried out it becomes part of the large pool of available compositional resources, to be used freely and at will in appropriate but often unexpected contexts. Thus the harmonic and melodic content of Ives' more mature pieces takes full advantage of a wide range of resources, from tonal through to totally chromatic, and many works are touched to a greater or lesser extent by the results of the experiments so far discussed.

But although a number of later pieces show Ives experimenting further with pitch (and, indeed, these will be discussed in due course) his interests from about 1901 onwards move increasingly towards other parameters. Simple polyrhythms and polymetres, both real and implied, had already been used in a number of works, while 'Lord of the Harvest' featured both complex polyrhythms and the structuring of elements other than rhythm and pitch. The implications of this work are more fully explored in *From the Steeples and the Mountains* (W3) (1901–?02) for one or two trumpets, trombone, and four sets of bells.[17]

The form of this piece is basically simple (figure 2.3), but beneath its surface

Figure 2.3. Structure of Ives' *From the Steeples and the Mountains* (W3)

section	[Intro]	A [exposition of canons]	B [retrogression of canons]	C [coda / conclusion]		
				link	cadenza	cadence
bars	1 - 14	15 - 27	28 - 40	41-42	43-45	46-48
dynamics : bells	*pp* ‹	*mf* ‹ *(f)* ‹	*ff* ‹	*fff*		
brass	*ppp*	*p* ‹ *f* ‹				

lies a wealth of intricate detail. The four sets of bells are arranged polytonally, each set playing a simple major scale:

<pre>
set 1: c″ b′ a′ g′ f′ e′ d′ c′
set 2: db c Bb Ab Gb F Eb Db
set 3: b′ a#′ g#′ f#′ e′ d#′ c#′ b
set 4: c′ b a g f e d c
</pre>

During the introduction, each set presents its descending scale in minims, in the order 1–2–4–3; each new entry coincides with the final minim of the previous entry. When not articulating its scale, each set plays a tremolando on its lowest pitch, giving the chord Db–c–b–c′. Dynamically, each scale is presented *mp* (except the last, which is *mf*), but the tremolando background is *pp* throughout. Against this, the brass have isolated but increasingly insistent fanfare-like gestures featuring chains of rising fourths.

Starting at bar 15 the bells perform a rhythmic canon: the order of entries is as before (i.e. 1–2–4–3) and the distance between entries is minim–semibreve–semibreve. The material of the canon's exposition consists of eight statements by each set of bells of each of the following rhythmic values:

minim-dotted crotchet-crotchet-dotted quaver-quaver-dotted semiquaver-semiquaver

(no. of semiquavers)   8   6   4   3   2   1½   1

(i.e. the values are arranged as a contracting arithmetic sequence). The process of exposition of this rhythmic material lasts for 51 crotchets per set of bells, the pitch materials assigned to it consisting of the descending scale patterns heard in the introduction (i.e. each set of bells performs a descending scale of minims, then dotted crotchets, then crotchets, and so on).

After each set of bells completes its exposition, the process is reversed: the rhythmic values are now arranged in an expanding series (i.e. 1–1½–2–3–4–6–8 semiquavers), each set of bells again giving eight statements of each rhythm.

The pitch material, however, is new; rather than playing the expected rising scales, the bells change to a pattern well known to campanologists:

set 1: c″ a′ f′ d′ b′ g′ e′ c′
set 2: d♭ B♭ G♭ E♭ c A♭ F D♭
set 3: b′ g♯′ e′ c♯′ a♯′ f♯′ d♯′ b
set 4: c′ a f d b g e c

This provides variety, as well as demonstrating once again that for Ives the various parameters of a musical idea are quite separate: the rhythms here are retrograded exactly, but the pitches associated with them are not. The overall result of this mathematical (and yet capricious) canonic structuring is that the 'bell-backcloth' accelerates from rhythmic simplicity to extreme polyrhythmic complexity and motivic duality – see example 2.12 – before the decelerating return to simplicity. The sound is at all times polytonal.

Example 2.12. Ives: *From the Steeples and the Mountains* (W3); bars 27–29 (bells only)
© Copyright 1965 by Peer International Corporation. Used by permission.

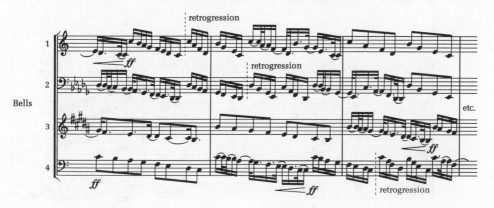

Against this backcloth the brass instruments have their own separate canon, which starts in bar 17. The trombone follows the trumpet at one bar's distance, and at the interval of a minor tenth below. The music is dissonant both vertically and horizontally, in rhythm as well as pitch.[18] The canon continues in the trombone until the end of bar 24 and is succeeded by two bars of freely invented material reminiscent of the fourths and fifths of the introduction. In bar 27 – a kind of upbeat to what follows – the trumpet plays a descending chromatic scale (disguised through octave displacement), counterpointed against a freer rising chromatic scale in the trombone.

In bars 28–37 the brass re-present bars 17–26 in reverse order (i.e. as in 'Lord of the Harvest' the order of bars is retrograded, but the material within each bar is not). Thus new horizontal relationships between existing ideas are created without any traditional form of reworking or development being employed. An additional refinement in the brass parts of sections A̲ and B̲ is that the ends of the canon are disguised by free materials linking them to the introduction and conclusion (i.e. in bars 14–16 and 38–40).

What is particularly interesting about the music of sections A and B is that the two musical layers – brass and bells – are essentially unrelated. The two canons are quite logical within themselves, but are written using different materials. Furthermore, while each canon is arranged as a palindrome, that of the brass reflects bar by bar about bar 27; the bells, however, have individual points of rhythmic reflection from bar 27 onwards, their pitches being newly invented. Thus the music of section B is in no sense a simple retrogradation of that of section A. Rather, Ives' adoption of separate (and asymmetrically related) organising principles for each of the two musical layers causes new textures to be created both microcosmically and macrocosmically through the simple vertical realignment of existing materials: the music of bars 18 and 25 is quite different from that of bars 36 and 29 (example 2.13).

Example 2.13. Ives: *From the Steeples and the Mountains* (W3); bars 18 and 36/25 and 29
© Copyright 1965 by Peer International Corporation. Used by permission.

The final bars of the piece are an early example of Ivesian pandemonium. In bars 40–42 the bells complete their canon, though with the *caveat* that from the third crotchet of bar 40 onwards each pitch is played tremolando. Each set then seems to take up a new canonic idea, now at a minim's distance, consisting of jangling two-note chords (derived from superimposed descending and ascending scales) played in triplet minims. Over this the brass have a freely invented bar (40), a repeat of the pivotal bar 27 (41) and a development of its basic ideas (42).

Bars 43–45 (example 2.14) are a quasi-cadenza: the bells abruptly halt their
canon, each instead jangling their lowest and highest but one pitches (i.e. each
plays the interval of a major seventh, though the score also provides for an alternative 'fast slide up and down of scales'). The brass continue their frenzied
playing, which climaxes in improvised converging glissandi at the end of
bar 45.

Example 2.14. Ives: *From the Steeples and the Mountains* (W3); bars 43–45
© Copyright 1965 by Peer International Corporation. Used by permission.

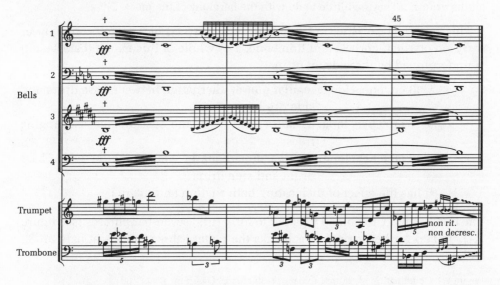

† A roll of these two notes or a fast slide up and down of scales.

Finally, bars 46–48 are a polytonal cadence: the brass hold octave Cs (a high
d‴ being added 'if [there are] two trumpets'), while bell-sets 2–4 have plagal
cadences in their respective keys. Set 1 has a decelerating final statement of Ḇ's
pitch pattern which incidentally outlines its cadential chords of F, G and C.

Paradoxically, although *From the Steeples and the Mountains* could easily
have been inspired by something heard in reality (the bell-ringing of different
churches colliding during a band practice) its theoretical complexity and
degree of (polytonal and polyrhythmic) dissonance are unusual even by Ives'
own standards.

More typical of this period – because of its quotation of extant melodies[19] – is
the *Overture, 1776* (V13) (1903). This work is fundamentally tonal, though its
adherence to any particular tonality at any given moment may be tenuous. The
Overture starts relatively normally: march rhythms for the strings lead to an
oboe recitative which is supported mainly by bitonal augmented chords. Bars
10–13 include some hints of metric instability (oboe and clarinet phrases) as
well as an early example of 'piano-drumming' (example 2.15). Ives describes the
invention of this technique in *Memos*:

Example 2.15. Ives: *Overture, 1776* (V13); bar 10 (piano only)

When I was a boy, I played in my father's brass band, usually one of the drums. . .In prac-
tising the drum parts on the piano. . .[I] got to trying out sets of notes to go with or take-
off the drums. . .They had little to do with the harmony of the piece. . .[20]

This introduction is abruptly halted by the arrival of a march, one quaver
early, on clarinet, cornets and trombone. The whole of this march (bars 14–39)
is underpinned by three drum ostinati:

> i 10 crotchets long: regular quaver alternation between bass drum and
> side drum;
>
> ia 6 crotchets long: as above, but with the instruments exchanging
> rôles;
>
> ii 12 crotchets long: regular dotted-quaver alternation between bass
> drum and side drum.
>
> (ii has the effect of dislocating both rhythm and metre.)

The three ostinati are joined together to form (in $\frac{4}{4}$) seven-bar phrases (see figure
2.4). To add further variety, Ives breaks the pattern three times – at bars 21, 32
and 39.

Figure 2.4. Combination of ostinati in bars 14–39 of Ives' *Overture, 1776* (V13)

bar	14–16;16–17	18–20	21–23;23–24	25–27	28–30;30–31	32–34	35–37;37–38	39
ostinato	i : ia	ii	i : ia	ii	i : ia	ii	i : ia	only one quaver long
comments	S.D. : B.D. on : on beat : beat	B.D. starts	B.D. : S.D. on : on beat : beat	B.D. starts	B.D. : S.D. on : on beat : beat	B.D. starts + Cymbal→	B.D. : S.D. on : on beat : beat	

[i.e. variation on first phrase]   [coincides with 'climax' to 'Hail, Columbia']

The music over these ostinati falls into three parts. Bars 14–19 are a kind of
introduction: the double bass continues its opening music while the initial
brass fanfare (bars 14–15) is succeeded by a typically dislocated rendering of
'The British Grenadiers'. The strings and piano initially help the flute but then
attempt to trip it up with their anticipation in bar 18 (see example 2.16). A brief
examination of this flute melody will illustrate many of Ives' methods of treating
borrowed material. Particularly important are the metric instability of the quotation itself, and its polymetric relationship to the given metre; the omission of

Example 2.16. Ives: *Overture, 1776* (V13); bars 16–22 (flute, piano, upper strings, then flute, only)
© 1975 Merion Music, Inc. Used by permission of the publisher.

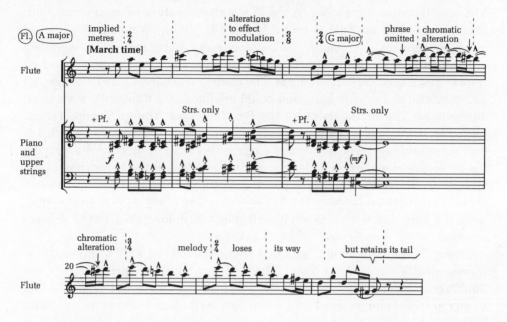

fragments of the quotation; the final peroration to 'fade out'; and the deliberate use of tonal ambiguity (small chromatic alterations and larger transpositions).

The borrowed and invented melodies of the second part of the march (bars 20–31) fare little better, though the opening phrase of 'Hail, Columbia' is allowed to remain in the given $\frac{4}{4}$ metre (bars 28–31). However, this sub-section is underpinned by an additional rising ostinato pattern played by the 'cellos, whose entries are reinforced by *sforzandi* on the double bass, piano and trombone. The ostinato is initially seven quavers in length, implying a metre of $\frac{7}{8}$; but its ninth to fifteenth appearances are first contracted to five quavers ($\frac{5}{8}$) then further reinforced on the third quaver ($^{2+3}_{8}$). The sixteenth and final appearance (at the end of bar 31) is contracted to three quavers ($\frac{3}{8}$). Consequently, what little stability might have been given to the music by the regularity of 'Hail, Columbia' is entirely lost.

Rather than releasing the tension built up during this passage, Ives increases it further during the remainder of the march. Bars 32–33 are a polyrhythmic climax to 'Hail, Columbia', the tune itself being played by the cornets and underpinned by pedal Ds on viola and piano. Against this the winds have descending, then ascending, chromatic scales with 'rag' rhythms and secundal dissonances; the violins have ascending, then descending, whole-tone chords with 'on-beat' rhythms; and the remaining instruments alternate dotted-quaver triads of D and A♭. As a final decoration, the cymbal is added to the drum ostinati (see figure 2.4). Following this, five bars of minor pandemonium finally cadence onto G major (bar 39), before immediately slipping down to the dominants of B major (bar 40) and B♭ major (bar 41).

The basic material of the trio (bars 40–56) is a 'performance' of 'Columbia, the Gem of the Ocean' in which the two cornet players get their crooks mixed up. The tune therefore appears in B♭ and A simultaneously, and commences with the upbeat to bar 42. This is probably a further fixing in music of an actual event, as is the regular dropping of a quaver every fourth bar 'which was often done in parades'.[21] This ensures that the tune becomes increasingly detached from its given metrical surroundings. The melody is accompanied by a bass part (on trombone and double bass) and counterpointed by a differently mismetred amalgam of 'The Battle Hymn of the Republic' and 'Tramp, Tramp, Tramp', played by the flute with help from bells, clarinet and occasional oboe. What is both remarkable and typical in this passage is Ives' skill in successfully weaving the unrelated quotations of melody and countermelody into a believable whole. Many other examples of multiple quotation occur in his work, of which those in *He is There!* (Z104a) (30 May 1917), *Old Home Day* (Z97) (?1913) and particularly the barn-dance section of *Washington's Birthday* (V26) (1909) deserve mention.

Underpinning the melody, bass and countermelody of 1776's trio are three independently organised ostinati. The first, for all of the strings except the double bass, also commences in bar 42. Two bars long, it features a melodic line in quaver triplets (on violin 1 and viola) answered canonically by violin 2 and 'cello. While each of the voices is consonant (being based on the alternation of falling fifths and rising fourths, and therefore having a whole-tone feel) their combination is dissonant (alternating harmonic minor ninths and minor seconds).

The second ostinato, for the drums, commences one bar before the cornet and flute melody/countermelody and string ostinato, in bar 41. It consists of a 4 + 2 bar, standard $\frac{12}{8}$ drumming pattern, repeated two and a half times. The third ostinato, for piano, is a similar drumming pattern, 2 + 4 bars long, but commencing one bar after the main melody and countermelody, in bar 43. Thus appearances of its larger second component coincide with those of the smaller second component of the drum ostinato, at bars 45 and 51.

If the trio is viewed as a whole, we find Ives using both polymetre (in the regular $\frac{4}{4}$ of the ostinati against the irregular 'dropped quaver' melody and countermelody) and polyphrase (in the varying lengths of the ostinati and their differing points of commencement). There is also, almost incidentally, the polytonality and polytexture of the melody, countermelody, bass, 'wrong' tune, and ostinati. The entire section resembles an intricate mechanism with independent – yet interdependent – components, which Ives can switch off (with the conclusion of the main melody) as abruptly as he switched it on.

The final part of the *Overture* commences with a reminder of the opening music. Indeed, the strings (now with bass drum) continue to play a variant of their opening idea right up until bar 70, while the oboe melody and clarinet answering phrases of bars 9–12 now occupy bars 59–63. However, from bar 63 onwards the situation becomes more complicated: over the strings' two-bar 'march' ostinato is laid the same rhythm, but as if in a faster tempo, an effect used also in *Putnam's Camp* (V30,ii) (1912). Ives achieves this by having the 'drumming' piano and side drum move in minim triplets (example 2.17). The

Example 2.17. Ives: *Overture, 1776* (V13); bars 63–64 (piano, strings, percussion only)
© 1975 Merion Music, Inc. Used by permission of the publisher.

tempo ratio of 3:2 thus created is made more complex through the 'faster' tempo commencing on the half-bar. This texture continues until bar 72, each march-tempo having borrowed melodies laid over it. Firstly, a bitonal variant of 'Hail, Columbia' in $\frac{4}{4}$ (bars 61–66, flutes) is counterpointed against 'The British Grenadiers' 'in' $\frac{4}{12}$ (bars 63–66, clarinet, etc.). 'Hail, Columbia' is in B♭ and D, 'The British Grenadiers' in A. Subsequently these keys remain while the melodies change to 'Columbia, the Gem of the Ocean' (bars 67–71, in $\frac{4}{4}$, but commencing on the half-bar) and 'Yankee Doodle' (bars 67–69, 'in' $\frac{4}{6}$, but very much off-beat). Again, Ives makes rhythmic alterations to 'Hail, Columbia' (bars 64–65), 'The British Grenadiers' (bar 64) and 'Columbia, the Gem of the Ocean' (bars 70–71); and he cleverly welds 'The British Grenadiers', 'Yankee Doodle' and the subsequent bugle calls(?) into a single melodic line, as 'John Bull gets weaker and finally gives'.[22]

From bar 71 the music disintegrates into total pandemonium: rising and falling scales of triads are thrown together with falling, then rising, chromatic scales (piccolos, in fourths), bugle calls (cornets) and uneven drum patterns. Finally, in bars 75 and 76, a polytonal reference to 'The Star-Spangled Banner' – played as if in $\frac{3}{4}$, and across the bar – leads to a dissonant explosion.

Many of the points made above regarding the *Overture, 1776* also apply to the contemporary *Country Band March* (V14) (1903). It, too, spoofs an amateur performance of a march which moves from relative simplicity, via a contrasting middle section, to eventual chaos. Indeed, so similar in spirit are the two works that Ives was later able to amalgamate them in *Putnam's Camp*.

Also humorous in intent are the second movement of the *Trio* (W9,ii) (1904–05, rev. 1911) and the *Scherzo: Holding Your Own* (W15,ii) (1903–14). The *Trio* movement is a *Presto*, generally known as 'Tsiaj' (This Scherzo Is A Joke) and subtitled 'Medley on the Campus Fence'. The joke lies not only in the humorous succession of popular and sacred melodies, but also in their settings. The form of the piece is generally rhapsodic, though there are some elements of recapitulation. Most notable among these are the two intrusions of 'In the Sweet Bye and Bye', the first coming at bars 84–87, and the second near the end.

Perhaps more typical are the settings of 'Marching through Georgia' (bars 43–64) and 'My Old Kentucky Home' (bars 68–83). The former is accompanied by ostinato figures on 'cello and piano (marked 'as a bass drum'); the latter (in the piano right hand) is accompanied by a 'cello countermelody and polyrhythmic ostinati for violin and piano left hand, separate dynamic levels being allocated to each textural layer. This leads directly to the first of the appearances of 'In the Sweet Bye and Bye', which in turn is succeeded by a passage (example 2.18) whose piano part makes overt reference to music better known in its later incarnations – in *Hawthorne* (X19,ii) (1911) and the corresponding second movement of the Fourth Symphony (V39) (1911–16).[23] There, however, it does not underpin 'The Sailor's Hornpipe'.

Example 2.18. Ives: *Trio* (W9),ii; bars 88–92
© Copyright 1955 by Peer International Corporation. Used by permission.

A similar combination of humour and complexity distinguishes the *Scherzo: Holding Your Own* whose dissonant outer sections conceal references to a number of melodies including 'Massa's in the Cold Ground' (bars 5–9), 'My Old Kentucky Home' (bars 10–13), 'The Sailor's Hornpipe' (bar 14) and – possibly – 'Rule, Britannia' (bar 14). Most of these melodies appear in the 'cello, accompanied by music of an uncompromisingly acerbic nature. The transition to the middle section is achieved through a canonic (and polytonal) setting of 'The Streets of Cairo' (otherwise known as the 'Hootchy Kootchy Dance'). This middle section is utterly different and consists essentially of what Hitchcock has termed a mensuration canon:[24] each player attempts to 'hold his own' rhythms and scales against the polyrhythmic distractions of the others (example 2.19). In

Example 2.19. Ives: *Scherzo: Holding Your Own* (W15,ii); bars 22–28
© Copyright 1958 by Peer International Corporation. Used by permission.

fact the music is not truly canonic: the rhythmic imitations between violin 1 and viola/'cello and violin 2 last only one bar, and the pitch imitations not much longer. More important is the acceleration of the violins' writing against the deceleration of the lower instruments.

Canon proper is a substantial feature of the *Trio's* last movement, the strings being in imitation between bars 86 and 125; but a more interesting aspect of the work lies in the construction of its first movement (figure 2.5). This *Andante*

Figure 2.5. Structure of Ives' Trio (W9),i

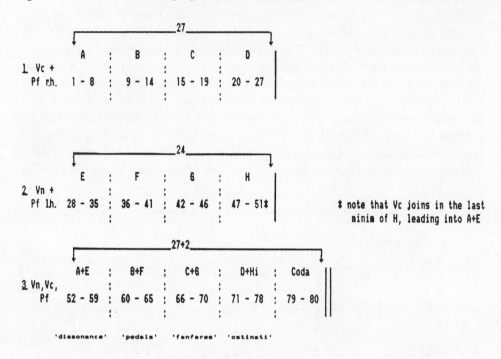

moderato is generally recognised as being a prime example of Ives' 'layering' techniques.[25] Each of the stringed instruments in turn plays a duet with one of the piano's hands; the two duets are then superimposed to produce a quartet (or, rather, trio, as the pianist's two hands now work together). Note that H is only five, rather than the expected eight, bars long. Ives must have felt it unnecessary to employ here the full number of repetitions of the prevailing ostinato ideas. Consequently in the fuller texture of D+Hi three extra bars are included in the violin part, and three extra repetitions of the varying ostinato in the piano left hand.

Each duet progresses from relative dissonance to relative consonance: thus sections A and E – which are predominantly dissonant – when superimposed produce a complex, polyphonic and polyrhythmic texture (example 2.20).

Both B and F use pedal-notes to control this music. In all parts there is less polyrhythmic and polyphonic movement, and more harmonic consonance. In C and G the two stringed instruments have 'bugle calls', while the piano's two hands come together to play a chordal counterpoint. Thus the two original duets are now combined to produce a new two-layered texture. Although the layers are polyrhythmically separate, both move in a harmonic orbit close to C major.

In D and H(i) all four lines have quasi-ostinati which decorate a basic bitonality of B♭ and C, with pedal C root. All of the rhythmic materials are extremely simple, while the final coda refers to the opening bars of each duet (example 2.21). The radiant circling of this passage is reminiscent of the more complicated endings of the Second String Quartet (W19,iii) (1911–13) and Fourth Symphony.

Example 2.20. Ives: *Trio* (W9),i; bars 52–55
© Copyright 1955 by Peer International Corporation. Used by permission.

Example 2.21. Ives: *Trio* (W9),i; bars 71–72; 77–80
© Copyright 1955 by Peer International Corporation. Used by permission.

While being related to the 'accidental' polyphony of the early *Psalms*, *Over-ture, 1776*, *Country Band March* and so on, the kind of polyphony found in this movement – where the two halves of a whole are at first introduced in isolation from each other – is actually quite different. For while in those works Ives was merely fixing in music an experience of reality, in the bifurcation of the *Trio's* opening movement and in the canons of *From the Steeples and the Mountains* he has moved to the realm of pure invention. The accidental independence of a band-player or a singer is one thing; the deliberate independence of musical ideas or parts, or of their component parameters, is quite another.

The implications of this total polyphony were substantially worked out in a series of chamber works dating from 1906 onwards. Before these, however, standing as a kind of preliminary squall to Ives' experimental storm, comes the *Three-Page Sonata* (X14) (Sep. 1905), which is conceived in one multi-section movement.

The opening *Allegro moderato* section (bars 1–30), though very dissonant, equates to a normal sonata movement. There is a first subject (with bass pedal pitches, dissonant harmony, and B–A–C–H motif) (bars 1–4); a second subject (with 'ragged' syncopated rhythms and inverted pedals on g″ in bars 5–6 and d‴ in bars 8–9) (bars 5–9); and a codetta (in which the bass pedal is restored, as is the B–A–C–H motif in retrograde inversion and transposition) (bars 10–11).

This whole exposition is then repeated exactly (except for the extra d pedal-note in bar 12) and is followed by a kind of development (bars 22–30). The relatively slow-moving left hand of bars 23–25, and disguised B–A–C–H in bars 23 (right hand) and 24–25 (left hand) refer to the first subject. The 'ragged' rhythms and inverted f♯″ pedal of bars 26–28, followed by the polyrhythms of bars 29–30, refer to the second.

Of note in this music are its rhythmic complexity, both horizontal and vertical (see especially bars 5–7) and the frequent harmonic use of fourths and tritones, both exclusively and in combination with each other (see especially bars 1–7 and 10–11). Rather than including a recapitulation, however, Ives moves straight into his slow movement, an *Andante* (bars 31–42) followed by an *Adagio* (bars 43–61). The left-hand pattern seen in bars 31–35 (example 2.22) is a persistent and unifying feature throughout the *Andante* and *Adagio*. It always retains its shape, though the details of its rhythmic and intervallic content are variable. Both it and the music above it are tightly organised (see figure 2.6). The base pitches of the left-hand pattern move progressively downwards by whole-tone steps, and are coupled with higher pitches to produce either triadic or quasi-triadic formations. The first four base pitches are also associated with specific rhythmic patterns having a polymetric relationship to the given time signatures. Pattern $\underline{x}$ uses quaver movement and implies a metrical sequence of $\frac{5}{8}, \frac{5}{8}, \frac{5}{8}, \frac{3}{8}, \frac{5}{8}, \frac{1}{8}$. Pattern $\underline{y}$ uses semiquaver movement and implies a metrical sequence of $\frac{3}{16}, \frac{5}{16}, \frac{4}{16}, \frac{4}{16}, \frac{3}{16}, \frac{6}{16}, \frac{3}{16}, \frac{8}{16}$. These two patterns can be seen in bars 31–33 and 34–35 respectively of example 2.22. The music given to the right hand is more freely organised: textures $\underline{l}$ and $\underline{m}$ can again be seen in example 2.22. $\underline{l}$ consists primarily of slow-moving two-part writing, and $\underline{m}$ of harmonic fifths and major

Example 2.22. Ives: *Three-Page Sonata* (X14); bars 30–35
© 1949 & 1975 Merion Music, Inc. Used by permission of the publisher.

Figure 2.6. Structure of the *Andante* section of Ives' *Three-Page Sonata* (X14)

sub-section	i		ii		iii		iv		v	
bars	31 – 33		34 – 35		36 – 38		39 – 40		41 – 42	
r.h. texture				bar 36 / 3rd crotchet		bar 38 / 2nd quaver		bar 40 / 4th crotchet		
	l		m		n		o		p	
l.h. 'metres'	x		y		x		y		regular $\frac{5}{8}$ [1+1+3] x 3	
base pitch	G		F		Eb		C#		B	
overlying pitches	d	b	c	g	Bb	g	G# d; G#	d#	F#	d#
							bar 39 / last semiquaver			
consequent intervals	5	M6	5	5	5	M6	5 T; 5	5	5	M6

third grace notes. (Note also the bitonal relationships between the hands; an additional refinement lies in the concealed inverted B–A–C–H in the right hand of bar 34 – b♭–c♭″–a♭′–a′.) After this, however, the changes of right-hand texture and left-hand pattern become increasingly unrelated: texture n̲ commences two crotchet beats 'late', on the third beat of bar 36. Consisting of three-to five-pitch chords, arranged into two varied statements of a three-crotchet rhythmic pattern, it is soon succeeded by texture o. This consists of five-pitch chords having identical intervallic structures (rising intervals of Π–m3–m2–M3); it, too, is arranged into two statements of a five-attack rhythmic pattern (dotted crotchet–two quavers–two dotted quavers) followed by an extension of five attacks (quaver–four dotted quavers). Texture p is a preparation for the *Adagio*, as is the regular ⅝ left-hand pattern underneath it; it contains hints of 'Westminster Chimes', plus oscillating tritone-plus-fourth chords.

The *Adagio* itself falls into two main parts, plus coda. In the first of these (bars 43–48) right-hand texture q continues the oscillating chords of p, but now arranged into a regular rhythmic pattern (in an implied ⅔ metre). Over this a wide-leaping melody implies metres of ¾, then ⁵⁄₄. The left-hand pattern has by now stabilised onto a base pitch of B (coupled with F♯ (5↑) and then d♯ (M6↑) or d (m6↑)) and into an implied metre of ⅝. But the subdivision into rhythmic units within each 'bar' is far from regular (see example 2.23). The first ⅝ 'bar' com-

Example 2.23. Ives: *Three-Page Sonata* (X14); bars 43–45
© 1949 & 1975 Merion Music, Inc. Used by permission of the publisher.

†*Note:* The notation given in the published score for this passage – ⌐⌐ etc. – has been rationalised here.

mences on the last quaver of the *Andante*. This and all subsequent 'bars' are arranged in one of the following patterns:

> 2 + 1 + 2; 1 + 2 + 2; 2 + 2 + 1;
> 1 + 1 + 3; 3 + 1 + 1; 1 + 3 + 1
> (i.e. all possible permutations are used).

The second part of the *Adagio* is more mobile: starting from the fourth crotchet of bar 49, the left-hand base pitches move sequentially (figure 2.7). The accompanying pitches are always a fifth and then major sixth higher.

The oscillating chords now shadow this bass sequence: each ⅝ 'bar' is matched by two chords (the root of the second a semitone lower than that of the first) having an intervallic content of fourth over tritone, and major third over tritone. The middle pitch of the first chord of each pair is the same as that of the base root. The top layer (constituting the remainder of texture r) is a rhythmically and metrically unrelated rendition of 'Westminster Chimes'; 'in' ⅝ metre, its second and fourth phrases each slip down by a semitone (example 2.24).

Figure 2.7. Base pitches of bars 49–60 of Ives' *Three-Page Sonata* (X14)

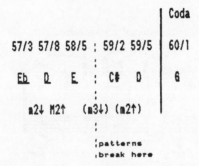

bar / quaver	49/7 50/4 51/1 51/6		52/3 52/8 53/5 54/2		54/7 55/4 56/1 56/6
base pitch	C B♭ C♯ B♭	:	A G♯ B♭ G	:	F♯ E G E
interval sequence	m2↓ M2↑ m3↓ m2↓	:	÷	:	÷

	Coda
57/3 57/8 58/5 : 59/2 59/5	60/1
E♭ D E : C♯ D	G
m2↓ M2↑ (m3↓) (m2↑)	
:	
patterns	
break here	

Example 2.24. Ives: *Three-Page Sonata* (X14); bars 49–52
© 1949 & 1975 Merion Music, Inc. Used by permission of the publisher.

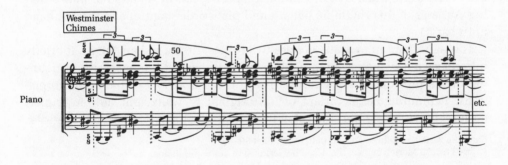

The final phrase is succeeded by a free variant, but at the end of bar 58 returns in augmentation. Under this, in bar 59, the left-hand pattern and its right-hand shadow are broken, leading to a two-bar coda (bars 60–61) which recalls the opening of the *Andante* as well as completing 'Westminster Chimes'.

The beauty of this ending is shattered by the arrival of a march-time *Allegro*, whose introduction first uses eleven of the available semitones of the octave, and then settles onto a strident tritone motif. The subsequent 'march and waltz' section divides into a number of parts: in the first of these (bars 69–71) elements from the introduction are reworked in a harmonised form, the right-hand chords Ives uses here having an intervallic structure very similar to that of bars 38–40 of the *Andante*.

In bars 72–73 the existing oom-pah bass is transposed up a minor third, from C♯–G♯/G♯ to E–B̲/B, and accompanies third-based chords of irregular lengths. Next, in bars 74–76, the right hand has a 'waltz' phrased in ¾. Its melody uses all twelve pitches of the chromatic octave (though in an order different to that of the introduction) and each pitch is harmonised identically – here by tritone over fourth (c.f. the oscillating chords of the *Adagio*, etc.). The melody itself is a minor third higher, this harmony having also appeared in the two 'upbeats' of bar 73. The oom-pah bass is again transposed upwards, this time by a minor sixth (example 2.25).

Example 2.25. Ives: *Three-Page Sonata* (X14); bars 74–76
© 1949 & 1975 Merion Music, Inc. Used by permission of the publisher.

In bars 77–79 this waltz is repeated verbatim; but the left hand now has a *second* waltz, in crotchet triplets, with a different rhythmic shape. It, too, makes use of all twelve pitches of the chromatic octave, but in yet another new ordering. Variants of this rhythmic pattern and pitch order continue in the left hand until bar 85.

The right hand in bars 80–85 does two things: firstly, in bars 80–81, it briefly introduces a new march rhythm which soon throws off the intervallic structuring of the previous 'waltz-chords'. Then, using a variety of harmonic formations, it reintroduces a variant of the original '¾' waltz, but now in triplets (example 2.26). Note the concealed transposition of B–A–C–H which straddles

Example 2.26. Ives: *Three-Page Sonata* (X14); bars 80–85
© 1949 & 1975 Merion Music, Inc. Used by permission of the publisher.

bars 82 and 83 (a′–g♯′–b′–bb′), the whole-tone melodic progression of bars 84–85, and the white-note diatonic clusters of bar 85.

Viewed as a whole, bars 69–85 are remarkable for their accelerating metrical progression from march to waltz, achieved through the superimposition of polymetres (see figure 2.8).

Figure 2.8. Structure of bars 69–85 of Ives' *Three-Page Sonata* (X14)

bars	➔73	74 – 76	77 – 79	80 – 81	82 – 84	(85)
polymetric relationship	$\frac{4}{4}$	$\frac{3 \times 4}{4}$	$\frac{3 \times 4}{4}$	$\frac{2 \times 4}{4}$	$\frac{3 \times 6}{6}$	$\frac{3 + 1}{4 \quad 4}$
		$\frac{4}{4 \times 3}$	$\frac{3}{6 \times 6}$	$\frac{3}{6 \times 4}$	$\frac{3}{6 \times 6}$	$\frac{3}{6 \times 2}$
basic perceived units of motion	semibreve	dotted minim / semibreve	dotted minim / minim ÷ 3	minim / minim ÷ 3	minim ÷ 3 / minim ÷ 3	dotted minim + crotchet / minim ÷ 3
	UNITY (march)	D I S P A R I T Y / A C C E L E R A T I O N			UNITY (waltz) :	

Dance rhythms and polymetre also combine in the music which follows – a 'ragtime' in $\frac{2}{4}$ (right hand) and '$\frac{3}{6}$' (left hand). This, too, is partially organised: the bass pattern of bars 86–87 is reversed (though not internally) as bars 88–89 and then repeated verbatim as 90–91. The melody, meanwhile, seems to oscillate between three adjacent pitches, though it actually includes rhythmically dislocated elements of recapitulation. This music is halted by a polytonal cadential passage; the two hands are in syncopated rhythmic unison, and the melody features the extreme leaps first encountered in the *Adagio* (bars 92–94). The 'ragtime' polymetric music is then repeated but with a newly invented melody in the right hand (which squeezes in a concealed B–A–C–H during bars 99–100). Its final chord is held for an extra quaver, so the subsequent repetition of the polytonal cadence is dislocated by an equal amount across bars 101–103.

Ives now repeats virtually all of the *Allegro* music heard so far. However, the alterations he makes conceal, articulate and vary this repetition. Firstly, the chromatic melody of the introduction is counterpointed by new material, while the strident tritone motif is accompanied by bitonal writing (bars 104–105; 106–110). Bars 111–118 are a literal repeat of bars 69–76. But the 'march and waltz' are now interrupted by the ragtime; bars 119–127 thus repeat the music of bars 95–103. There is no place, however, for a repetition of either the original ragtime (bars 86–94) or the 'polytemporal waltz' of bars 77–79. The ragtime interruption is therefore followed by a repetition of bars 80–85 as bars 128–133. The short coda consists of a tremolando chord (intervallically constructed as minor third over tritone over fourth – c.f. bars 73–80, etc.) plus pedal pitch, and a rather surprising C major triad, the whole resembling a kind of plagal cadence.

Thus, in the *Three-Page Sonata*, as in some earlier works, Ives experiments with the independent organisation of simultaneous musical layers (in the patterning of the *Andante* and *Adagio*, and 'march and waltz' of the final *Allegro*) as well as with the reordering and occasional metric dislocation of extant successive musical ideas (especially in the second half of the *Allegro*).

Very few of his later keyboard works are as systematic in their exploration of new compositional techniques. The norm, rather, in both the two large sonatas and the numerous smaller pieces, is of rhapsodic invention, generally making free use of resources devised elsewhere. Indeed, as the piano was the instrument closest to Ives' heart, mind and fingers this is exactly what one would expect. His general attitude to keyboard composition is admirably expressed in his specific comments regarding the *Concord Sonata*:

[you] don't have to. . .play every thing and piece and measure the same every time. . .
    Play it before breakfast like — !
     "   "   after   "   " — !
     "   "   "   digging potatoes like — !
In fact, these notes, marks, and near pictures of sounds, etc. are in a kind of way a platform for the player to make his own speeches on.[26]

If the *Three-Page Sonata* was the preliminary squall to the experimental storm of 1906, then the outer movements of the *Set for Theatre or Chamber Orchestra* (V22,i,iii) written respectively in July and June of that year, must be among its first thunderclaps. The first movement – 'In the Cage' (known also in a version for voice and piano (Z75)) – again attempts to fix in sound an experience from reality, in this case the observation of an animal in Central Park's menagerie. The song's text reads:

A leopard went around his cage from one side back to the other side; he stopped only when the keeper came around with meat; A boy who had been there three hours began to wonder, 'Is life anything like that?'

The pacing of the leopard is heard in the regular – but often metrically unrelated – drum beats. But the piece also has a technical point to demonstrate, being

a study of how chords of 4ths and 5ths may throw melodies away from a set tonality. . .a song does not necessarily have to be in any one key to make musical sense.[27]

The cor anglais melody (commencing in bar 5) consists of a series of wholetone melodic phrases, each pivoting about a different pitch. The rhythmic movement (derived from the words) is mainly in quavers, and the melody is shadowed throughout by an oboe. This shadowing – almost invariably at the fourth above, except in bar 14 – is also a distinctive colouring, *pp* against the melody's *f*. The phrases of the melody are further articulated through changes in the whole-tone scale being used: each of the second, third and fourth phrases (bars 7–10, 10–12, 13–16, respectively) commences a semitone higher than the final pitch of the previous phrase. This upward movement is balanced by a downward descent of a minor third, from the end of the fourth phrase to the opening of the fifth (which recapitulates the first).

The barring of this melody is dictated by the accompaniment, for strings and occasional piano, whose five sections only partially coincide with the melodic phrases. The first section is a repeated introduction (bars 1–4) featuring a rising sequence of fourths chords. These are arranged rhythmically as a diminishing arithmetic series, and completed by an unrelated chord with additional piano dissonances. The whole passage falls into two parts (see example 2.27).

Example 2.27. Ives: 'In the Cage' (V22,i); bars 1–4 (strings and piano only)

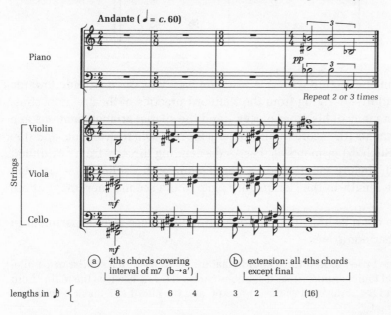

The second section (bars 5–9) transposes the whole of this sequence a fourth higher, while the fifth section (bars 16–17) is a similar transposition of its first part. The degree of transposition, like the rhythmic content, is related to the overlying melody. The third section (bars 10–13) is an extended and transposed variation of the first part of the basic sequence, with new melodic pitches being inserted into the line. The degree of transposition is now a minor tenth higher than at the start.

Section 4 (bars 14–15) matches the fifths of the melody and shadow with its fifth-derived chords, while the 'wondering' of the boy, in bar 15, is represented by a rolled ten-pitch piano chord. The boy's question is answered affirmatively by the return to the opening music in bars 16–17.

The timpani's ostinato pattern, representing the pacing of the leopard, is constantly present. Like the caged animal, this ostinato is divorced from its surroundings, in both pitch (alternating A and d♯) and metre. However, occasional changes in pattern – presumably representing the leopard's change of direction – *do* generally coincide with important moments in the music: the end of the introduction, start of melodic phrases 2, 3 and 4, and the rolled chord at 'wonder'.

The third piece in the Set – 'In the Night' – is composed almost entirely of superimposed ostinati. But it does have a basic form (figure 2.9). Two important

Figure 2.9. Structure of Ives' 'In the Night' (V22,iii)

section	Intro,	Horn tune 'verse 1' : 'verse 2'	'Hymns' and Conclusion	
bars	1-2	3 - 6 : 7 - 10	11-(17) / (15)-19	
key of main melodies		E	Db , Bb	

points to note in connection with this work are Ives' very open attitude towards its instrumentation – deriving from the standard practice of theatre orchestras, and reflected in many of his other pieces – and the spatial arrangement of some of these instruments (the score includes parts for off-stage instruments and distanced bells). Such experiments as these – descending directly from childhood memories, and already mentioned in connection with *Psalm 100* – are discussed at some length in the Conductor's Note to the second movement of the Fourth Symphony.

However, the main technical point underlying this piece is an experiment in harmony and harmonic area:

In this little piece I tried to find three chords that might be used in a similar or parallel sense to the usual tonic, dominant, and subdominant. . .Db was taken as the main chord (or the tonic), and Bb. . .was used as the dominant, and the chord of E major. . .was used as the subdominant.[28]

Thus the usual cycle of fifths is replaced by a 'cycle of minor thirds' – the three key-notes together form the diminished triad often favoured by Ives. The three chords are linked by shared pitches; but whereas in conventional harmony the key-note of the subdominant is the 'dominant seventh' pitch, or (suspended) fourth, here it becomes the 'blue third' of the 'tonic' (i.e. E = Fb in Db major). Much use is made of such ambiguities in the present piece.

The three tonalities feature in both the harmonic ostinati and the overlaid melodies. The horn 'verses' are in E (with flattened seventh) and the two 'hymns' are in Db ('Abide with Me') and Bb ('Massa's in the Cold Ground'). All three melodies are to a greater or lesser extent polymetrically related to the given metre and underlying ostinati, but the horn tune's rhythms are complicated even by Ives' usual standards (example 2.28). Paradoxically, the score carries a note that 'It is not essential that the time indicated. . .against the main 3/4 be kept too literally, if the phrases of this part sufficiently overlap the general time.' Here, as in so many other places in Ives, 'it's more important to get the "gist and swat" agoing than to slow up to get the written notes'.[29]

Example 2.28. Ives: 'In the Night' (V22,iii); bars 3–11 (horn only)

† *Note*: (1) This bar has been renotated rhythmically to correct the mistakes in the published score;
(2) 'fright' is where some of the ostinato lines momentarily or permanently change their patterns.

The various harmonic ostinati are as follows:

1   Piano r.h.; violins; violas
    Six crotchets long; dotted quaver units, presenting triads of Db–E–
    Bb–Db–E–Bb–E–Db
2   'Cellos
    Linked to 1, but only three crotchets long; dotted quaver units, adding
    a 'false fifth' under the final chord(s) of each bar
3   Piano l.h.; double basses
    Two crotchets long; regular pattern of crotchet followed by two
    quavers; outlines Db and Bb
4   Low bells
    Six crotchets long; two dotted minims; plays Db and Bb. (The low
    bells actually form part of the group of distanced instruments, but
    unlike the other components of that group are given a short repeated
    pattern.)
5   Piano ('middle hand' – the part is for two players)
    Three quavers long; compresses E, Db and Bb into one chord, plus
    'melodic' cb addition

The music of the offstage instruments and distanced bells is freer. (See example 2.29.)
    The combination of these various layers produces an extremely polyrhythmic
– and quasi-polymetric – 'wash' of sound, similar to those found later in
The Housatonic at Stockbridge (V30,iii) (1908–?14) and *From Hanover Square
North. . .*(V37,iii) (1915). The use of foreground and background further links
'In the Night' with the Fourth Symphony's first, second and fourth movements
(1910–16).

Example 2.29. Ives: 'In the Night' (V22,iii); bars 1–2 (ostinati and distanced instruments)

† *Note:* See Ives' note re. the instrumentation of these lines in the published score.
‡ *Note:* Low bells are actually part of group of distanced instruments: see text.

All of the ostinati except 4 are affected by the horn's 'fright' of bar 9: particularly noteworthy is the piano's two-octave-plus white-note cluster, remarkable at
this early date. But generally they continue unaltered until the dissolution of
the final bars. The distanced instruments' music, however, both changes and
begins to dissolve from this point onwards. As the piece 'dies away as a Bell
tolling in the distance',[30] the programmatic nature of the work is more clearly
revealed: '. . .the heart of an old man, dying alone in the night, sad, low in
heart – then God comes to help him – bring him to his own loved ones'.[31]

The centre piece of the *Set for Theatre or Chamber Orchestra* – 'In the Inn'
(V22,ii) (1906–11) – is an early example of a collage form resulting from stylistic
diversity within a single movement. This self-styled *pot-pourri* is substantially

the same as the 2nd verse and chorus of the First Piano Sonata (X17,iib) (1902–
?08), itself derived from the first of the *Four Ragtime Dances* (V12/X13) (1902–04).
In the sonata, Ives makes 'punning' use of three motivically related hymn melodies – 'I Hear Thy Welcome Voice', 'Bringing in the Sheaves' and 'Oh Happy Day'
(also known as 'How Dry I Am').[32] But the *Theatre Orchestra Set* version also
includes a wealth of overlaid melodies, both extant and invented. These, too, are
musical puns, for many share intervallic shapes in common with both the three
hymn tunes and the ragtime music which follows the opening piano-drumming
(example 2.30).

Ives often distinguishes these various layers of melody through the use of
implied polymetre. (Indeed, in later, more complex pieces, *actual* polymetre
and polytempo are used to distinguish the layers.) In the present work bars
28–33 provide a typical instance of such use (example 2.31).

The given $\frac{2}{4}$ metre is maintained only by the timpani. Against it are placed
the following layers:

1 Clarinet: 'ragged' $\frac{3}{16}$ (bars 29–30).
2 Piano r.h.: a different 'ragged' $\frac{3}{16}$ (bars 28–30), though sharing the
   clarinet's accents. Then $\frac{2}{8}$ (bars 30–32), $\frac{3}{16}$ (bar 32) and $\frac{2}{4}$ (bar 33).
3 Violins and violas: 'After the Ball is Over', mainly in a disjointed $\frac{6}{12}$
   waltz-time (bars 28–31), then $\frac{7}{12}$ (bars 31–32), then $\frac{3}{4}$ (bars 32–33). (For
   Ives' methods of distorting extant melodies, compare with the earlier
   discussion of *Overture, 1776*.)
4 Bassoon, 'cello, piano l.h. (plus violas until the first quaver of bar 29):
   mainly $\frac{3}{8}$ 'waltz' bass, but with intrusions of $\frac{4}{8}$ (bars 29–30) and $\frac{2}{8}$
   (bar 33).

Of these various layers, the timpani $\frac{2}{4}$, plus 2 and 4, were present before bar 28.
From bar 34, the timpani still emphasise the given $\frac{2}{4}$, but in a different way;
variants of layers 2 and 3 continue, though the quoted melody in 3 is no longer
'After the Ball is Over'. Note also here how each layer has a separate dynamic
shape.

The form which contains this Joycean stream of invention would, in conventional terms, be described as rhapsodic: the general progression is towards the

Example 2.30. Ives: 'In the Inn' (V22,ii); melodic network (all melodies transposed to C major)

Example 2.30. (cont.)

Example 2.31. Ives: 'In the Inn' (V22,ii); bars 28–33 (renotated and simplified)*

† Piano has E♯: error?
* An asterisk following the caption indicates that accidentals apply only to those pitches they immediately precede.

final chorus (bars 125–129) but within this progression a number of ideas recur (figure 2.10):

<u>A</u> can be defined as ragtime music, generally pinned harmonically to
G major or g minor on the piano, with A or c as pitches in the bass
<u>B</u> starts similarly, but the bass (except in the timpani) moves much more freely; the rag becomes displaced
<u>C</u> is less well defined. But much of it refers to a motif (M3↑–m2↑–m2↓) first announced in the bass at bar 59

Figure 2.10. Generalised structure of Ives' 'In the Inn' (V22,ii)

```
section  | Intro | Ai ; ii ; iii | Bi ; ii ; iii ; iv | Aiv    | Ci ; ii ; iii

tempo    | Allegro| Allegro moderato| più mosso    poco ten,| A tempo| meno mosso

bars     | 1 - 8 | 9-19;20-25;26-33| 34-37;38-40;41-46;46-49| 50 - 55| 56-60;61-66;67-72

comments | Piano-|               |   Piano-drumming   |        |
         | drumming|
```

```
 [: Di & ii  ; ''; ]2° iii;    iv    | Ei ;  ii  ;  iii

 Meno allegro ; Presto  ; a tempo         meno mosso
 (con moto)   ;         ; (con moto)

 [:  73 - 77  ;78a; ] 78b-80;  81 - 83 | 84-85 ; 86-89 ; 90-94

               Piano - drumming
```

```
 Dv  ;    iiia    ;    vi    | Ciiia | Eiiia ; link |      F

 con ; Presto ; a tempo                              | Refrain - Meno
 moto;                                               | mosso con moto

 95-101; 101-104 ; 105 ; 106-109 ;110-111|112-116|117-119;120-124| 125  -  129

               Piano - drumming
```

D – except for its *Presto* interruptions – is almost exclusively based on variants of the opening of 'Oh Happy Day'

E, again, is less well defined except by its countermelodies

F is a short refrain on the chorus of 'I Hear Thy Welcome Voice'

It is clear, however, that this sectionalisation is unsatisfactory: with the exception of blatant changes of texture or tempo, most of the edges between sections are very blurred. Thus the form, as defined above, is not necessarily perceptible to either listener or score-reader.

An alternative way of viewing pieces like 'In the Inn' is to consider them not as simple one-dimensional forms, but rather as multi-dimensional objects – as collages not only of musical materials but also of possible paths through these materials and their interrelationships.[33] Although 'In the Inn' is a relatively simple work, it can be experienced in many different ways – i.e. it suggests many alternative and yet equally viable formal plans. As has already been seen, the piece includes a large number of melodic fragments which are interrelated through their intervallic shapes. In one sense it would be possible to hear 'In the

Inn' simply as the succession of these melodies, at the expense of other material. But it is also possible to perceive structures based on only *some* of the melodic fragments. If we restrict ourselves to the consideration of the three hymn tunes, each through its appearances defines one or more sectional forms (figures 2.11–2.13). But the combination of these three tunes provides a network

Figure 2.11. Appearances of 'Bringing in the Sheaves' in Ives' 'In the Inn' (V22,ii)

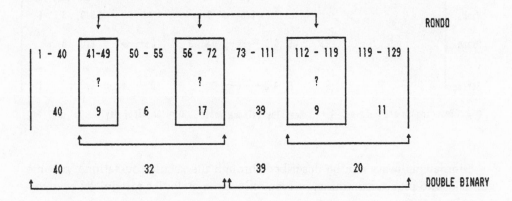

Figure 2.12. Appearances of 'Oh Happy Day' in Ives' 'In the Inn' (V22,ii)

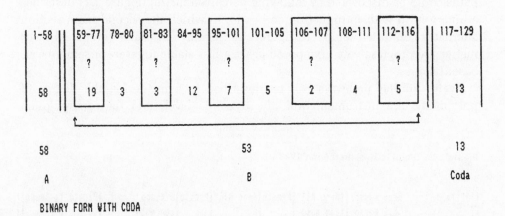

Figure 2.13. Appearances of 'I Hear Thy Welcome Voice' in Ives' 'In the Inn' (V22,ii)

of references, through which the listener may wander at will – see figure 2.14, which can also be interpreted sectionally as a binary form, or as a secular introduction plus sacred 'prose' movement.

Figure 2.14. Appearances of sacred melodies in Ives' 'In the Inn' (V22,ii)

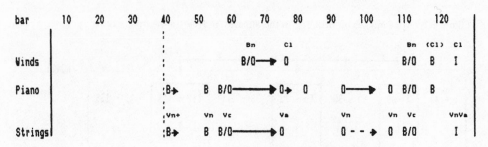

B = 'Bringing in the Sheaves'   I = 'I Hear Thy Welcome Voice'   O = 'Oh Happy Day'

Similar pathways can be described through the secular quotations, ragtime music, and piano-drumming, or even only those melodies recognised by a particular listener.

On a quite different level it is possible to provide sectional analyses based on tempo and given metre, as in figures 2.15 and 2.16 (though, of course, different paths could be discovered by following perceived metre). Figure 2.15 describes a binary form with introduction and coda, in which the second main section alternates contrasted tempi. In figure 2.16, meanwhile, stable (crotchet-based) metres are progressively juxtaposed against less stable (quaver- or semiquaver-based) metres.

Again, similar pathways can be described by considering the degree of polyphony, the instrumentation, the dynamic level, and the tonality/pitch

Figure 2.15. Tempi of Ives' 'In the Inn' (V22,ii)

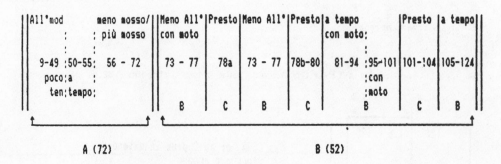

BINARY FORM, WITH INTRODUCTION (bars 1-8, All°) AND CODA (bars 125-129, Meno mosso con moto)

Figure 2.16. Given metres of Ives' 'In the Inn' (V22,ii)

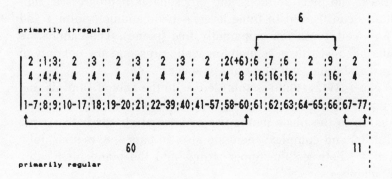

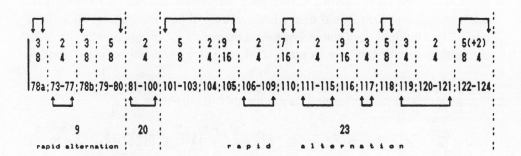

5

centre. But just as the melodic fragments discussed earlier provide unity despite their diversity of style and pitch, so on the largest scale do these various pathways through 'In the Inn', despite their differing structural implications, provide an overall sense of direction and purpose. The inexorable and irresistible progression here is from stability through instability to the final unity of the chorus at bars 125–129.

In a continuation of the ideas tried out in *From the Steeples and the Mountains* and the first movement of the *Trio*, many of the other experimental pieces of 1906 also find Ives working with different musical layers, often in combination with canonic techniques. In *Halloween* (W11) (1 Apr. 1906) the structure (three or four sections plus coda), instrumentation (optional bass drum) and, occasionally, musical content are all determined by the players. Furthermore, like 'Lord of the Harvest', the piece loudens and quickens as it progresses. *Halloween* is essentially constructed in three layers – two canonic (violin 1 and viola; violin 2 and 'cello) and one apparently free (piano). The canons are bitonal, their material consisting of semiquaver scalic runs, and are 'not only in tones, but in phrases, accents, and durations or spaces. . .'[34]

Largo Risoluto No. 1 (W12) (1906) is subtitled 'as to the Law of Diminishing Returns',[35] as its repeated main section is a proportional canon. The dissonant nine-bar introduction to the piece makes use of interval chords both simple (fourths, major thirds) and complex; there are also, in bars 4–8, regular polyrhythmic ratios of 4:3 between the upper strings and the piano plus 'cello, though the metre changes.

The canon itself is based on an extension of the 'cello theme of bars 1–3; announced first by the piano, subsequent entries (or 'returns') on viola, 'cello and violin 2 are diminished to rhythmic values of (approximately) 75%, 50% and 25%. The final 'free' entry, however – on violin 1 – brings in a bonus, with rhythmic values of 150% (example 2.32). Each voice eventually comes to rest on

Example 2.32. Ives: *Largo Risoluto No. 1* (W12); bars 10–22
© Copyright 1961 by Peer International Corporation. Used by permission.

Example 2.32. (*cont.*)

an ostinato figure; but though these are dissonantly related, three are based
on low Cs. Surprisingly, this texture finally resolves into the string ostinato
underlying bars 42–56 of the *Overture, 1776*, plus a simple descending piano
line. After the second performance of the canon, however, bars 24–25 are
replaced by an expanded chordal version of the preceding ostinati.

In later works, Ives generally shied away from the particular kind of rhythmic
and metric complexity found here, preferring instead the employment of
unrelated polyrhythms within a fixed common metre (for example in *All the
Way Around and Back* (W14) (1906) and *The Gong on the Hook and Ladder*
(V28) (?1911)). Alternatively, separate groups of polymetrically or polytemporally related instruments are each assigned their own conductor (for example
in *The Unanswered Question* (V23,i) (1906), *Central Park in the Dark* (V23,ii)
(Jul.–Dec. 1906) and the second and fourth movements of the Fourth Symphony
(V39) (1911–16)).

Thus while the *Largo Risoluto No. 3* (subtitled 'a shadow made – a silhouette')
(W13) (1906) also makes use of a proportional canon, it is in only two relatively
simple voices, the rhythmic values of the second (string quartet) voice being
50% larger than those of the first (piano) – see example 2.33. (Each voice is tonal
in itself, but the relationship between the voices is bitonal.)

An obvious consequence of the rhythmic arrangement found here is that the
strings' music becomes increasingly distanced from that of the piano it imitates
(i.e. the strings' 'shadow' of the piano's 'object' becomes longer). Thus Ives omits
the strings' imitation of piano bars 11–13, allowing them to catch up slightly, and
provides a final unimitated piano 'codetta' (bars 22–27) over which the strings'
imitation is completed.

Example 2.33. Ives: *Largo Risoluto No. 3* (W13); bars 1–5
© Copyright 1961 by Peer International Corporation. Used by permission.

In the scherzo *All the Way Around and Back* (W14) (1906), Ives attempts to describe the hectic backtracking of a baseball player caught on third base by a foul ball. His chosen form of palindrome plus introduction and conclusion is thus quite appropriate, as is the accumulation of chromatic, polyrhythmic layers of material which fills the palindrome's exposition (bars 7–18). By bars 17–18/19–20, which lie at the apex of the process of accumulation, there are polyrhythmic ratios (relative to a semibreve) of

$$1(Pf):2(Pf):3(Pf):5(bells):7(C1):11(Pf+Vn)$$

The extreme chromaticism of *All the Way Around and Back* is combined with other elements in the more expansive scherzo *Over the Pavements* (V20) (1906–13). This, too, had an extra-musical inspiration:

In the early morning, the sounds of people going to and fro, all different steps, and sometimes all the same – the horses, fast trot, canter, sometimes slowing up into a walk. . .an
occasional trolley throwing all rhythm out (footsteps, horse and man) – then back again.
I was struck with how many different and changing kinds of beats, time, rhythms, etc.
went on together – but quite naturally, or at least not unnaturally when you got used to
it. . .[36]

Thus the piece is in essence an exercise in polyrhythm and implied polymetre.
    The form of *Over the Pavements* is a kind of arch, arranged as

A–B–C–(D)–Bi–Ci–Ai

though with each large section subdivided into many smaller parts. The musics of A and B are developments of the idea of 'the sounds of people going to and fro, all different steps'. A is a specific study of two against three, both rhythmi-cally and metrically, derived from an earlier work (*Take-off No. 3: Rube Trying to Walk 2 to 3!!* (W10) (1906)).
    B is more interested in building polyrhythms: two fairly constant features are

a 'ragging' figure implying $\frac{3}{16}$, and marching triads, ostensibly in the given $\frac{5}{8}$. Both of these – which also appear in the 3rd verse and chorus of the First Piano Sonata (X17,iva(2)) (?1909) and *'Gyp the Blood' or Hearst!? Which is Worst?!* (V32,ii) (?Oct. 1912) – are played by the piano at the start (bars 32 +) while other lines throw in other ideas (example 2.34).

Example 2.34. Ives: *Over the Pavements* (V20); bars 35–37 (omitting trombones)
© Copyright 1954 by Peer International Corporation. Used by permission.

Like *Halloween*, *Over the Pavements* includes some optional instruments: B̲i differs from B̲ only in its *ad libitum* addition of three trombones (which in the passage quoted in example 2.34 double the piano left hand at the octave below). Bars 32–45 alternate 'simple' statements of the $\frac{3}{16}/\frac{5}{8}$ music with more complex passages like that of the previous example. Bars 46–48, perhaps related to the 'trolley throwing all rhythm out' act as a kind of fulcrum, for their music is succeeded by increasingly wild and polyrhythmic attempts at ousting the basic $\frac{3}{16}/\frac{5}{8}$ complex. This is achieved by bar 61 (example 2.35).

Much of C̲ is concerned with *Rube's* two against three, though from bar 73 this is expanded to four against three: here Ives re-uses material from bars 3–9 of *Largo Risoluto No. 1*, though there are many small changes of detail.

The final component of *Over the Pavements* is section D̲ (bars 81–95) which, following on from the variable form of *Halloween*, is an optional cadenza 'To play or not to play' as Ives puts it. While it is still concerned with poly-rhythm and implied polymetre, an additional feature is 'a "little practice" that I did with Father, of playing the nice chromatic scale not in one octave but in all octaves – that is, 7ths, 9ths, etc.'.[37] (Ives' description is of the piano part, only one of the three musical layers present here. He uses similar effects in the songs *Soliloquy* (Z79) (1907) and *Vote for Names* (Z87) (Nov. 1912).)

Example 2.35. Ives: *Over the Pavements* (V20); bars 59–61
© Copyright 1954 by Peer International Corporation. Used by permission.

† Trombone f, rather than a?

The cadenza is subdivided into six small sections followed by a link which appears whether the cadenza is used or not:

a: bars 81–82   e: bars 89–90
b: bars 83–84   f: bars 91–93
c: bars 85–86   link: bars 94–95
d: bars 87–88

Present throughout is a regular drum beat (quaver attack–quaver rest) which often has an implied polymetric relationship to the two overlying layers. These – for piano, and for clarinet, trumpet and bassoon – are metrically related, as in each sub-section the phrase lengths of the piano's arpeggii and the durations of the winds' chords are equal. However, these common durational units contract from sub-section to sub-section: in a the unit is seven semiquavers long, in b six, in c̲ five, and so on, through to f̲'s two-semiquaver units. By increasing the number of units per sub-section, though, their total lengths are approximately equal (a̲ and d̲ are 28 semiquavers in length; b̲, c̲ and e̲ 30 semiquavers).

The pitch material allocated to these two metrically related layers is quite different. In each sub-section, the piano plays the first half of an ascending chromatic scale (B♭–F), in semiquavers, but with the interval between adjacent pitches being a minor ninth rather than a minor second. The pattern is then reversed (downward return to B♭) and then completed (upward, then downward, chromatic ascent from B♭ to A and beyond). In sub-sections b̲, c̲ and e̲ the final semiquaver attack consists of a four-pitch black-note cluster rather than one specific pitch. As a consequence of Ives' overall system, the piano pitches of sub-sections a̲ and b̲ recur exactly (but with new phrasings) in sub-sections d̲ and e̲.

Against these arpeggiations, the winds have interval chords: each sub-section is allocated a specific interval, these intervals together forming a contracting series. Thus in a̲ the chords are built from major sevenths, in b̲ from minor and major sixths, in c̲ from fifths, d̲ fourths, e̲ minor and major thirds, and f̲ minor and major seconds. Additionally, in a̲, b̲ and c̲ the final durational unit is broken into two chords of shorter lengths (though phrased together) and in d̲ and e̲ this arrangement is found in each bar.

Putting the three musical layers together, we find an overall 'acceleration' in the winds and piano, against a regular crotchet pulse on the drum. All of the above points are illustrated in bars 87–90 (sub-sections d̲ and e̲; see example 2.36).

The experience here is not only of polyrhythm and polymetre, but also of the superimposition of subjective (or pure) and objective (or clock) time, something more usually recognised in the work of such later composers as Harrison Birtwistle (b.1934).

Sub-section f̲ is slightly different. It commences as expected but on the last beat of bar 92 the winds have individual polyrhythmic lines which lead into their held octave Gs of bar 93. Under this the piano line goes haywire, in turn leading to the link of bars 94–95 which features alternating interval chords and black- and white-note clusters. Finally, descending triads (winds) and clusters (piano) lead back to B̲i.

This experiment in accelerating and static musical layers clearly follows on from the accumulating and accelerating polyrhythms of *All the Way Around and Back*, the proportional and mensural canons of the two *Largo Risoluto* pieces, *Holding Your Own* and *From the Steeples and the Mountains*, the polytemporal marches of *Overture, 1776* and, ultimately, Ives' experience of musical accidents and his father's experiments in his youth. The sequence reaches its logical conclusion in the superimposition, in two linked pieces, of unrelated accelerating and static musics, each of which requires a separate conductor. The two pieces are a contemplation of a serious matter – *The Unanswered Question* (V23,i) (1906) – and a contemplation of nothing serious – *Central Park in the Dark* (V23,ii) (Jul.–Dec. 1906). In both, the accelerating and static musics are

Example 2.36. Ives: *Over the Pavements* (V20); bars 87–90
© Copyright 1954 by Peer International Corporation. Used by permission.

further characterised (literally and physically) as foreground and background, though in *The Unanswered Question* an extra third layer is also present, that of the 'questioning' trumpet.

The ever-present (but off-stage) static background layer in *The Unanswered Question* is string music of great beauty, representing 'The Silences of the Druids – Who Know, See and Hear Nothing'. The opening sequence (bars 1–13) is repeated as bars 14–27 and varied as bars 28–44; subsequently its outer lines are quasi-retrograded as bars 46–61, though the middle (harmonic) parts are further varied. So slow are the tempo and rate of harmonic change of this music, and so restricted is its rhythmic movement, that what seems to be 'clock-time' is actually timeless. This effect is further emphasised by the overall ambiguity of harmonic centre: the music is written as if it were in G, but much of it leans towards C.

The second layer – that of the questioning solo trumpet – is placed on-stage; though related polyrhythmically and (in effect) polymetrically to the string background, it keeps to the same tempo (example 2.37). All but one of the

Example 2.37. Ives: *The Unanswered Question* (V23,i); bars 14–19
© Copyright 1953 by Southern Music Publishing Company, Inc. Renewed by Peer International Corporation.
© Copyright 1984 by Peer International Corporation. Used by permission.

six subsequent questions have this exact rhythmic shape, though the 'two bars of $\frac{6}{9}$ metre' shown here are positioned in various ways across the $\frac{4}{4}$ of the strings. These pitches all reappear in subsequent questions, many holding a 'blue' relationship with the underlying string harmony; note, however, that questions 2, 4, 6 and 7 close on b' rather than c".

Each question except the last is answered by a quartet of flutes which constitutes the third – accelerating – musical layer. Each of the first five answers is of roughly the same rhythmic and metric length but speed, dynamics, degree of activity and dissonance all increase. Answer 1 (bars 20–21) is quiet, and at the same tempo as the strings and trumpet; but answer 5 (over bars 47–49)[38] is loud and fast. This answer is followed by a low, quiet cluster – Ives describes it as a 'secret conference' – held against question 6, and then by the fastest, loudest passage, which mocks the question and ends on a high and very dissonant cluster (example 2.38). After it ceases, ' "The Question" is asked for the last time, and "The Silences" are heard beyond in "Undisturbed Solitude".'[39]

Central Park in the Dark has a less mystical portrait to paint, being 'a picture-in-sounds of the sounds of nature and of happenings that men would hear some thirty or so years ago. . .when sitting on a bench in Central Park on a hot summer night'.[40] The static (off-stage?) background music, again for strings, represents 'the night sounds and silent darkness'. The tempo is as slow as that of *The Unanswered Question*; but the music has more movement, rhythmically and harmonically, and is arranged cyclically (example 2.39). Note here the use of

Example 2.38. Ives: *The Unanswered Question* (V23,i); bars 47–53 ('answer' – secret conference – question – mocking of question)

Example 2.39. Ives: *Central Park in the Dark* (V23,ii); bars 1–10
© Copyright 1973 by Boelke-Bomart, Inc. Copyright assigned 1978 to Mobart Music Publications, Inc.
Used by permission.

interval chords (major thirds and tritones in bars 1–2, fourths in bars 3–5, fifths
and tritones in bars 6–8, fifths in bars 9–10). In addition, the spaces the chords
occupy (2, 3, 3, 2 semibreves), rhythm (semibreves divided 2, 3; 2, 3, 4; 3, 4, 5;
4, 3), and phrases (asymmetrically placed over interval sequences, forming
phrases of 3, 3, 4, 4, 6, 7, 5 chords) are also structured, and together emphasise
the cyclic nature of the music. This background layer is repeated verbatim
throughout: there are ten appearances of the ten-bar phrase, with the final bar of
the piece sustaining the first chord of the sequence, so as to complete the cycle.

Similar 'square-root' forms were developed by Henry Cowell and his pupil John Cage some thirty years later (see chapters 4 and 5). A final point to note is the 'cyclic' progression of the bass line (A♭–B♭–G♭–E♭) and the alteration of violin 1's final pitch (bar 10: d♭″ rather than the expected f♯″) to similarly seek resolution in the opening c″.

In complete contrast, the accelerating foreground music is very much goal-orientated. It represents 'sounds from the Casino over the pond – of street singers coming up from the Circle singing, in spots, the tunes of those days' and so on. Written for winds, brass, pianos and solo violins, it starts like the trumpet part of *The Unanswered Question*: in the same tempo, but distanced by implied polymetre. Thus the clarinet, in bars 11–17, has an 'off valse'[41] 'in' $\frac{3}{5}$ placed over the regular $\frac{4}{4}$ of the strings' background. This reappears in bar 24 (over the third string cycle) with a new ending, and is joined by flute ('from Columbus Circle!') and oboe, who continue through to bar 34. The third interruption of the string music coincides with the start of the fifth cycle: clarinet, flute and oboe are again the initial culprits, but then a solo violin '(over from Healy's)' and ragging piano join in at bars 44 and 47 respectively. This new texture persists until bar 51.

The fourth and final interruption commences in bar 59, still 'in tempo', on clarinet and piano. But the off valse suddenly livens up in bar 64, the clarinet playing ragged $\frac{3}{16}$ groups in a new metre ($\frac{2}{4}$) and tempo (*Più mosso*). From here until bar 118 the two musical layers move at quite separate speeds, the foreground winds and pianos accelerating against the static background strings (bar numbers here referring to the faster, foreground layer). The clarinet break leads to a dissonant canon, based on the oboe's earlier fragment, between oboe and flute (bars 65–70); this in turn is succeeded by more freely imitated arabesques (bars 71–75) and $\frac{3}{16}$ hoots (bars 76–77). Under this, piano 1 provides more interesting material: from bar 67 (*Allegretto con spirito*) it reveals that its earlier rag is the left-hand accompaniment to a setting of 'Hello ma Baby'. This, with its extension, forms a kind of twelve-bar cantus firmus for the rest of the foreground music. Both it and the oboe/flute music are repeated fairly exactly, but now *Allegro moderato*, as bars 79–90. The E♭ clarinet also has 'Hello ma Baby', in canon with the piano, one bar behind and an octave up.

From bar 91 (*Allegro con spirito*) things become more complicated, and the noise level higher. Piano 1 continues its twelve-bar ostinato, but now at the octave; its left hand is supported by bassoon and trombone. The oboe and E♭ clarinet follow on from the previous flute and oboe dissonances, 'in' $\frac{9}{16}$ and marked 'keep up off beat as a drum'. The flute leads into variants of 'The Campbells are Coming' (bars 93–99), while piano 2 has 'drumming' (bars 91–94) followed by music marked both as 'old Metcalf banging on the door' and 'another Piano from another floor pushes Freshmen in Park'.

The foreground texture becomes faster and increasingly complex: extra lines are piled on whose rhythmic and metric structures are unrelated to those of existing parts. In the inevitable pandemonium of bars 114–118, a 'runaway smashes into the fence'; the shrill policeman's whistle is heard on flute and oboe (and Eb clarinet?) and the fire engine siren on trombone.

Suddenly, at bar 118, the foreground is erased and the calm of the background is restored (similar moments occur in the second movements of the *Concord Sonata* and Fourth Symphony, and elsewhere). By this time the strings have completed their eighth cycle, and at bar 119 commence their ninth. The join to the tenth and final cycle is slightly concealed by a recapitulation on clarinet, flute and solo violins of some of the earliest foreground materials, as 'an echo over the pond' (see note 40), but the peace is little disturbed by this intrusion 'and we walk home'.

One result of writing polytemporally is that major difficulties of notation and coordination arise. Ives was well aware of both of these problems, as the Note to *Central Park in the Dark* makes clear. Without reverting to the scales of tempi postulated by Cowell in his *New Musical Resources* (see chapter 4), but in full knowledge that

the relation of the string orchestra's measures to those of the other instruments need not and cannot be written down exactly, as the gradual accelerando of all but the strings cannot be played in precisely the same tempi each time,

Ives provides both a fairly accurate relative notation for the superimposed musics and (conversely) a contingency plan should the notated relationship not be borne out in performance.

The strings play louder with the rest of the orchestra to measure 118 – that is, until the rest of the orchestra reaches measure 118. Here the strings will decrescendo down to ppp and before the rest of the orchestra has stopped playing the chord in measure 118. The strings finish their ten-measure phrase, wherever they may be in it, when the rest of the orchestra stops playing measure 118, and then the strings go to measure 119 and the piece finishes as indicated.

The only possible development of polytempo beyond this is found in the second and fourth movements of the Fourth Symphony, where separate tempi proceed and change quite independently, though a simpler – and freer – use of polytempo occurs at the beginning of *The Swimmers* (Z100) (1915, rev. 1921).

Earlier, mention was made of the concept of total polyphony: the creation of complex textures through the deliberately independent treatment afforded to different musical ideas or parts, or to their component parameters. Many of the works subsequently examined achieve this degree of polyphony through their implied, or actual, use of polytempo. In the former category can be included the two *Largo Risoluto* pieces, with their proportional canons, and *Over the Pavements, All the Way Around and Back* and *The Gong on the Hook and Ladder* (V28) (?1911) which feature rhythmic acceleration and deceleration over a static pulse or pulses. The most obvious members of the latter category are *The Unanswered Question, Central Park in the Dark,* and the second and fourth movements of the Fourth Symphony.

Often found in these works as an almost accidental consequence of their metric complexities is a second type of total polyphony: that created purely through the contrapuntal superimposition of dissonant, rhythmically unrelated lines.[42] This variety of total polyphony is more fully explored in the two *Tone Roads*. Ives speaks of No. 1 (V38,i) (1911) in *Memos*:

> If horses and wagons can go sometimes on different roads (hill road, muddy road, rocky, straight, crooked, hilly hard road) at the same time, and get to Main Street eventually – why can't different instruments on different staffs?[43]

Thus the tone roads are independent voices in a polyphonic work. The note at the end of the published score – 'All roads lead to the Centre – in a race to Town Meetin'' – implies not a palindromic form, but rather a short middle section – or rhythmically unified 'Main Street' – surrounded by polyphony (see figure 2.17).

Figure 2.17. Structure of Ives' *Tone Roads No. 1* (V38,i)

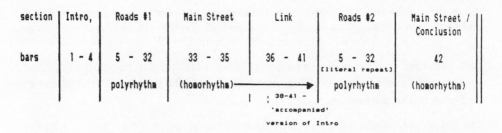

Among the roads appearing in the music are the following.

1 Regular rhythmic motifs or patterns (see example 2.40)

There are five of these, plus their variants. The most common (and extended) is announced by the 'cellos in bars 1–4; it has two distinct halves (1a: bars 1–2; 1b: bars 2–4). In bars 3–5 the bassoon introduces motif 2 as a counterpoint. Each of the five motifs/patterns may use the same pitches on subsequent appearances (2: violin 2, bars 5–7) or be transposed (1a + 1b: flute, bars 5–8) or inverted (1a: bassoon, bars 6–7).

Other possibilities include metric dislocation (1a + 1b: flute, bars 5–8) or harmonisation (2: violin 1 + viola, bars 5–7).

2 Regular harmonic interval patterns (see example 2.40)

These can be applied to an existing rhythmic idea (as in the treatment of 2 by the violins and viola in bars 5–7) or to rhythmically free material ('cellos and double bass, bars 5–13).

There are also more irregular harmonisations of existing patterns, particularly those applied to the five variants of rhythmic pattern 5, which underlie bars 20–31.

Example 2.40. Ives: *Tone Roads No. 1* (V38,i); bars 1–8

Example 2.40. (*cont.*)

3 Regular melodic interval patterns

There are a few appearances of quartal and quintal melodies; more frequent, however, is the regular use of two unrelated series of pitches, each of which is totally chromatic. The first of these – here called x – is composed as follows:

> f–f#–c′–d#–e–b♭–g–c#–d′–g#–b–a

It appears first in the low strings (bars 9–13), harmonised by fourths chords. Following this, in bars 14–19, it is used in quasi-isorhythmic combination with rhythmic pattern 4, again on low strings. Its final incomplete presentation is continued by the clarinet in bars 20–21 (first appearance of harmonised rhythmic pattern 5).

Series x also appears in the bassoon (bars 20–25), transposed up by a major third, and again in isorhythmic combination with rhythmic pattern 4.

The second series – here called y – is composed as follows:

> e″–g#″–d#″–c#″–f#″–g″–f″–b♭″–a″–c‴–b″–d″

It appears mainly in the flute (in bars 13–32), initially combined isorhythmically with rhythmic pattern 3. The series appears simultaneously – in retrograde – on the clarinet (bars 13–19), again combined with rhythmic pattern 3, but a bar later than the flute (example 2.41). This clarinet line is doubled by the violins

Example 2.41. Ives: *Tone Roads No. 1* (V38,i); bars 13–19 (flute and clarinet only)
© Copyright 1949 by Peer International Corporation. Used by permission.

and violas in bars 17–19. The violins also have a partial retrogression of series y (pitches 12 to 3) allied to free material in bars 22–24.

The flute's presentation of series y is interrupted in bars 19–20 by rhythmic pattern 1a; but between bars 20 and 32 it has five complete presentations of the series (though pitch 4 – c♯″ – is missing in the fourth of these) and begins a sixth. All are accompanied by free rhythmic material.

Ives' use here of two separate, totally chromatic series, with transposed and retrograded forms, is remarkable for its early date; nor was this the first appearance in his work of totally chromatic melodic lines (c.f. the *Three-Page Sonata*). But typically they are used unsystematically even here. It was not in Ives' nature to be inhibited by his inventions: the totally chromatic roads here are, after all, only two among many.

The above examples convey something of the complexity of *Tone Roads No. 1*, and of its dissonant, polyphonic, 'organised chaos'. Each part literally proceeds along its own melodic road, though some may be paralleled, or even dual carriageways. The sudden meeting, therefore, of these various roads in the (comparative) rhythmic unison of 'Main Street' (example 2.42) comes as something of a surprise. Note here the fourths and fifths of the main melody – but also the shadowing of violin 2 and the rhythmically unrelated tremolando background chords which already hint at the imminent return to polyphony. Indeed, the 'unison' has failed by bar 35 (the bassoon now doubles the shadow and the clarinet branches off from 'Main Street' onto a side road).

Similar concerns also predominate in *Tone Roads No. 3* (V38,iii) (1915), though its form is slightly more complicated (figure 2.18). The piece commences with a twelve-pitch totally chromatic melody, played by the chimes in bars 1–7:

e♭′–d′–e′–f♯′–f′–d♭′–g♯′–b′–g′–b♭–a′–c″

Example 2.42. Ives: *Tone Roads No. 1* (V38,i); bars 33–35
© Copyright 1949 by Peer International Corporation. Used by permission.

Note the gradual intervallic expansion from semitone (bar 1) to major seventh (bar 6). This series is varied in bars 7–12; against it the trombone has a counter-melody in quintuplet crotchet rhythms, and in bars 10–12 the trumpet adds a five-pitch motif (c″–f′–g′–a′–b′).

The two <u>A</u> sections are identical but for two details: <u>Aii</u> includes a part for flute omitted in <u>Ai</u>, and moves at a faster speed than its twin. Ives obviously considered that material could be varied by restatement at different tempi as well as by more conventional methods (c.f. the second *Harvest Home Chorale*, etc.). Various 'roads' are present here (example 2.43).

1 The chimes' series is presented twice: in bars 13–18 it is reasonably intact, but in bars 18–21 it disintegrates. Rhythmically, it moves in minim triplets (bars 13–17 and 20–21) and in crotchets (bars 18–19).

2 The clarinet moves in semiquavers, making use of two recurring and related groups of pitches.

3 The flute (playing in <u>Aii</u> only) is freely arranged.

4 The trumpet, too, is basically free. However, in bars 13–15 it refers to its earlier motif, in 19–21 collaborates with the piano, and at the end of 21 doubles the flute at the fifth below.

Figure 2.18. Structure of Ives' *Tone Roads No. 3* (V38,iii)

||TRIO

section	Intro || Ai	Intro :	Bi :	Bii
bars	1 - 12	13 - 24	25-26 :	27-35 :	27 - 35
tempo	Andante con moto			: Allegro :moderato :	Allegro vivace
details		[no Fl]		:[Vns]+Tbn :	[Fl,Cl,Tpt]+Tbn
	Chimes 'theme'→	,22-24 :Cod^ta		: Chimes+Pf 'theme'	
dynamic	[p] <	f		: f	: ff
metre	4 / 4	,10-19, 3 : 4 / 4 : 4			
no.of bars	12	12 score unclear	? : ?	←—— 11 ——→	

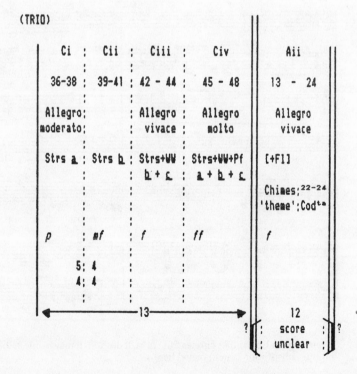

(TRIO)

	Ci :	Cii :	Ciii :	Civ	Aii
	36-38 :	39-41 :	42 - 44 :	45 - 48	13 - 24
	Allegro :moderato:		: Allegro : vivace	Allegro molto	Allegro vivace
	Strs **a** :	Strs **b** :	Strs+WW : **b** + **c** :	Strs+WW+Pf **a** + **b** + **c**	[+Fl]
					Chimes;22-24 'theme':Cod^ta
	p :	*mf* :	f :	ff	f
		5: 4 / 4: 4 :			
	←————————— 13 —————————→				12 score unclear

Example 2.43. Ives: *Tone Roads No. 3* (V38,iii); bars 18–21
© Copyright 1952 by Peer International Corporation. Used by permission.

† *Note*: Piano also doubles chimes from here, if desired (it may in any case be playing the chimes' part, but this substitution is not notated here).

5 The piano, entering at bar 17, plays mainly dotted quaver rhythms;
its pitch material consists of harmonic major sevenths and minor
ninths. In bars 19–21 these chords are added to by the trumpet, and
in bar 21 the line divides into two parts. (Note also that the piano
may be playing the chimes' part; this doubling is not shown in example 2.43.)

6 The trombone repeats its earlier phrase, though this is surrounded by
newly invented material.

The codetta (bars 22–24) consists of a series of rhythmically accelerating
interval chords, interspersed with isolated pitches, which culminates in a
quarter-tone cluster.

Like the two A sections, Bi and Bii are identical but for some changes of
detail: Bii again moves at a faster speed and contains a new melody (on trumpet). Additionally, one voice is differently instrumented on its two appearances
(see below) and the dynamics also are varied (example 2.44). The simplest layer

Example 2.44. Ives: *Tone Roads No. 3* (V38,iii); bars 30–33
© Copyright 1952 by Peer International Corporation. Used by permission.

here is the chimes' three-pitch pattern (derived from the trumpet's motif of
bars 10–11), emphasising C as pitch centre and harmonised by the piano using a
regular intervallic structure. The 'cello has a theme consisting initially of a
descending chromatic scale (bars 25–30); but after two 'free' bars this is answered by an ascending white-note scale (bars 33–34) plus 'cadence' (bar 35).
The trombone enters at bar 31. It plays in sextuplet crotchet rhythms, at first

with free pitches, but later (counterpointing the 'cello) has a descending whole-tone (bar 33) then chromatic scale (bars 34–35).

The trumpet part is fairly free throughout (though it appears only in Bii), while the final layer is written for violins in Bi and flute plus clarinet in Bii. Its material consists of interval patterns both melodic and harmonic, descending in pitch level during bars 28–30 and ascending in bars 31–35. The system partially breaks down from bar 33 onwards. In the three-quaver groupings of these patterns, Ives is making use of implied polymetre as well as polyrhythm; this is borne out by the chimes/piano ostinato, written 'in' $\frac{3}{2}$.

Section C is organised quite differently, as an accumulation process (example 2.45). Its first layer or component – a, announced by the strings in bars 36–38, but eventually given to the piano (bars 45–48) with its rhythms slightly altered – seems to be that described by Ives in *Memos*:

Example 2.45. Ives: *Tone Roads No. 3* (V38,iii); bars 45–48
© Copyright 1952 by Peer International Corporation. Used by permission.

Over the top is 'Rondo Rapid Transit'. This was about the time the Subway was started, and 'blocks' were regular things – getting out of the block and back into it again. So – half-tone chords opening up [into] wider and wider chords, and back again:

This may not be a nice way to write music, but it's one way![44]

The second component (<u>b</u> – strings, bars 39–41; 42–44; 45–48) shows a freer organisation of pitch and rhythm, though there is an overall expansion and contraction of both parameters. The opening and closing pitches ($b'–a\sharp'$; $f'–e'$) sandwich those of the piano's cluster.

The final layer (<u>c</u> – winds, bars 42–44; 45–48) is arranged similarly, its opening and closing pitches enclosing those of both the strings and the piano. Thus the initial chord of bar 45 and the closing chord of bar 48 both contain all twelve pitches of the chromatic octave, compressed into a semitonal cluster. The local expansion and contraction of rhythm and pitch are matched by an overall accumulation in sections <u>Ci</u> to <u>Civ</u> of harmonic width, rhythmic complexity, number of voices, amount of material, dynamic, and speed.

However, the degree of organisation found here is slight in comparison to that of *In Re Con Moto Et Al* (W20) (1913):

. . .a wild idea came to me (it seemed wild then, but not now) – to make a piece that no permanent-wave conductor (of those days) could conduct. I stuck in some of my old piano cycle rhythm studies – 2–3–5–7–11–7–5–3–2 – etc. . . .[45]

Elsewhere in this passage, Ives subtitled the piece 'Studies in space, time, duration, accent, pulse'. Significantly, he does not mention pitch: despite some use of interval chords, and of two regular punctuating chords, this parameter is generally freely (though very chromatically) arranged. The piece has a rhapsodic form which falls into the sections shown in figure 2.19.

Figure 2.19. Structure of Ives' *In Re Con Moto Et Al* (W20)

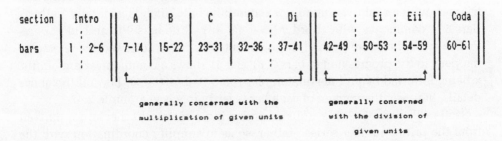

The introduction is in two parts. In the $\frac{10}{4}$ bar 1, each of the four strings has simple rhythms derived from compounded quavers (violin 1: quavers; violin 2: crotchets; viola: dotted crotchets; 'cello: minims) though violin 1 quickens in the final two beats. Harmonically (and to a lesser extent melodically) it is possible to detect quartal and quintal formations.

Bars 2–6 contain a series of interval chords; their durations are derived from the multiplication of a common quaver or semiquaver unit, by a series of prime numbers (11, 7, 5, 3; 2, 3, 5, 7). However, the series breaks down in bar 6, and a number of the interval chords are altered after their initial presentation (see example 2.46).

Example 2.46. Ives: *In Re Con Moto Et Al* (W20); bars 2–6 (in short score)*
© Copyright 1968 by Peer International Corporation. Used by permission.

Apart from the octave Cs shown here, the piano is silent until section B. Section A introduces the two main punctuating chords, here termed x and y, as well as a number of procedures followed elsewhere. The metres of A are formed by multiplying a common six-semiquaver unit by the prime number series. Here, though, the series is presented as Ives actually described it in *Memos* (2, 3, 5, 7, 11, 7, 5, 3) yielding bars of $\frac{6}{8}$, $\frac{9}{8}$, $\frac{15}{8}$, $\frac{21}{8}$, $\frac{33}{8}$, $\frac{21}{8}$, $\frac{15}{8}$ and $\frac{9}{8}$ respectively. The palindromic nature of the series and these metres is reflected in the music: bar 11 ($\frac{33}{8}$) acts as a fulcrum, bars 8/14, 9/13 and 10/12 being identical pairs (bar 7 has no equivalent). But as in earlier Ivesian palindromes the music *within* each bar is not reflected. Furthermore, the palindrome is disguised by the changed dynamic patterns of bars 12–14 and their initial tremolandi.

Bar 7 consists solely of chord x, which is constructed from alternate fifths and tritones, with an intervening minor second; its base pitch is generally 'cello C. Bars 8/14 commence with chord y (Eb–f–f#'–b') while bars 9/13 and 10/12 commence with the more normal arrangement of x being followed by y (as also happens in the progression of bars 7–8). Bar 11 shows a common variant of this, x being followed by an interversion of y (here B–eb'–f#'–f"). Beyond the above details, however, the content of each bar is fairly free: see example 2.47.

Section B (bars 15–22) is unusual in having a metrical scheme not derived from the prime number series. Rather, so as to simplify coordination with the piano, the metre of bars 15–21 is $\frac{4}{4}$ and that of bar 22 is $\frac{9}{8}$. However, 'durations' or 'spaces' – defined by appearances of x and y and derived from the prime number series – can still be discerned. Here the common unit is five semiquavers long, and is multiplied by 3, 5, 7 and 11 to produce cross-rhythms against the given metre. The second and fourth appearances of y are interverted in various ways; furthermore, successive 'spaces' show an increasing tendency towards

Example 2.47. Ives: *In Re Con Moto Et Al* (W20); bars 7–12*
© Copyright 1968 by Peer International Corporation. Used by permission.

polyphony and polyrhythm, the unusual rhythmic device of three quavers played in the time of five semiquavers being used. An additional feature here is the appearance of interval chords in bars 19–22.

The strings' section $\underline{C}$ (bars 23–31) is similar to $\underline{A}$, though the common unit is now only four semiquavers long and the prime number series arranged in reverse (i.e. 11, 7, 5, 3, 2, 3, 5, 7, 11) yielding metres of $\frac{11}{4}$, $\frac{7}{4}$, $\frac{5}{4}$, $\frac{3}{4}$, $\frac{2}{4}$, $\frac{3}{4}$, $\frac{5}{4}$, $\frac{7}{4}$ and $\frac{11}{4}$. Once again the music is arranged quasi-palindromically about the central $\frac{2}{4}$ bar (bar 27) though there are no internal retrogressions of material. Each initial $\underline{x}$ chord is given a specific length (bars 23/31: minim; 24/30: crotchet; 25/29: dotted quaver; 26/28: quaver) while each subsequent variant of $\underline{y}$ initiates increasingly polyphonic and polyrhythmic activity. The central bar 27 consists simply of $\underline{x}$ and (interverted) $\underline{y}$, each of crotchet length.

Under sections $\underline{B}$ and $\underline{C}$ the piano has a single stream of music, arranged differently. The right hand plays two chords, each five semiquavers long. The first (1) has the pitches b′ and b♭, and the second (2) b♭′ and a. Their order of presentation seems to be related to the prime number series (figure 2.20). (In section $\underline{B}$ the piano has the same metric pattern as the strings, but in section $\underline{C}$ it plays in $\frac{4}{4}$ throughout, and therefore holds a polymetric relationship with them.)

Figure 2.20. Structure of the right hand of the piano part, in sections B̲ and C̲ of Ives' *In Re Con Moto Et Al* (W20)

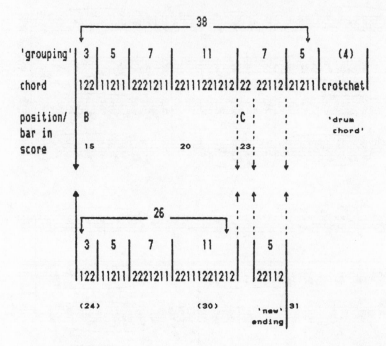

The piano's left hand also has an ostinato texture, but this is melodic rather than harmonic. In bars 15–(24) the pattern is four crotchets long, in bars (24–31) five; the change in length coincides with the right hand's 'drum chord'. The four-crotchet pattern consists of a sequentially-rising element (two 'rhythmicised' crotchets: D–Eb, D♯–E, etc.) and a static element (two crotchets: F–gb); in the five-crotchet pattern the sequential element falls in pitch (as a quasi-reflection) while the static element has a third beat added (two-pitch chord: G–ab). The final four crotchet beats of this pattern (under bar 31) present an accelerating descending chromatic scale to complete the quasi-reflection of the sequential element.

The combination of these various layers creates music of great rhythmic complexity (see example 2.48).

Section D̲/D̲i̲ is similar: the strings' metres in D̲ are derived from a three-semiquaver unit multiplied by 11, 7, 5, 3 and 2; and in D̲i̲ from a two-semiquaver unit multiplied by 2, 3, 5, 7 and 11. Thus the metric pattern of bars 32–41 is $\frac{33}{16}, \frac{21}{16}, \frac{15}{16}, \frac{9}{16}, \frac{6}{16}; \frac{2}{8}, \frac{3}{8}, \frac{5}{8}, \frac{7}{8}, \frac{11}{8}$. Chord x̲ and variants of chord y̲ open every bar, and there is some use of interval chords in the comparatively homorhythmic D̲. D̲i̲, though, tends more towards polyrhythm.

The piano's music in D̲ is unbarred, and in D̲i̲ is written in $\frac{4}{4}$ and $\frac{6}{4}$, creating polymetre with the strings. Under bars 32–39 the left hand (in octaves) has pairs of chromatically rising minor thirds, moving in regular crotchets; this process is reversed in bars 40–41.

Example 2.48. Ives: *In Re Con Moto Et Al* (W20); bars 24–25*
© Copyright 1968 by Peer International Corporation. Used by permission.

The right hand, meanwhile, starts with a rising chromatic scale, disguised by octave displacement and also moving in regular crotchets. The harmonic interval between the hands is either a major seventh or a minor ninth. After rising through all twelve pitches to b♭, a new pattern emerges. The scale is now regularly interrupted, as follows:

(b)–c′–g♯ – (d♭′)–(d′)–(b♭) – (e♭′)–e′–(c′) etc.

(Pitches in brackets are displaced by one or more octaves.) Rhythmically, this pattern alternates variants of two ideas, the first based on two dotted quavers plus quaver, the second on triplets. As in the left hand, there is a retrogression from bar 40 onwards, though some pitches are altered. The combination of strings and piano again creates very complex textures (example 2.49).

In sections <u>E</u>, <u>Ei</u> and <u>Eii</u> the relationship between the strings and the piano becomes even more tenuous. The process seen in sections <u>A</u>–<u>D</u>, by which the strings' metres (or 'spaces') were created through the multiplication of a given durational unit (6, 5, 4, 3, 2 semiquavers) by the prime number series, reaches its logical conclusion here. Both strings and piano have short sections whose durations are prime number compounds of a single semiquaver unit. This is seen in the first three bars of <u>E</u> (bars 42–(44)) in the piano. Once again the music

Example 2.49. Ives: *In Re Con Moto Et Al* (W20); bars 39–40*
© Copyright 1968 by Peer International Corporation. Used by permission.

is quasi-palindromic (see example 2.50). The main focus of attention here, however, is a new process: the rhythmic *division* of a given unit by the prime number series. The strings' basic semibreve unit is divided by 2, 3, 5 and 3. Note, however, that further subdivisions are made against these basic rhythms, and that from bar 44 the strings and piano are related polymetrically. In bars 42–44 x and (variants of) y are transposed, while in bar 45 y is replaced (rather surprisingly) by a C major chord.

During the remainder of E, the strings subdivide a minim unit (2, 3, 5, 7, 11, 7, 5, 3) (bars 46–49) and the piano a dotted minim unit (2, 3, 5, 7, 11, 7, 5) (against bars 45–49). The strings commence each subdivision with x and (variants of) y, the piano with three distinct chords (two in its initial bar); both layers are arranged quasi-palindromically, though the vertical relationship between them changes through realignment in the 'reflection'.

In Ei (bars 50–53) the piano's right hand subdivides a regular minim unit (2, 3, 5, 7, 11, 7, 5, 3). Its pitches are dictated by a six-note cyclic ostinato (c⁗–b″–b♭″–a′–b♭″–b″), an isorhythmic relationship being created between the two patterns. The left hand, meanwhile, alternates two crotchet-length chords (A♯–b; d♭–c′). Over this the strings' durations are prime number compounds of a single semiquaver unit (c.f. piano, bars 42–(44)), arranged quasi-palindromically. The two violins move in phrased semiquavers, but the viola and 'cello have held notes of the 'correct' length (2, 3, 5, etc., semiquavers). The pitch material of these held notes consists of transpositions of the lower parts of x. The pitches of violin 1 are derived from an extended intervallic series, featuring minor thirds and major seconds, which rises sequentially (and consequently falls in the 'reflection'). Its line is mirrored by violin 2, the starting interval between the two instruments being either a major seventh or a minor ninth.

Example 2.50. Ives: *In Re Con Moto Et Al* (W20); bars 42–45*
© Copyright 1968 by Peer International Corporation. Used by permission.

The strings' bar 53 is a polyrhythmic codetta which shows some pitch correspondences to the music of the preceding three bars.

In Eii the prime number compounds of the semiquaver unit are again played by the piano (bars 54–56). Its right-hand pitches are quasi-palindromically arranged and are derived from the same intervallic series as those of violin 1 in bars 50–52. But here each group starts on d″ and is matched by a two-pitch chord (c♯′–d♯′: c.f. piano-drumming). The left hand, like the viola and 'cello in bars 50–52, plays chords of the 'correct' length: these alternate low and high register, but are not arranged quasi-palindromically. Over this the strings divide a regular semibreve unit (2, 3, 5, 7, 11) in bars 54–58. Only bar 54, however, contains x and (interverted) y, though interval structuring is discernible both horizontally and vertically from bar 56 onwards. Furthermore, each bar contains polyrhythmic subdivisions of its basic units.

From the last beat of bar 56 to bar 58 the piano divides a regular crotchet unit (3, 5, 7, 11, 7, 5, 3, 5, 7). Its right-hand pitches are those of bars 54–56, but with the first pitch and chord alternating between the expected d‴–d♯″–c♯″ and an identical unit a semitone higher. The left-hand pitches are also arranged as a repeated intervallic series – which freely mirrors that of the right hand – plus octave Gs to complement the right-hand chords. Note, however, that the initial pitch of each left-hand group alternates between f and a; and that when the right hand has a subdivision of 3 its pitches are freely arrived at.

The relentless but independent structuring of strings and piano seen so far has created a massive amount of pent-up tension. The breaking point comes in bar 59 as the music bursts out of its prime-number straitjacket into an orgy of polyrhythm and polyphony. In bars 59–60 the piano accelerates through clusters to seemingly impossible chords and scales, while the strings climax in polyrhythmic glissandi, notated graphically. The final 'cadence' consists of a twelve-pitch chord and octave Bs, with x added *pp* as an afterthought (example 2.51).

In Re Con Moto Et Al is without doubt Ives' most organised small-scale work: both the degree of structuring found here, and the integral nature of that structuring (with its basis in a single palindromic series of prime numbers) are without musical precedent. The form of the work – with its 'double acceleration' through increasingly short compounded, then subdivided, units – is remarkable, as are the extremes of polyrhythm, chromaticism and dissonance it contains. Ives never again approached the almost claustrophobic complexity and intensity of *In Re Con Moto Et Al*. Yet its breadth of technical vision, and its questing, questioning experimentalism, are qualities which continue to animate later works, both large and small. Among these we might mention three large-scale songs – *Majority* (Z131) (1921), *On the Antipodes* (Z145) (1904; 1915–23) and *Aeschylus and Sophocles* (Z146) (1922); and the *Three Quarter-Tone Pieces* (X22) (1923–24) for two pianos. But finally, let us examine *Psalm 90* (Y40) (1894, rev. 1924) which in many ways summarises Ives' development and achievement as a composer of experimental music. It also encompasses a particularly wide spectrum of techniques and styles in its sectionalised – though essentially text-derived – form. Part of the reason for its musical diversity must, however, be its unusually long gestation period:

Example 2.51. Ives: *In Re Con Moto Et Al* (W20); bars 59–61*

© Copyright 1968 by Peer International Corporation. Used by permission.

There must have been two earlier versions, both now missing – one that his father knew, and one that he left. . .in. . .the Central Presbyterian Church when he resigned in 1902. . .he evidently started to reconstruct the 90th Psalm in 1923, but actually he recomposed it.[46]

Consequently the piece combines the freshness of youth with the maturity and vision of (comparative) old age – as well as benefitting from the practical insight of the organist-choirmaster.

As was mentioned above, the form of the piece is highly sectionalised, as is shown by the simplified formal figure 2.21. This patchwork arrangement is held together in two main ways: firstly, by the constant low C pedal of the organ (c.f. a number of earlier works) with its slow but regular minim pulse; and secondly, through the use of a number of recurrent harmonic/textural musical 'types'. Five are announced in the introduction, and given specific characters (see example 2.52).[47] Others grow out of these five, while a sixth appears only later.

Verse 1 commences with the chorus singing a diatonic melody in octaves: its natural speech rhythms syncopate against the regular minim pulse of the accompaniment. This, for organ, consists mainly of type 1 harmony, though its regular semibreve alternation of e and c′ is reminiscent of the progression from 1 to 2. This feeling is strengthened by the appearance of the a of type 2 in a descending line in bar 10, while bar 12 contains a specific progression from 1 to 2. However, this cadences onto a mixture of 2 and C major.

In bars 13–15, over the C pedal and to the words 'to another', the voices present three transpositions of chord 3, separated by similar chords. This whole sequence constitutes a distinct, recurrent idea, 3a. The progression in this first verse from 1 through 2 to 3a may suggest 'God's wrath against sin' both being eternal and developing 'from one generation to another'.

The chanted verse 2 is set mainly in variants of 2 (2a: quartal and quintal chords) while verse 3 commences with 3a. But the change of tempo and texture (to *Adagio* and solo tenor) reflect the words, set to a cadential figure (4a) based on augmented triads. Verse 4's accompaniment consists of two presentations of the four-chord sequence of 4, though with a cadence at the end of each into C major; the chorus sings in homorhythmic octaves, mainly on Gs.

Verse 5, however, is quite fragmented, and introduces a musical type (6) not encountered in the introduction. Its outward choral expansion by semitones from c′ recalls verse 1 of *Psalm 24*. It culminates in a compressed version of 3a and is followed by a new female melody over a variant of 4a. The voices now pair off: at first their music is in fourths and imitative (2b: bars 41–43), then in homorhythms (c.f. 2a). Imitation is momentarily restored at bar 44 with the arrival of verse 6, but this disintegrates into homorhythmic polyphony over the first two chords of 4. Bars 46–49 seem to recall 4a, under a dying melody for tenors and basses.

Much of verse 7 consists of type 3b (a variant of the progression of 3a). But it is opened by music similar to 2a and 2b, underpinned by 'gongs, irons or bells' which support the organ's minim pedal Cs, and is closed by a sentimental

section	[Intro]	: [A]			: [B]			: [Ci]				: [Cii]			: [D]				
verse		1	2	3		4	5	6	7	8	9	10	11	12	13	14	15	16	17
bars	1 – 5	6 – 15	16–20	21–23	24–25	26–34	35–43	44–49	50–54	55–59	60–65	66–75	76–79	80–87	88–92	93–98	99–104	105–110	111–133
type of music	1 2 3 / 4 5	1 2 ; 3a	2 2a	3a	4a	4	6 3a / 4a 2b	4 4b	(2b) 3b		6a	2a	3c	6b	(4)	(1 2) / 5			
tempo	Freely	Largo			Adagio			:				: Tempo 1			:				

Figure 2.21. Generalised structure of Ives' *Psalm 90* (Y40)

Example 2.52. Ives: *Psalm 90* (Y40); bars 1–5
© 1960 Merion Music, Inc. Used by permission of the publisher.

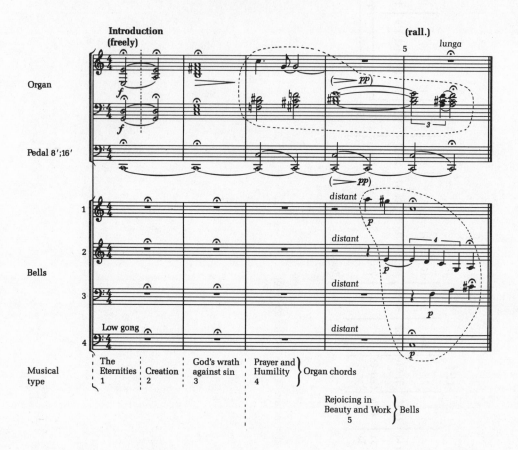

cadence which seems to pre-echo bars 118–120. Verse 8, in contrast, resembles little else in the piece: both organ and basses have descending melodies, followed by a rising chordal figure which cadences onto a chord of G11 (though underpinned by the ever-present C pedal).

This serves as a preparation for the unison c′ opening of verse 9. From here the chorus pans out by whole-tones (6a) reaching a massive twenty-pitch whole-tone cluster at the end of bar 62. This also has two dissonant outer pitches – g″ and E♯. The durations of the chords leading to this cluster are arranged in a decreasing arithmetic series, written out by Ives in the manuscript. Furthermore, the whole process is retrograded in bars 63–65, giving the verse a palindromic shape (example 2.53). Ives ignores here the musical implications of the text: its mention of 'God's wrath' suggests that a progression based on 3 would be appropriate. Instead, the wedge-shaped expansion of texture recalls bars 35–36 of the present work (6), and verse 2 of *Psalm 24*; the massed seconds of the central climactic chord further remind us of bars 150–152 of *Psalm 25*, and the use of palindrome of many other works.

Example 2.53. Ives: *Psalm 90* (Y40); bars 60–65

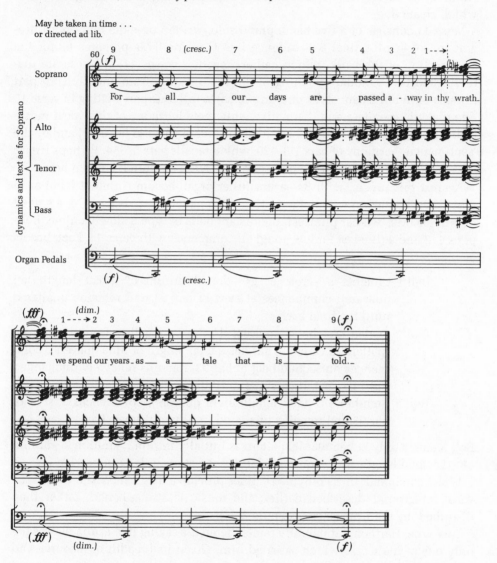

The opening of verse 10, with its chanting and interval chords, recalls verse 2 (bars 16–18), as does the return to Tempo 1. But the organ part here develops the basic harmonic idea of <u>2</u>, as a sequence of fifths gradually rises away from the pedal C. This texture reappears in the final sections of the work.

The vocal chanting is temporarily interrupted by the free polyphony of bars 71–75 – with its pictorialism at 'we fly away' – but resumes in verse 11. Here the main chanting pitch rises from f'/f to g♯'/g♯, though the words 'pow'r', 'anger', 'fear' and 'wrath' are all set to rising <u>3</u> chords. Verse 12 is again palindromic: the triadic harmony moves downwards by whole-tone steps (minor chords of c, b♭, a♭, g♭, e, d and c) before climbing back up again. It reminds us of verses

13–14 of *Psalm 135* and the organ part of the second *Harvest Home Chorale*. However, its harmonic shape is disguised by the rising, then falling, melodies which create it.

Verse 13 consists of a five-bar soprano solo, written over the four-chord progression of 4, plus final 6–5 cadence into C major. This prepares us for the final section of the work, which gathers together verses 14–17. These are distinguished by a gradual widening of the vocal texture from one (unison) part in verse 14 (reminiscent of the opening verse) to full four-part writing in verse 17. The diatonic evenness and distinctive white-note harmony of this vocal music is disturbed only twice – by a 3 chord at the end of verse 15 (at 'evil') and by the 'sentimental' harmony of bars 118–120, which recalls bars 53–54. Perhaps Ives is unconsciously remembering a phrase from a hymn or church anthem here.

Against this music, with its earlier fuller organ accompaniment (similar to that in bars 66–69 but with the repeating fifths pattern c–g, d–a, e–b, d–a spread in minims over two-bar phrases), the distant bells of type 5 slowly chime. Bell-parts 1, 2 and 4 (the last for low gong) all commence with verse 14. Each has its own pattern:

> Bell 1 Crotchet a″–crotchet g♯″–dotted minim c″ (total length ten quavers); commences at start of bar 93 and remains unaltered until the final bar.
>
> Bell 2 Dotted crotchet e′–quavers d′–c′–g–a, together lasting a minim (pattern is variable, but has a total length of nine quavers); commences on second beat of bar 93, remains relatively unchanged until bar 125, then slows until the end.
>
> Bell 4 Semibreve c (total length eight quavers); commences at start of bar 93 and remains unaltered until penultimate bar.

Bell 3 enters only at bar 103: its pattern is initially minim f′–minim a′–minim c♯″ (i.e. total length twelve quavers) but it soon starts to lengthen.

When combined, these polymetric lines provide a magical background to the vocal foreground described earlier; the music is strengthened, rather than disturbed, by their presence (example 2.54).

Ives' wife, Harmony, apparently remembered his saying that *Psalm 90* was the only one of his works which satisfied him. Given its breadth of resource and style this is understandable: certainly it contains much that is best in Ives, and in various ways recalls music of his both old and new, conventional and experimental. One hears the resonance in this piece of early psalms and late songs, wild chamber music and transcendental orchestral works, acceptable diatonicism and unacceptable chromaticism.

But if this view of *Psalm 90* is correct, what were Ives' feelings towards his other works, particularly those featuring the most extreme experimentation? Verses 5 and 6 of *Majority* (Y37/Z131) (1914–15/1921) are omitted from all its available versions, both published and recorded. According to the *Temporary Mimeographed Catalogue* of Ives' works, the music of these verses was highly structured rhythmically, and totally chromatic in melody and harmony: 'The

Example 2.54. Ives: *Psalm 90* (Y40); bars 121–133
© 1960 Merion Music, Inc. Used by permission of the publisher.

plan of this in orches [*sic*] parts is to have each in different rythm [*sic*] group
complete the 12 notes (each on a different system & end & hold last (of 12). . .
as finding its star'.[48] This description is suggestive of the kinds of structuring
found in a variety of works, including *From the Steeples and the Mountains*, the
Three-Page Sonata, *All the Way Around and Back*, *Over the Pavements*, *Central
Park in the Dark*, *Soliloquy*, *The Gong on the Hook and Ladder*, *Tone Roads
Nos. 1* and *3*, *Vote for Names*, *In Re Con Moto Et Al* and, ultimately, the pro-
jected *Universe Symphony* (V43) (1911–28).[49] However, the sketches of verses 5
and 6 of *Majority* also contain remarks – surrounding the above description –
which seem to utterly condemn the processes used there:

something made in this calculated, diagram, design way may have a place in music, if it
is primarily to carry out an idea, or part of a program. . .but generally or too much or
alone as such it is a weak substitute for inspiration or music. It's too easy, any high-
school student (unmusical) with a pad, pencil, compass & logth table and a mild
knowledge of sounds, & instruments (blown or hit) could do it. It's an artificial process
without strength though it may sound busy & noisy. This wall paper design music is not
as big as a natural mushy ballad.[50]

Elsewhere, though, Ives passed a more qualified and considered judgement
on some of his extreme ideas and works:

Right or wrong, things like these – some hardly more than memos in notes – show how
one's mind works. The only value probably of some of these things was that, in working
these sound-pictures out (or trying to), it gave the ears plenty of new sound experiences
– it strengthened the ear muscles, and opened up things naturally that later were used
naturally and spontaneously – that is, without thinking of it as 'this chord' or 'this way'
– good bad, or nice! But some of these things I did take more seriously when they were
written, and so copied [them] out and had [them] played.[51]

Ives' mention in this paragraph of 'working these sound-pictures out' is significant. For, as we have seen, the majority of his musical experiments were based
in a desire to fix in music an experience of reality. Among these experiences
were the excited singing at a camp meeting, the accidental polyphony of a barn
dance, the baseball player caught out by a foul ball, and the sounds reaching the
ears of a night-time visitor to Central Park. As a consequence of this approach,
Ives' experimentation is generally unsystematic, both within individual works
and between successive works (though an exception might be made for the
series of experiments in accelerating and static musical layers, etc., of 1906).
Nor, overall, do his experiments follow any ordered theoretical or abstract path.
Rather, they were improvised, literally made up as he went along, so that the
experience or idea of the moment might best be encapsulated in his music:
'many of those things were started as kinds [of] studies, or rather trying out
sounds, beats, etc., usually by what is called politely "improvisation on the
keyboard" '.[52] The legacy of this unorthodox approach to composition is music
of genius.

3 'On Dissonant Counterpoint'

The development of a new polyphony, primarily by Charles Seeger (1886–1979), Carl Ruggles (1876–1971) and Ruth Crawford (1901–53)

The conventional thus became a thing to be avoided. . .
Charles Seeger, 'On Dissonant Counterpoint'

Ironically, by the time that Ives' improvised experimentalism was becoming better known – initially through the circulation of the *Concord Sonata* and *114 Songs* in the early 1920s – a new, more systematic experimentalism was already coming to the fore. The key figure in its development and dissemination was Charles Louis Seeger. Seeger is nowadays remembered principally as an ethnomusicologist, but in the years before the Second World War he was known also as a composer, teacher, critic and government administrator. Seeger was chairman of the Music Department at the University of California at Berkeley from 1912 to 1919. He later lectured in New York at the Institute of Musical Art (1921–33) and the New School for Social Research (1931–35). His most prominent critical work was written for the New York *Daily Worker* under the pseudonym Carl Sand. From 1935 to 1938 Seeger served as Music Technical Adviser in Roosevelt's Resettlement Administration, from 1938 to 1941 as Deputy Director of the Federal Music Project of the Works Progress Administration and from 1941 to 1953 as Chief of the Music Division of the Pan American Union.[1]

Such was the regard in which he was held in the late 1920s and early 1930s that Henry Cowell could write of him:

Charles Seeger is the greatest musical explorer in intellectual fields which America has produced, the greatest experimental musicologist. Ever fascinated by intricacies, he has solved more problems of modern musical theory, and suggested more fruitful pathways for musical composition (some of which have proved of great general import), than any other three men.[2]

Cowell had studied with Seeger at Berkeley between approximately the autumn of 1914 and February of 1918[3] and had remained a close friend during the intervening years. His estimation of Seeger's importance was thus based on a particularly full knowledge of the man and his ideas.

For Seeger, music had to come from both the head and the heart if it was to succeed. Yet, paradoxically, while Seeger found little emotion in Ives' works, his own ideas on composition were far more scholastic in approach than Ives' had ever been. Apart from personal opinions expressed in articles on other composers (see, for instance, Seeger's contributions to Cowell's *American Composers on American Music*) and an early book on elementary composition, the only major published account[4] of Seeger's ideas is the article 'On Dissonant Counterpoint'. Although this article appeared only in June 1930 (in volume 7 of the periodical *Modern Music*) it was based on an interlinked series of compositional principles which Seeger had been developing since about 1914 or 1915, initially in connection with his teaching of Henry Cowell.[5] To quote Seeger himself:

Dissonant counterpoint was at first purely a school-room discipline – a link between the preparatory studies in harmony, counterpoint, canon and fugue of a regular composition course and the 'free' composition of the second decade of the twentieth century. . .It was based upon the perception of a difference, sincerely felt but also logically postulated, between consonance and dissonance. . .The essential departure was the establishment of dissonance, rather than consonance, as the rule. . .by definition the procedure was on the whole one of negation and contrariness.[6]

Seeger felt that European forms of tonally dissonant composition (he particularly mentions Skryabin and Schoenberg) were 'an elaboration and extension of the old diatonic and chromatic harmony rather than a revolutionary reversal of it' and that

The chief fault of the Schönberg school, as of all the others, seemed to lie not in the handling of dissonance, but of consonance. All went well as long as a thoroughly dissonant structure was maintained, but upon the first introduction of consonance, a feeling of disappointment, of defeat, frequently occurred. It was as if there were holes in the fabric.

In an attempt to alleviate this feeling, 'the conventional. . .became a thing to be avoided' and dissonant counterpoint was born.

Initially, the old rhythmic species were retained; in matters of pitch the octave, fifth, fourth, thirds and sixths were held to be consonant, and the tritone, seconds, sevenths and ninths dissonant. The novelty lay in the principle that dissonance rather than consonance was established as the norm. Thus in First species counterpoint (example 3.1) no consonance between the two

Example 3.1. First species dissonant counterpoint*

† The consonance is counteracted by the subsequent melodic dissonance.
* An asterisk following the caption indicates that accidentals apply only to those pitches they immediately precede.

parts was allowed; additionally, the melodies themselves consisted in the main of dissonant intervals. If any consonant melodic intervals *were* used, they were immediately dissonated (i.e. counteracted by the introduction of a pitch related dissonantly to one of the 'consonant' pitches).[7] In other species consonances had to be prepared and resolved by dissonances, preferably by leaping rather than stepwise motion (example 3.2). Apart from these purely intervallic con-

Example 3.2. Second species dissonant counterpoint (with an intrusion of fourth species)*

† The harmonic consonance is prepared by a leap to a dissonance, and resolved by a leap to a dissonant pitch which *also* counteracts both components of the previous consonant melodic interval.

siderations, it was also felt that the melodic repetition of any pitch (or the sounding of its octave) was unsatisfactory unless the two appearances were separated by at least five other pitches. In practice this often meant that there would be eight or more intervening pitches, resulting in the creation of a densely chromatic line. The only exceptions to this were the use of a pivotal tone and the occasional appearance of reiterated (or rhythmicised) single pitches, though Seeger criticised the clichéd use of the latter.

Difficulties accumulated, however, in direct relation to the number of voices employed; consistent application of the rules led to an increased dependence on homophonic rather than polyphonic textures. The solution to this problem came with the realisation that rhythm, as well as pitch, needed to be treated in a consistently dissonant way, both horizontally and vertically. Indeed, Seeger felt that the ability to rhythmically 'dissonate' a single melodic line was an essential prerequisite to the successful writing of dissonant counterpoint and identified a number of practices through which this ideal might be realised. These included successive (horizontal) rhythmic dissonation of a single line, simultaneous (vertical) rhythmic dissonation between lines, and also what he termed three species of dissonant counterpoint.[8] Thus rhythmically, as well as intervallically, the successive appearance of identical formulations was discouraged – regularity of pitch, interval or rhythm weakened the required dissonant effect.

Having described the development of the essential principles of dissonant counterpoint, let us now examine their dissemination and growth in finished compositions. In his 1932 article Cowell wrote:

While Seeger has worked out some of his findings himself, his greatest importance lies in his subtle influence in suggesting to others both a new musical point of view and specific usages in composition.[9]

Although the biographical section in Cowell's book (on page 215) includes reference to a number of works by Seeger, it fails to explain that most of them were destroyed in the Berkeley fire of 1926. However, it does mention a series of *Studies in Single, Unaccompanied Melody and in Two-line Dissonant Counterpoint* written between 1915 and 1932. Although the fate of these studies is not known, what would seem to be two of them – *Psalm 137* (1923) and *The Letter* (1931) – were published in *New Music* in 1954.[10]

From an examination of *Psalm 137* it is obvious that – the demands of sympathetic text setting notwithstanding – the techniques of dissonant counterpoint were fairly well advanced by 1923. Rhythmically, the piece proceeds almost exclusively through the irregular subdivision of regular metrical units, a practice clearly defined in Seeger's article. This is demonstrated in the opening verse (example 3.3). Even when a pitch is repeated the rhythm generally

Example 3.3. Seeger: *Psalm 137*; bars 1–8
© 1958 Theodore Presser Company. Used by permission of the publisher.

dissonates the line, as is the case at the opening of verse 6. However, there are exceptions to this consistency of rhythmic dissonation. Verse 4, for instance, has a predominantly triplet feel, while at the join between verses 8 and 9 the quaver and its multiples are used almost exclusively over a seven-bar period. Furthermore, there are very few ties both across and within the bar, leading to a stronger feeling of regular pulse than might be expected.

Intervallically *Psalm 137* is not exceptionally well dissonated, as an examination of example 3.3 shows. Both the relatively large number of thirds and sixths and the relatively small number of major seconds/minor sevenths are important factors here. Note how, though, in the opening phrase Seeger follows most beautifully his rules for the preparation and resolution of consonance. The rule of non-repetition of pitches is also applied less than strictly: for although the use of reiterated pitches was covered by Seeger in 'On Dissonant Counterpoint', in the present work it does become something of a mannerism. Additionally, there are many instances of pitches being repeated before six or more other pitches have intervened. These 'holes in the fabric' cannot be explained completely by either of the following of Seeger's statements:

The present writer feels that the repetition [of a given tone] can be made, provided it is skilfully done, at rare instances as soon as the fourth progression, though normally it can only be done easily at the sixth or seventh.[11]

. . .one may recommend. . .the alloting of a flat and a sharp to each of the seven tones A, B, C, D, E, F, G, theoretically [giving] a twenty-one tone scale. With even a little composition 'away from the piano', differences such as that between the augmented octave and the minor ninth grow upon one.[12]

Perhaps the major factor influencing Seeger's choice of pitches and rhythms is, therefore, the need for effective (and affective) word setting in combination with an overall sense of melodic flow. Certainly, the most cursory examination of the rhythms shows that in general Seeger follows the natural stresses of the spoken text rather than any more abstract considerations. In the matter of pitch, too, he shows a remarkably musical attention to detail, as for instance in his setting of the words 'we wept' (example 3.3) and elsewhere in his perhaps symbolic use of both chanted pitches (verses 3–4, and 5–6) and large intervals (verses 7, 8 and 9).

The requirements of sympathetic (and accurate) text setting would also seem to have been of prime importance to Seeger in *The Letter*, written some eight years later. One is again surprised by the freedom with which the rules of dissonant counterpoint are applied, especially given that this piece was written only one year after 'On Dissonant Counterpoint'. As in *Psalm 137* there is a surprisingly large number of reiterated pitches; additionally, there are many occurrences of repetitions of pitches before the appearance of five or more intervening pitches. Both of these points are illustrated in the opening bars (example 3.4). Note that while the use of a reiterated pitch may separate two

Example 3.4. Seeger: *The Letter* (first version); bars 1–3
© 1958 Theodore Presser Company. Used by permission of the publisher.

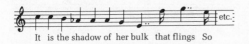

appearances of a repeated pitch by a substantial distance in *time*, this situation does not necessarily excuse the reappearance of a pitch before five or more other pitches have intervened – see for instance the Gs of bars 1 and 2, which are separated by only four intervening pitches. The use of reiterated pitches has two other main consequences. Firstly, certain pitches come to be stressed more than others, leading to the establishment of two specific pitch centres for the piece – c' and e'. Secondly, as the unison was considered by Seeger to be a particularly consonant interval, the otherwise well dissonated intervallic content of this piece becomes somewhat compromised. Although there are some (intervallically) very dissonant passages, the norm is of dissonance being tempered to a greater or lesser extent by the consonance of reiteration.

Any discussion of the rhythm and structure of this song is complicated by the fact that it was published in two alternative versions, the second of which is rather more complex than the first (c.f. the strophic aria 'Possente spirto' in Monteverdi's *Orfeo*). Seeger probably saw the simpler version as being a kind of pitch blueprint which would be brought to life only by a (rhythmically) rubato performance. Evidence for this is found in the tempo marking – *Tranquillo, quasi sotto voce e rubato* (crotchet = 60–90) – the comparative rhythmic simplicity of the first version, and the following note to the second version: 'One possible rendition of the song, with or without a soft, toneless, unaccented, beat'. The difference between the versions is clear if one compares example 3.4 with the corresponding passage from the second version (example 3.5). The first version's simple crotchets, disturbed only by occasional triplets or dottings, have been replaced by a complex dissonated relationship between the sung line and its implied accompaniment: four against three, three against two and syncopation now become the norm. Even here, though, the choice of rhythms is partially restricted by the composer's desire to match the natural stresses of the spoken text. Consequently the rules are again compromised and the degree of successive rhythmic dissonance is at times less than might be expected: see, for instance, the repeated triplets of bars 1–2, and the quadruplets and dotted patterns of bar 3 in example 3.5.

Example 3.5. Seeger: *The Letter* (second version); bars 1–3
© 1958 Theodore Presser Company. Used by permission of the publisher.

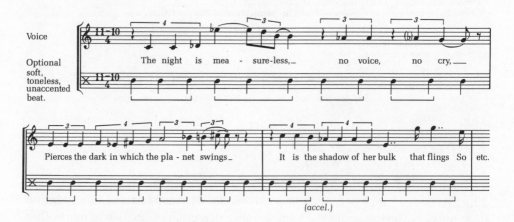

Structurally, the song – at least in its second version – would appear to be an example of another technique (probably) invented by Seeger: phrase balancing.[13] The purpose of this technique is to structure the form of a monody (or other work) through the careful proportioning of its phrases. Thus the four sections of the second version of *The Letter* – defined by double bar-lines and changes of tempo – are divided into phrases as shown in figure 3.1. This struc-

Figure 3.1. Phrase structuring of Seeger's *The Letter*

(crotchet = 60-90)   (each phrase equals one bar in the score)

1	2	3 Poco più mosso (crotchet = 72)	4 Meno mosso (crotchet = 69)
phrases, in crotchets 11 + 10 + 10 + 11	11 + 10 + 10 + 11	11 + 10 + 10	10 + 10 + 11

bar	1	2	3	4	5	6	7	8	9	10	11	12	13	14

turing is highlighted – for singer, listener and score-reader – in a number of ways:

1 through each section being allocated a single page in the printed score;
2 through each phrase (bar) being allocated a separate system in the printed score;
3 through the physical lengths of these systems being directly proportional to their metrical (phrase) lengths;
4 through the use of punctuating rests, particularly at the ends of sections;
5 through the almost tonal use of the pitch centres (c' and e' plus their octave transpositions) mentioned earlier, these being reinforced through their preparation via quasi-cadential melodic formulae (example 3.6).

Example 3.6. Seeger: *The Letter*; abstraction from second version, showing pitch centres and cadential writing [*Note*: 1 system: = 1 section of original; 1 bar = 1 phrase (bar) of original.]

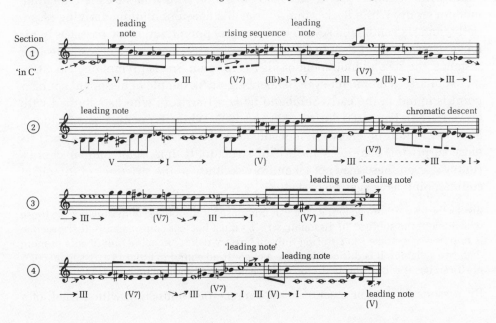

Although phrase balancing is not mentioned specifically in 'On Dissonant Counterpoint' it would seem to be one answer to the need recognised by Seeger for organic structure within dissonant compositions:

Only the shorter compositions have pronounced good form. Diffuseness of inner organisation in modern music, where a maximum of material is spread over a minimum time, contrasts unfavorably with the music of Bach and Beethoven. . .We need to give special attention to the question of organic structure, for without it the dissonant texture is made far more difficult to sustain. Tonal and rhythmic centricity, though of a different kind from that in the old music, must be established and maintained, if compositions of more than a few minutes' duration are to be made.[14]

The lack of further published examples of Seeger's own practical realisations of his theories is regrettable. Fortunately, however, many of his ideas were taken up and developed more fully by his friends and pupils, in ways as diverse as the characters of the composers themselves. Indeed, so individual, radical and wide-ranging was the reaction of Henry Cowell – Seeger's earliest successful protégé – that it will be discussed separately in chapter 4. However, Seeger's influence was felt also by those less directly connected with him, as was suggested by Cowell: 'most of those who use his ideas do not know his name and believe themselves to have originated the ideas'.[15] An obvious example of this 'subtle influence' would be Cowell's own work as a teacher and new music entrepreneur in the 1920s and 1930s, through which two composers as different in outlook as John J. Becker (1886–1961) and Lou Harrison (1917–   ) were introduced to the disciplines of dissonant counterpoint.[16]

Becker spent most of his adult life in the mid-west of America, primarily as a teacher and administrator.[17] Following a chance encounter with Cowell in 1927, a lively correspondence ensued between the two composers in which many ideas were exchanged. By November 1929 the formerly conservative Becker could write to Cowell that he was ready to march with what he called the ultra-modern group. While Becker himself saw his new-found idiom deriving essentially from sixteenth- and seventeenth-century polyphony, many passages in his music show an overt debt to the principles of dissonant counterpoint: see, for instance, the second movement of his *Symphonia Brevis* (Symphony No. 3).

A similarly Teutonic (or even Schoenbergian?) example of dissonant counterpoint is found in the early *Saraband* by Lou Harrison, who had studied with Cowell in San Francisco during 1934 and 1935. While its opening bars include a high proportion of intervallic consonances (both horizontal and vertical) its most surprising feature is its use of structurally important bitonal chords. However, even these may not be entirely contrary to the strictures of dissonant counterpoint, as Seeger suggested:

Just as the greatest music of the past was composed without fear of dissonance, so those who attempt the sublime in dissonant writing must not fear consonance. Otherwise one is hopelessly restricted to painting only in tertiary colors, to using only words of more than two syllables. It is difficult to make a major triad sound in order in a dissonant composition, but if it is properly dissonated it is not only possible but good.[18]

By 'dissonated' Seeger meant the appearance in conjunction with a triad, of a pitch (or pitches) holding a dissonant relationship with one or more of the triadic components – for instance, triads of C and G can both be dissonated by an F♯, particularly if it appears in the bass. However, it is also possible that Harrison's use here of bitonal chords might be related to Cowell's concept of polyharmony, which is discussed in chapter 4.

The companion piece to this *Saraband* – a *Prelude for Grandpiano* – is quite different in style. A number of the ideas it employs show a strong debt to its dedicatee, Cowell. But the running semiquavers (in octaves) which open and subsequently punctuate it resemble much more clearly the dissonated lines proposed by Seeger, as well as recalling a particularly fine extended example of such a line: the *Piano Study in Mixed Accents*, by Ruth Crawford, which had been published in *New Music* in October 1932. The majority of the intervals in Harrison's line are dissonant, while those consonances which do appear are generally prepared and resolved correctly. And on no occasion are there more than two consonances in succession.

Elsewhere, however, Harrison disregards the 'rules' by writing descending chromatic lines which rather conflict with Seeger's statement that 'not more than two consonant or three dissonant intervals of the same kind can occur in succession with dissonant effect'.[19]

A rather more personal and sustained development of Seeger's ideas is found in the music of Carl Ruggles (1876–1971). The two composers probably met in 1920, Cowell again providing the initial contact: 'Henry Cowell came over to Grantwood and brought Charles Seeger who saw me working on *Angels* and said "There – that's the way music should be!"'[20] A mutual musical respect soon developed between them which later blossomed into a lifelong friendship: Seeger dedicated *Psalm 137* 'To C.R.', wrote the chapter on Ruggles for *American Composers on American Music* (1932), and in 1972 (following Ruggles' death) contributed an 'In Memoriam' to *Perspectives of New Music*. Likewise, Ruggles dedicated both versions of *Angels* (1921; 1938) to Seeger.

Only one published work – the tiny song *Toys* (May 1919)[21] – predates Ruggles' meeting with Seeger. Its language is already dissonant, but this dissonance derives from a conscious spicing of traditional tonal harmony and an acute ear for musical imagery. Indeed, much of the dissonance is created through the simple device of shadowing the (piano or vocal) melody at the distance of a seventh. But in the first version[22] of *Angels* (written in 1921 for the unusual combination of six trumpets) we can already see Seeger's influence coming through most notably in the voice-leading, in the clearly dissonant relationship between treble and bass, and in the way that both of these parts – as well as the subsidiary middle line – are shadowed quite consistently by secondary parts, often at the third or sixth (example 3.7).

The song cycle *Vox Clamans in Deserto* (1923) and the orchestral triptych *Men and Mountains* (first version – 1924) are both significant steps along the musical path which in 1925 led to the full maturity of Ruggles' dissonant style in *Portals*, for string ensemble.[23] Here, the striving lyricism of Ruggles' earlier music is tempered by a quite strict adherence to the principles of dissonant counter-

Example 3.7. Ruggles: *Angels*; bars 1–8, renotated*
© 1960 American Music Edition. Used by permission of the publisher.

point. Again there is a basic distinction in the musical fabric between melody, subsidiary melody and bass, each of these lines being fairly consistently shadowed at the third/sixth or – more usually in the outer parts – seventh.

Portals is cast in two roughly equal parts, framed by introduction and coda. The unison opening is a fine example of the mature Ruggles melody, well dissonated in terms of pitch, slightly less so in interval and rhythm. Its arched shape is typical. Indeed, the wave-like accretion of such melodic shapes is the principal building block in many of Ruggles' formal schemes. Thus, the first of *Portals'* two main sections can be further divided into six sub-sections, in each of which the principal melody or melodies grows organically (or prosaically). These sub-sections are further defined by changes in tempo (example 3.8). Note particularly in the example the dissonant relationship established rhythmically and intervallically between melody and bass, as well as the shadowing of the principal parts mentioned earlier. The major result of this kind of writing is that a complex web of interrelated dissonances is built up; the harmony shows a high degree of asperity and at no time do we perceive the 'holes in the fabric' which so troubled Seeger.

However, *Portals* contains relatively little imitative polyphony, either free or strict: this is compensated for in Ruggles' subsequent works, most notably the orchestral piece *Sun-treader* (1926–31) and the piano collection *Evocations* (1934–43; revised 1954). In all of these works, except the *Evocation* dedicated to

Example 3.8. Ruggles: *Portals*; abstraction of bars 6–13* (sub-sections A and opening of B)
© 1930 American Music Edition. Used by permission of the publisher Theodore Presser Company.

Principal melodies

Subsidiary melodies

(Subsidiary) basses

Principal basses
[where marked as such in score]

his wife Charlotte,[24] Ruggles makes use of the quasi-ternary form of *Angels*. In *Sun-treader*, this is vastly expanded into a kind of sonata, whose development section makes substantial use of canonic techniques. After the initial reworking of the main subject (bars 42–49) the music proceeds as shown in figure 3.2. The simplest version of the canon comes last (bars 138a–148), three strict entries following each other at a bar's distance and the interval of a major second above. Each entry is accompanied (or shadowed) by a second part whose imitations are free after their initial bar (example 3.9). (Note that only the initial instrumentation of each line is given, that the violins and violas are divided, and that the canon is partly concealed by unrelated instrumental parts.)

The pitches and intervals of each entry are well dissonated, but the rhythms (especially after bar 141) less so. A number of details of pitch and rhythm differ

Figure 3.2. Structure of bars 51–168 of Ruggles' *Sun-treader*

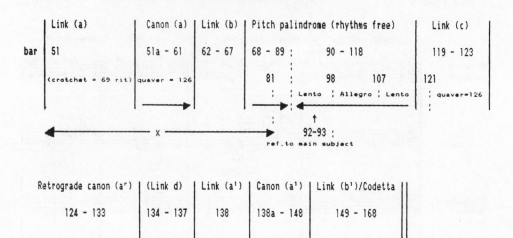

Example 3.9. Ruggles: *Sun-treader*; abstraction of bars 139–148*
© 1954 Theodore Presser Company. Used by permission of the publisher.

Example 3.9. (*cont.*)

in both the original version of the canon (bars 52–61) and its retrograde (final beat of bar 124–bar 133); and on each occasion the canon is both reorchestrated and dovetailed into the surrounding music.

The large-scale pitch palindrome which reflects about bars 89–90 is less obvious to the score-reader or listener, especially on those occasions where the notation of the initial and reflected presentations of the pitches is substantially different (compare, for instance, bar 80 with bars 100–103). Generally it is only the pitches of the principal melodies which are reflected, though other lines may also reappear (e.g. the double bass line at bars 79–82/98–105; and the trumpet line at bars 73–74/110–111).

As with the canon, this palindrome is dovetailed into the surrounding music. Thus its opening (bars 68–71) does not reappear in the reflection; rather, a closing phrase based on the pitches of bars 71–73 appears in three variants at bars 111–112, 113–114 and 115–116. Bars 117–118 continue this process of evaporation; following the caesura and pause, a short link leads to the retrograded canon.

The centre of the palindrome (fourth quaver of bar 88 to fifth quaver of bar 91, inclusive) consists of three short, non-retrograded, and interlocking phrases which, in the manner just described, virtually extinguish the line through their repetition. This evaporation – together with the quasi-recapitulation of the principal subject's timpani strokes at bars 92–93, and the *Allegro* interlude of bars 98–106 – helps to disguise the second half of the palindrome. This ensures that musical coherence does not become equated with simple repetition. Indeed, so cleverly does Ruggles conceal the technical devices described above that an 'emotional' analysis of the development section, based on the rise and fall of its melodic arcs, comes out quite differently.[25]

Elsewhere in *Sun-treader* the 'rules' of dissonant counterpoint apply as far as Ruggles lets them. The openings of both the principal and secondary subjects show good dissonation of pitch and interval, but again a less consistent dissonation of rhythm (see example 3.10) though more dissonant rhythmic lines occur

Example 3.10. Ruggles: *Sun-treader*; abstracted openings of principal and secondary subjects (bars 1–4; 44–45)*

© 1954 Theodore Presser Company. Used by permission of the publisher.

later in the piece, for instance at bars 61–66 and 74–78. The harmony of the work – whether resulting from homophonic or polyphonic textures – is characteristically dissonant throughout.

In *Sun-treader* Ruggles most successfully resolves a number of points raised by Seeger in 'On Dissonant Counterpoint'. He shows firstly that it is possible to build a large formal structure without reference to tonality; and while this form is based on an existing prototype, Ruggles adapts it to the demands of a dissonant texture. Seeger had spoken of the need for organic structure; here the exposition and recapitulation are surprisingly short in comparison to the development, as the emphasis is on the growth of the material rather than its fragmentation and/or traditional development. It is interesting to note, incidentally, that the work's striking opening melody is subjected to extensive (and extended) transformation only in the coda (bars 221–241): up to that point its appearances have been effectively limited by its purely functional rôle as a structural landmark. (It introduces each of the four main sections – exposition (bars 1–4), development (bars 42–45), recapitulation (bars 169–172) and the coda itself (bars 221–224). It also makes a partial appearance near the point of reflection in the development's pitch palindrome (bars 92–93), as mentioned earlier.)

However, the potential proliferation of materials engendered by adherence to processes of melodic growth is checked by Ruggles' use of imitative devices both strict (e.g. the three varied appearances of the canon) and free (e.g. the pitch palindrome). Aided by these devices Ruggles approaches in this work Seeger's ideals of economy of melodic resource, and of tonal and rhythmic centricity: a minimum of material is made to cover a maximum time.

Almost all of the above points relating to *Sun-treader* can also be applied to the first three *Evocations*,[26] though with the *caveat* that fifteen years had by now passed since Ruggles' initial introduction to the disciplines of dissonant counterpoint. His consequent familiarity with these techniques is reflected in the flexibility with which he uses them.[27] Thus in the short *Evocation 1* ('to Harriette Miller') the degrees of intervallic and successive rhythmic dissonance are not particularly high. Much of the harmonic content both here and in the more consonant *Evocation 3* ('to Charles Ives') is obtained through a technique first used at the opening of *Sun-treader*: some, or all, of the melodic pitches are sustained to create chords.

Evocation 2 ('to John Kirkpatrick') is quite different, showing a high degree of dissonance of both pitch and interval. The principle of non-repetition of tones is extended to such a point that in the introduction (bars 1–7) the melody virtually consists of three statements of a twelve-note set (example 3.11). During this

Example 3.11. Ruggles: *Evocation 2*; bars 1–7*
© 1945 & 1956 American Music Editions. Used by permission of the publisher Theodore Presser Company.

phrase the norms are of major intervallic dissonance, and of a minimum of nine intervening pitches before any pitch is repeated. However, this music is in no sense serial: its total chromaticism is a consequence of its unaccompanied nature. Any exposed melody of this kind is particularly susceptible to weakening through the early repetition of any pitch and it therefore follows that the more dissonated a melody is, the stronger it will be. Of course, the present melody would be even stronger were its rhythms not so consonant.

Larger and smaller fragments of the melody are re-used, in transposition, at a number of points in the piece, notably the openings of the recapitulation of the A section (bar 42) and of the large canon which occupies most of the middle section. Although this canon starts strictly (bar 19) it becomes increasingly free in its rhythmic imitation; however, it follows to a greater or lesser extent the conventions of dissonant counterpoint. Thus the pitches, intervals and rhythms of the two main lines are all quite well dissonated, as is the contrapuntal relationship (vertical rhythmic ratio) between them. Additionally, the rhythmically consonant free parts combine with the canonic voices to produce a particularly dissonant harmony.

But the degree of dissonance found in *Evocation 2* is as extreme in Ruggles' work as is the degree of consonance found in some passages of *Evocation 3*. The reality of Ruggles' later mature style lies somewhere between these two poles: dissonant counterpoint was for him only the boldest of a wide range of compositional colours. Its principles were fully assimilated into his overall and very personal musical language.

A markedly more radical view of the possibilities inherent in Seeger's ideas was taken by a pupil who eventually became his second wife – Ruth Crawford (1901–53). Born in Ohio, Crawford was educated in Florida and from 1920 at the American Conservatory in Chicago. Her musical preoccupations lay initially with the keyboard but, encouraged by Adolf Weidig, Djane Lavoie-Herz and (after 1925) Dane Rudhyar and eventually Cowell, she became increasingly interested in composition. The works she wrote before 1930 are freely chromatic and essentially European in style, this perhaps reflecting her admiration of the musics of Skryabin and Bartók. In 1929, however – and undoubtedly at Cowell's persuasion – Crawford moved from her native mid-west to New York, where six preliminary lessons had been arranged for her with Charles Seeger. These, and the many others which followed, proved to be the turning point in her compositional career.[28]

Among the first fruits of her studies were the four *Diaphonic Suites* of 1930. In essence these works are exercises in dissonant counterpoint, though it should be stated that their musical qualities are far greater than this description might imply. In 'On Dissonant Counterpoint' (on page 28) Seeger points out that the logical consequence of dissonant counterpoint is a new kind of polyphony – heterophony – in which the individual lines are truly independent:

. . .the parts must be so different in themselves and the relation between them (which makes their simultaneous sounding agreeable) must perforce be such that their difference rather than their likeness is emphasized. This is possible upon a basis of dissonance; but with the slightest error in the handling of consonance, our homophonically over-educated ears will infer chordal structures not intended and the polyphony will be lost. So it becomes necessary to cultivate 'sounding apart' rather than 'sounding together' – diaphony rather than symphony.

Thus Crawford's *Diaphonic Suite No. 2* – for bassoon and 'cello[29] – takes a standpoint rather different from the late-Romantic view of dissonant counterpoint afforded us by Ruggles. In the first movement's opening 'cello solo pitch, interval and rhythm are all well dissonated; yet the line grows quite naturally (example 3.12). When the bassoon enters it is with a rhythmic variant of this melody, though the pitches are newly invented. Against this, the 'cello counterpoints fresh material; then (at bar 27) it introduces the first of a series of extended trills, over which the bassoon continues its melody. These trills (which, especially towards the end of the movement, are on Ds) have a quasi-

Example 3.12. Crawford: *Diaphonic Suite No. 2*, i; bars 1–23*

harmonic function, giving stability to the music. They gradually come to dominate the texture: from bar 49 to the end (bar 69) there is a continual trill on one or other of the two instruments. The diaphony of the closing bars could not be greater, as trilled Ds provide the backcloth to rising, dissonant scales which at all times avoid this very pitch.

The lyrical second movement of this suite is constructed similarly, though here held single pitches – rather than trills – are the increasingly prominent backcloth against which gentler dissonant melodies unfold. The third movement, however, contains virtually no counterpoint, except in bars 16–18 and 33–35. Elsewhere the music consists almost exclusively of an asymmetrically phrased bassoon melody written predominantly in staccato quavers. The phrase-endings of this melody are defined by descending major seventh leaps, often followed by rests. The 'cello, meanwhile, exposes a series of twelve very dissonant and *sforzando* four-pitch chords, separated by rests of irregular length. These chords punctuate the bassoon's melody, most often appearing during its rests; their harmonic width gradually expands from a thirteenth to almost three octaves (nine of the chords have the low C string as their bass). There is also an overall acceleration in the frequency of their appearance (c.f. the trills of the first movement and the held pitches of the second) especially towards the end.

In the first and third movements of the *Diaphonic Suite No. 3* for two B♭ clarinets a more complex relationship between the two parts is encountered. This relationship is explained in a rubric appearing in Crawford's manuscript of the first movement: 'The first Clarinet carries the melody. Its rhythms, however, are determined by the changing meters in the second Clarinet, which must follow throughout.' What this means in practice is that the second clarinet moves in almost relentless irregularly grouped quavers; against this the first clarinet plays a melody which irregularly subdivides the metric units thus created. This rhythmically complex contrapuntal relationship is illustrated at the outset of the work (example 3.13). Note here the high level of dissonance of both pitch and interval: the only exception to this lies in the repeated pitch of the first clarinet's opening phrase, which reappears (sometimes transposed) as a kind of motto at various points.

Example 3.13. Crawford: *Diaphonic Suite No. 3*, i; bars 1–10* (written, not sounding, pitch)

In the third movement there is again a clear division of rôles between the instruments: but here it is the second clarinet which carries the (generally) higher-voiced, rhythmically awkward melody, while the first has the (generally) lower-voiced, plodding quaver accompaniment. The qualification is, however, important, for towards the end of each of the movement's three (A–A + –B) sections, the first clarinet rises frantically into its top register to obscure the underlying melody. In A + this tendency is held back somewhat so that in the B section (where the accompaniment *twice* rises and quickens in pace) it appears with more force. The pitch content of this first clarinet part is interesting for its frequent re-use, in transposition, inversion and retrogression, of material taken from the opening twenty bars. Thus most of section A + (bars 27–38) is a variant of bars 2–13, transposed upwards initially by a major, and later by a minor, second. Furthermore, bars 45–56 of section B are a retrograde of bars 2 to (first quaver of) 14, transposed upwards by a major seventh or downwards by a minor second (example 3.14).

Through such varied re-use of pitch material, Crawford provides a simple solution to Seeger's demands for economy of melodic resource, and for tonal centricity. In brief moments elsewhere, however (e.g. bars 20–22) clarinet 1 represents pitch material which is disassociated from its original rhythms. The fundamental implication of this – as in some of Ives' works – is that the pitches and rhythms of any given musical fragment are quite separate, and that either can reappear without the other. Here, and also in the opening movement of the

Example 3.14. Crawford: *Diaphonic Suite No. 3*, iii; bars 1–5, 26–30, 53–56* (written, not sounding, pitch)

String Quartet, the technique is applied in only a loose fashion. But the result of applying the idea rigidly has important consequences for Crawford's later work.

By contrast, the second clarinet melody has no apparent pitch or rhythmic structuring. The first half of the A section melody is varied in the first half of the A+ section (see example 3.14) but the two second halves, along with the B section, are unrelated both to the opening and among themselves. Overall, this melody often has an off-beat $\frac{3}{8}$ feel to it; this is in marked contrast to the accompanying line, which rigidly enforces the irregular metrical pattern by strongly accentuating the first beat of each bar. Once again there is a portent here of Crawford's later work: the disparate rhythmic relationships between the parts in these outer movements confound any perception of harmony. Rather, one is aware only of a new kind of heterophony – the co-existence within the same time-plane of quite separate lines.

From the first *Diaphonic Suite* (for solo flute) onwards, Crawford steps beyond the elementary disciplines of dissonant counterpoint and concerns herself instead with some of the larger issues raised by Seeger: the need for tonal and rhythmic centricity, for economy of melodic resource, and for organic structure.

Thus the first, second and fourth movements of this work all make use of the kind of phrase balancing discussed earlier in connection with Seeger's *The Letter*. The difference here, however, lies in the integration of this phrase balancing into an overall organic structure; and in the use of recurrent intervallic and rhythmic gestures to articulate this structure. A detailed examination of the first movement will clarify these points.

As is shown in example 3.15, the movement is constructed using a specific pattern of phrase-lengths. Thus, in <u>A</u>, the initial 5 + 4 melodic phrase consists of a five-bar dotted passage succeeded by a four-bar decelerating running passage. The difference in gesture between the two halves of the phrase creates tension. The second 5 + 4 melodic phrase is a variation of the first which starts as an inversion.

Example 3.15. Crawford: *Diaphonic Suite No. 1, i****

In section $\underline{B}$ – a kind of miniature development – two variations on the five-bar phrase are succeeded by an extension (by 100%) of the four-bar phrase which introduces an acceleration as well as a deceleration. Note the intensification caused by the overall expansion of the pitch range. The increased tension is released by the final crotchet rest. In section $\underline{C}$ only the acceleration remains in the opening six-bar phrase, which combines the two melodic ideas; the semitone rise between the six-bar phrase and the five-bar phrase hints at finality, and the music is evaporated by the elongated final note. The structure is further heightened by the dynamics.

While the second and fourth movements are constructed along similar lines, the third – a kind of passacaglia – uses quite different methods to create an integrated structure. Rhythmic centricity of a kind is ensured by the fact that the music proceeds almost entirely in relentless quavers in $\frac{7}{8}$. Tonal centricity and organic structure are guaranteed by the remarkably economic melodic resource of using a permutation process to generate the entire pitch content of the movement from a single short set.

At its simplest level (i.e. that which Crawford later employs in the oboe part of 'Prayers of Steel' from the *Three Songs*, and the piano part of the *Ricercar: Chinaman, Laundryman*) the process operates in the following way.

1   A short set of pitches is presented in its prime form:

    a b c d e

2a The first pitch of this group becomes the final pitch of the subsequent group, all other pitches remaining in order (apart from octave transpositions):

    b c d e a

2b This process is repeated until all five possible permutations have been presented:

    c d e a b
    d e a b c
    e a b c d

3   The original set is then re-presented, but now transposed up to the pitch level of its original second member:

    b c♯ d e f♯

(i.e. the original intervallic shape of the set is retained).

4   The process of permutation described in 2a and 2b is now applied to this new set, thus generating four more presentations:

    c♯ d e f♯ b
    d e f♯ b c♯
    e f♯ b c♯ d
    f♯ b c♯ d e

5   The processes of transposition and permutation described in 3
and 4 are repeated at the remaining pitch levels of the original set
(i.e. permutations are made of sets beginning on c, d and e). The
final group of pitches in this large-scale process will therefore be

b e f♯ g a

Thus a simple set of pitches can generate large quantities of material; specifically, an initial set of x pitches can be used to generate x^3 pitches.

However, the system used to generate the pitch material of the third movement
of *Diaphonic Suite No. 1* is slightly more complicated. This is based on a seven-
pitch set whose prime form is

g'   a'   g♯'   b'   c"   f"   c♯"

giving an intervallic series of

M2↑   m2↓   m3↑   m2↑   4↑   M3↓

The process starts as described above. Thus bars 1–3 replicate as bars 9–11 and
so on (example 3.16). But for the permutations based on the third and fourth

Example 3.16. Crawford: *Diaphonic Suite No. 1*, iii; bars 1–3, 9–11*

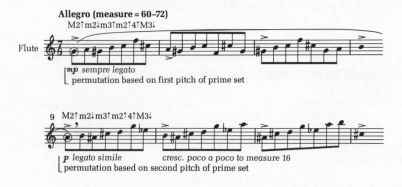

pitches of the original set (g♯' and b') the interval series of the prime set is
retrograded, and for those based on the fifth and sixth pitches (c" and f")
the interval series is inverted. The interval series used for the permutation based
on the seventh pitch (c♯") is a retrograde inversion, as is that of the additional
eighth permutation (based on the original opening pitch, g') which follows it.
Thus later 'equivalents' to bars 1–3 are rather different from those we might
expect (c.f. examples 3.16 and 3.17).

Then, to close the movement, the second presentation of the original set
(i.e. that starting with a') is stated in augmentation so that the first and last
pitches of the movement are both Gs. Thus, owing to a desire to vary the
material through the balanced appearance of *pairs* of permutations based on
each of the four possible versions of the original interval sequence (prime, retrograde, inversion, retrograde inversion) Crawford generates more than the
expected 7^3 (= 343) pitches. (And, in doing so, makes what is for her an

Example 3.17. Crawford: *Diaphonic Suite No. 1*, iii; bars 17–19, 38–40, 52–54*

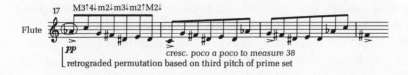

unusually frank acknowledgement of her interest in Schoenbergian serial techniques.)

A further complication is that the first and second 7^2 permutations (those based on g′ and a′) end unusually: each includes an *extra* final presentation of the original set upon which it was based (i.e. bar 8 equals bar 1, and bar 16 equals bar 9, except for octave transpositions). Additionally, the final pitch of bar 16 (e♭‴) is held over into bar 16a and succeeded by a minim rest, before the retrograded permutation on pitch 3 (g♯′) begins in bar 17.

These extra bars may have been included because Crawford wished to balance the additional eighth permutation (on g′, starting at bar 52) and the final augmented version. Any objection to the lack of rhythmic dissonance here can be countered by pointing out that the music is essentially arhythmic: its relentless quavers are as much anathema to conventional 'consonant' rhythms as are Crawford's more usual rhythmic dissonances. A final refinement lies in the shaping of the movement through phrasings, dynamic markings and tessiturae which emphasise its permutational framework (this can be partly seen in examples 3.16 and 3.17).

A number of other works from 1930 explore further the techniques so far described, as well as several of Seeger's other ideas. Both the *Piano Study in Mixed Accents* (December 1930) and the exactly contemporary first movement of the *Diaphonic Suite No. 4* for oboe and 'cello, achieve tonal centricity, melodic economy and organic structure through their use of large-scale pitch palindromes which reflect about free centres. In the *Piano Study* the pitch palindrome is disguised by a rhythmic palindrome placed asymmetrically over it (so that in the reflection pitches and rhythmic groupings are arranged, quasi-isorhythmically, into new configurations).[30] In the *Diaphonic Suite*, the pitch palindrome is disguised by being treated canonically between the two instruments, whose rhythms, however, are completely free.

More remarkable is the provision in the *Piano Study* of three quite separate sets of dynamic markings: two of these reflect the palindromic shape of the work as a whole (and therefore hold consonant relationships with its structure) while the third (*ff* throughout) does not. But the choice of pattern is left to the performer: like Ives in *Halloween* (W11) and *Over the Pavements* (V20), Crawford predicts the methods of much later music.

The third movement of the *Diaphonic Suite No. 4* takes even further the idea (first encountered in the finale of *Diaphonic Suite No. 3*, but also implicit in the *Piano Study* and the first movement of this fourth suite) that the various parameters of a musical line are not inextricably linked, and can easily be organised or articulated by quite different means. Thus both oboe and 'cello adhere to an overall four-part formal structure; but within this structure each instrument follows its own, partially organised, path. Traditional vertical musical relationships are being fundamentally changed, here: diaphony is indeed replacing symphony.

To a greater or lesser extent, however, the *Piano Study in Mixed Accents* and the four *Diaphonic Suites* all lack one thing – harmony. Crawford turns her attention more towards this parameter in the *Three Chants*, also of 1930.

Considering the restrictions of writing for (amateur) women's voices, these chants are remarkable for their use of advanced compositional techniques, and for the high levels of horizontal and vertical dissonance found in them. Furthermore, none of the chants uses a conventional text: rather, all three share a common invented language, composed of 'decorated' vowel sounds. A possible clue to their origin is provided by one of Crawford's daughters: 'She was very fond of making up nonsense syllables which delighted us children. . .'[31] The sounds are often grouped in a seemingly random way; but elsewhere sequences are repeated or varied. A typical example of text, taken from the third chant is:

OR U M RU NYA OR RU YONG OR RA NGO YONG O LYA CHE O NGYAH E NGYE RU KAH NGO YA ZA
LO RU CHYA E RA TE CHYAH

(Accents over individual letters have been omitted; Crawford gives detailed instructions for the pronunciation of these syllables in her manuscript.)

The first chant – 'To an Unkind God' – consists basically of the alternation of sections of dissonant counterpoint (melody against either a pedal point, or against one or two countermelodies) with sections of rhythmic or complete unison. Throughout the piece there is a distinct division of rôles between an ever-present melody and various types of accompaniment. This relationship is continued in the second chant – 'To an Angel' – though here the occasionally complex dissonant counterpoint of 'To an Unkind God' is replaced by a much simpler vertical texture.

In its original form 'To an Angel' was written for solo soprano, accompanied by two groups of voices (probably *a cappella* soprano and alto): there was no equivalent to the tenor/bass line which appears in the published/recorded version. The essence of the piece is revealed in the opening ten bars (example 3.18).

Example 3.18. Crawford: *Chant 2*; bars 1–10*
Used by permission of the Estate of Ruth Crawford Seeger

† Elsewhere given as 'sopranos', 'altos'.
‡ These details occur in one copy only.

The accompanying lines seldom stray from this regularity of rhythm and harmony (the latter based mainly on thirds and sevenths). Indeed, in the original manuscript Crawford asks for 'complete monotony of tempo and "white" tone throughout'. She also provides an extended rubric concerning the solo line:

In the solo part, one vowel should 'modulate' slightly to the next. The solo should sound as little as possible like a 'vocal exercise'. It must also seem to 'grow' out of the chorus, and not stand too much apart or too prominent.

The soprano's tessitura slowly weaves its way upwards (reaching gb″ at bar 39) before falling to its final f′ during the ensuing sixteen bars.

Interestingly, this becalmed middle movement ends on the same (transposed) three-pitch chord as 'To an Unkind God'. The dissonant intervals of this chord – tone and semitone – also act as the bases of the two cluster chords of the final (untitled) chant, for soprano and alto soli, accompanied by twelve-part chorus (probably divided equally between sopranos and altos, though not indicated as such in the manuscript). The simple form of this chant consists of two large accumulative sections (A and B) followed by a shorter, coda-like recapitulatory section (Ai). The basis of sections A and Ai is chord 1 from example 3.19, and the basis of section B is chord 2.

Example 3.19. Crawford: *Chant 3*; basic chords, plus added pitches*
Used by permission of the Estate of Ruth Crawford Seeger.

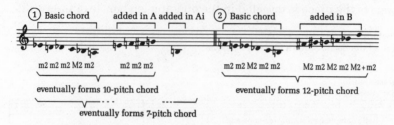

Within each of the two main sections, three processes occur:

1 the basic chord has pitches added to it (see example 3.19) (i.e. the harmony becomes increasingly dissonant);

2 individual pitches within the chord are progressively rhythmicised (i.e. the counterpoint between the lines becomes increasingly dissonant);

3 over the chord, a soloist weaves an increasingly complex melody.[32]

The result of combining these three processes is an increasingly dissonant overall texture. Thus in A the simple, homophonic, chordal opening is gradually transformed until it reaches a complex, polyrhythmic, climax. This then subsides before the transition to B, where the degree of accumulation is even greater, in terms of number of pitches involved, density of polyrhythmic activity, width of dynamic range, and sheer virtuosity of the solo part. The homophonic opening (chord 2) is completely transformed during the fifteen bars which lead to the climax (example 3.20).[33] Note that while the underlying chord now contains all twelve pitches of the chromatic scale, the high soprano soloist tends to emphasise those pitches which do *not* lie in the chord's upper regions, in particular b″, c″ and c#‴. The climactic nature of bars 48 + is further emphasised by the unexpected rhythmic homophony of the chorus. The process of subsidence here is achieved more rapidly than in A, leading to the pp reappearance of chord 1 as early as bar 53. The closing Ai section is very much an exhausted shadow of its former self.

The accumulative processes of this chant make no use of mathematical (or other) organisation, but rather are determined by purely musical, instinctive, considerations. Thus the progressive contrapuntal consonance/dissonance has a wave-like fluidity, while the elaboration of the two solos (the second of which, incidentally, is a very free variation of the first) is handled with an acute sense of melodic direction.

The kind of pulsating cluster heard here reappears in two later Crawford works – the third movement of the String Quartet, and 'In Tall Grass' from the *Three Songs*: but nothing else like it occurs in Western music until the 1960s and 1970s, notably in the works of György Ligeti (1923–   ) (c.f. particularly *Lux Aeterna* of 1966).

Example 3.20. Crawford: *Chant 3*; bars 46–49
Used by permission of the Estate of Ruth Crawford Seeger.

Example 3.20. (*cont.*)

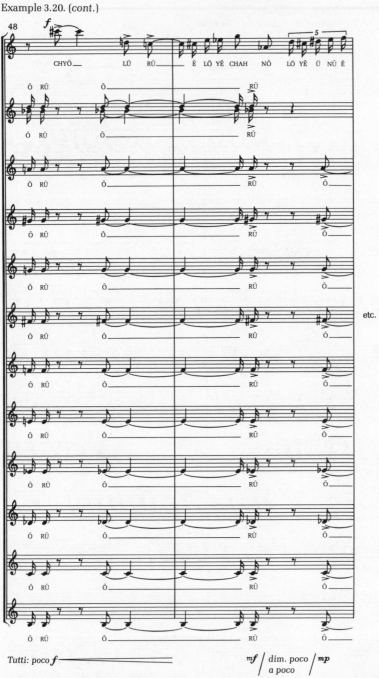

Between August 1930 and (approximately) July 1931, Crawford visited Europe on a Guggenheim Fellowship (she was the first woman to receive such an award). The major product of this period was her best-known work – the String Quartet. In a sense, the Quartet both summarises the new techniques she had worked with during 1930, and charts a chronological path through them, moving from free dissonant counterpoint to total organisation. It is also,

fundamentally, traditional, with four movements in the order opening sonata–
scherzo/rondo–slow movement–fast finale. One wonders how much effect
Europe had on the work, especially considering Crawford's long discussion in
Vienna with Berg, whose *Wozzeck* – with its new use of traditional forms – she
particularly admired. Certainly there are aural resemblances between the
Quartet and both Berg's *Lyric Suite* and the third of Schoenberg's Op. 16 *Orchestral Pieces*. Also present, in the middle movements, is the influence of Bartók,
whom Crawford had met in Budapest and believed to be the (then) greatest
living composer.

The first movement – *Rubato assai* – is a sonata in the sense that it has an
overall exposition–development–recapitulation shape; but whereas in European tradition the form is defined by harmonic area, here the tensions are
created by melodic type. Indeed, an almost continuous melody runs right
through the movement (and is designated as such by 'solo' indications in the
score). But it has two distinct – and alternating – characters, which might be
termed lyrical and frantic. These, with their extremely dissonated shared countermelody, are exposed at the start of the movement in a kind of double exposition (bars 1–15; example 3.21).

Example 3.21. Crawford: String Quartet, i; bars 1–9*
© 1931 Merion Music, Inc. Used by permission of the publisher.

† The melodic line, as indicated by 'solo' in each part, must be heard continuing throughout
the movement.

The development (bars 16–63) divides into four sections. In the first (bars 16–25) a frantic solo is superimposed on both the extant countermelody (or rather a variant of it) and a new, more lyrical countermelody. In the second (bars 26–43) a lyrical solo, set against both countermelody types, becomes increasingly agitated until the movement's trilled climax (section 3: bars 44–58). A short evaporation (section 4: bars 59–63) using the lyrical material leads to the varied recapitulation (bars 64–98).

Crawford's treatment of melodic material here resembles that of the third movement of the earlier *Diaphonic Suite No. 3* in that rhythmically altered statements of the basic melodies (and accompaniments) – together with inversions, retrogrades, etc. – are interspersed among unrelated materials. Thus in the development section of the present movement the first violin and later 'cello present (from bar 25 onwards) an inversion of the lyrical theme, followed by its retrogression, against which the viola plays a variant of the original countermelody. Again, from bar 40 the viola presents a quasi-inversion of the countermelody against new principal melodic material. In the recapitulation the frantic and lyrical melodies keep their characters but not necessarily their exact shapes, while the countermelody is entirely absent.

Apart from the above, much use is made here of what might be termed harmonic supports – long held pitches which act as a foil (and give stability) to the otherwise contrapuntally dissonant texture. (For instance, in example 3.21 see the violin 1 and viola lines in bars 6–7, and the 'cello line from bar 8 onwards.) As previously in Crawford's work one feels little sense of homophony here except at the climax. Rather, one is aware only of the heterophony of up to four unrelated horizontal lines.

The first movement's lack of imitation is compensated for in the next two movements – the second is freely imitative and the third strictly so. They also compensate for its horizontalism: the scurrying second movement – marked *Leggiero* – starts with a nine-pitch *ffz* chord. Formally, it is both rondo and scherzo, as shown in figure 3.3.

Figure 3.3. Structure of Crawford's String Quartet, ii

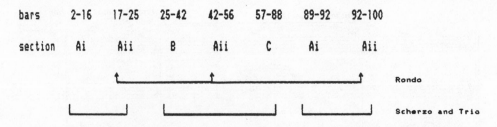

bars	2-16	17-25	25-42	42-56	57-88	89-92	92-100
section	Ai	Aii	B	Aii	C	Ai	Aii

Rondo

Scherzo and Trio

Both the A̲i material, and the inner voices of the B̲ material, are freely imitative, ranging from two to four parts. In A̲i this is juxtaposed with a recurring harmonic, quasi-cadential figure (example 3.22). In B̲ the imitation is sandwiched between two slowly changing, converging pedal points (or harmonic supports) on violin 1 and 'cello. In B̲'s short codetta, however (bars 40–42) the

Example 3.22. Crawford: String Quartet, ii; bars 1–4*
© 1931 Merion Music, Inc. Used by permission of the publisher.

poles are reversed and the pedals, now on violin 2 and viola, are sandwiched between the imitative lines. The A̲ii̲ material consists basically of a melody repeated almost verbatim on each appearance and accompanied by fragments of A̲i̲'s 'cadences', while section C̲ features a solo-plus-shadow on the two violins, accompanied by hocketing pizzicato viola and 'cello (perhaps reminiscent of Bartók). Before the return of the A̲ materials, this is thinned down to second violin melody with pizzicato viola accompaniment.

The first two movements were free of any kind of mathematical structuring; in the third movement the pitch content is still free, but the dynamics and rhythm are controlled. This remarkable *Andante* was, it seems, inspired by noises encountered one New Year's Eve[34] but its complete originality of sound and form cannot be totally explained by this. The form is built from the aggregation of short dynamic/rhythmic units, treated canonically (see example 3.23). The pat-

Example 3.23. Crawford: String Quartet, iii; bars 1–8*. (a) Conventional notation; (b) Translated to a graph of rhythm and dynamics
© 1931 Merion Music, Inc. Used by permission of the publisher.

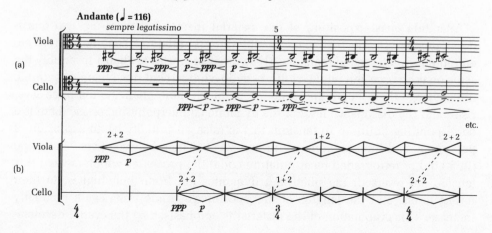

terns of the two instruments overlap – one loudens while the other softens; thus their relationship is dissonant rather than consonant. When the two violins are introduced at bars 13 and 19 respectively – creating a four-part canon – they have an identical relationship. But whereas the viola/'cello units begin on the odd-numbered beats of the bar, those of the violins start on the even-numbered beats (i.e. the level of 'dynamic dissonance' is increased) – see example 3.24.

Example 3.24. Crawford: String Quartet, iii; bars 19–22*. (a) Conventional notation (b) Translated to a graph of rhythm and dynamics
© 1931 Merion Music, Inc. Used by permission of the publisher.

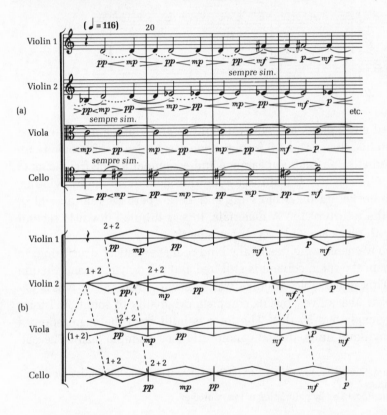

After this quasi-exposition of the material (bars 1–23) there are two quasi-developments. In the first (bars 24–48) various orders of canonic entries are employed; in the second (bars 49–74) the order of entries is almost invariably the same on each occasion (viola–violin 2–'cello–violin 1) but the dynamic/rhythmic units change their length and proportions much more often. As the pitch level rises, and the dissonance level of the dynamic counterpoint increases, there is a corresponding build-up in tension: this is released initially by an explosion of polyphony and then homophony in bars 75–76. Then, between bars 77 and 100 (in a kind of retrograded recapitulation/coda) the processes which created this tension are reversed: the pitch and dynamics fall from their highest to their lowest levels, and the lengths of the dynamic/rhythmic units again gradually increase. This evaporation of the material is emphasised by the overall deceleration from *Doppio movimento* (bar 77) to *Tempo primo* (bar 95) though there is an initial acceleration in bars 77–88. The shape of the movement as a whole is beautifully proportioned in terms of pitch level, dynamic level, length of dynamic/rhythmic units, distance between new entries, and so on: all climax at approximately three-quarters of the way through the movement, before subsiding back to their opening positions. But beyond this overall structuring, and the fact that the pitch content is concentrated in small cells, the piece is unordered except in terms of its dynamic/rhythmic canon: all other parameters are free.

This is certainly not the case in the last – *Allegro possibile* – movement, where everything except the pitch and rhythm of violin 1 is strictly ordered. Like the *Piano Study in Mixed Accents* this is a large-scale palindrome, though here the reflection is apparently transposed up by one semitone. Structurally, the movement is essentially a dialogue between the free, *concertante*, first violin and the ordered, *ripieno*, three lower instruments, who play in rhythmic unison and double octaves throughout. In the first half of the movement, violin 1 starts with a one-pitch rhythmic unit which expands arithmetically (1, 2, 3, etc.) to a twenty-one-pitch rhythmic unit. Its rhythms are free and almost rhapsodic. The *ripieni* start with a twenty-pitch rhythmic unit which contracts arithmetically (20, 19, 18, etc.) to a one-pitch rhythmic unit. Rhythmically they play only quavers, grouped irregularly (example 3.25). Some exceptions to this 'rule' occur in bars 32–44,

Example 3.25. Crawford: String Quartet, iv; bars 1–10*
© 1931 Merion Music, Inc. Used by permission of the publisher.

where each final pitch is held, presumably to provide textural relief and contrast. Even here, though, the elongations appear to be mathematically contrived.

The pitch content for the *ripieni* is derived from a ten-pitch set

$$d' \quad e' \quad f' \quad eb' \quad f\#' \quad a' \quad ab' \quad g' \quad db' \quad c''$$

permutated in a manner similar to that used in the third movement of *Diaphonic Suite No. 1*. After the initial (10^2) permutation (A) has been completed, a second (10^2) permutation (B) is made, based on the second pitch (e') of the initial set (i.e. the entire process is transposed up by one tone).[35] Just before the central point of reflection (which occurs in bars 57–60) the basic set – plus the first pitch (e') of permutation B, on which the reflection is made – is again played. The second half of the palindrome opens (at bar 63) with the retrograded basic set, transposed up by one semitone. It then continues by introducing two complete (10^2) retrograded permutations (C and D) which are based on the third and fourth pitches (f' and eb') of the original set (see figure 3.4). Thus the transposi-

Figure 3.4. Simplified pitch structure of *ripieni* in Crawford's String Quartet, iv

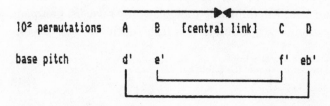

tion up by one semitone of this second half is only apparent: in reality the free first violin takes its cue from the ordered lower instruments. As in other works, Crawford makes a number of minor changes in the reflection.

The dynamics of both the *concertante* violin 1 and the *ripieni* are also structured. Violin 1 commences *ffz* and progressively quietens to *pp* at the centre; the three lower instruments commence *pp (sempre con sordino)* and progressively louden to the *ffzp<ffz* centre. These complementary processes are reversed in the reflection.

In this movement Crawford therefore utilises some of Seeger's most advanced ideas: we can identify dissonant dynamics (the complementary *crescendi* and *decrescendi* of the *concertante* and *ripieno* instruments), dissonant accents (the regularly articulated quavers of the *ripieni*, against the irregularly articulated dissonant rhythms of the first violin), and even a dissonant overall structure (the superimposition of two complementary, but different, forms). The mould for Crawford's remaining works of this period had been cast.

Despite being written over a period of two and a half years, the *Three Songs* – for contralto, oboe, piano, percussion, and optional orchestral ostinati – show a remarkable degree of homogeneity. This is all the more striking when one considers that the ostinati – consisting of clarinet, trumpet, horn, bassoon, four or more violins, two or more violas, one or two 'cellos and one or two double basses

– were added, at Seeger's suggestion, only after 'Prayers of Steel' had been completed in about November 1932.[36] The common factors which link the songs are their declamatory vocal style, the often 'vocal' nature of the oboe writing, and the generally accompanimental style of the piano, percussion and ostinato parts. But beneath their superficially descriptive surfaces, these songs conceal a wealth of pre-compositional plans. These should – by virtue of their independent, almost contradictory, methods of organisation – confuse and confound the work's directness and immediacy of communication. That they do not is both a vindication of totally dissonant composition and a tribute to Crawford's abilities as a composer.

'Rat Riddles' (completed as early as March 1930)[37] is in many ways the least complex of the songs, as is shown by the opening bars (example 3.26). Each of the *concertante* parts has its own repertory of melodic phrases and devices, varied on subsequent appearances. Their use compromises the norms of dissonant counterpoint, as pitches and intervals tend to reappear far more frequently than is usual.

With the exception of the ostinati all of the parts adhere basically to the verseform of the vocal line (figure 3.5). The vocal line itself is the least clearly defined in terms of melodic variation and repetition. This is a logical result of the composer's desire to set the words in a syllabic style reflecting the natural inflexions of the spoken voice. Despite this, there is a remarkable correspondence between the overall shapes of the four verses: each focusses on the range f♯'–a♯' (though there are excursions outside these limits) and generally progresses by punctuating more or less stepwise motion with large leaps, often of a seventh.

Example 3.26. Crawford: 'Rat Riddles'; bars 1–11*
© 1933 New Music Edition. Used by permission of the publisher Theodore Presser Company.

Example 3.26. (*cont.*)

† Percussion: 1 Chinese block
 2 Triangle
 3 Tambourine
 4 Cymbal
 5 Bass drum

Figure 3.5. Structure of Crawford's 'Rat Riddles' (*Three Songs*, i)

bars	1-17	18-32	33-39	40-53	54-57^1/$_2$	57^1/$_2$-62	63-77	78-84	85-89
section	Intro.	Verse 1	Interrupt^n	Verse 2	Interrupt^n	Verse 3	Recit.	Verse 4	Concl.
no. of bars	17	15	7	14	3^1/$_2$	5^1/$_2$	15	7	5

The oboe and piano also follow basic variation patterns, though with the complication that each employs different materials for the verse and instrumental sections. The oboe's main rôle is as a second 'voice' in the texture – a non-syllabic foil to the contralto's declamation. Consequently much of its material consists of held pitches separated by florid *gruppetti*. Its verse music, however, is distinguished most clearly by concluding elongated trills (e.g. at bars 26–31). The piano's verse music, by contrast, is notable for its extended, basically sextuplet, runs (e.g. bars 23–27). Otherwise both its verse and instrumental musics make elaborate, varied use of a small number of musical ideas, as can be seen from example 3.26. The percussion part uses only one germinal idea – a short figure for chinese block, tambourine and triangle (see bar 3 to first quaver of bar 4). This is repeated numerous times during the song, as well as being varied, shortened, and – particularly – interrupted by held triangle or cymbal rolls.

All of these various patterns among the *concertante* instruments are halted during the recitative section. Here, the interest lies primarily with the voice, at first accompanied only by a bass drum roll. Later the oboe and piano join in with long, held pitches, initially moving in contrary motion.

The orchestral ostinati, which – as has been noted – were written some time after the *concertante* parts, seem to fit into the overall formal plan of the song. But in fact their music (played *ppp* throughout) is determined by an entirely different – and much more highly organised – method. This is based on a 24-quaver rhythmic unit which is played ten times against bars 5–62, being sporadically varied to provide punctuation (example 3.27). Each attack is assigned one from a repertory

Example 3.27. Crawford: 'Rat Riddles'; ostinati's rhythmic pattern (c.f. example 3.26, bars 5–11)

Ostinati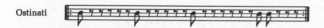

of twelve chords, though this repertory is exposed only slowly. The initial chord (see bars 5–10) is by far the most common; chord 2 makes its first appearance in bar 11 while chord 12 appears only immediately before the recitative, during which the ostinati are silent. The subsequent eleventh and final repetition of the rhythmic unit (played against bars 79–85) uses only chords 1 and 3.

When the two layers – *concertante* and ostinati – are superimposed, they therefore create an initially dissonant structure: the implied formal divisions of the two groups are essentially unrelated before bar 62. From here on, however, the structure becomes much more consonant as the formal divisions of the groups coincide almost exactly.

In the third song – 'In Tall Grass' (completed in January 1931) – both *concertante* and ostinati generally adhere to the structure implied by the text. The *concertante*'s music falls into four basic sections:

<u>A</u> (bars 1–19) – <u>B</u> (20–39) – <u>C</u> (40–64) – <u>D</u> (65–93)

The joins between these sections are emphasised by appearances of the lower ostinato instruments, and by changes in tempo.

In <u>A</u> the voice, oboe and piano lines all commence on, or near to, one central pitch – g' – before slowly expanding outwards. Under this music the percussion slowly reiterates a phrase on triangle and cymbal (example 3.28). The piano part here is particularly interesting: it consists of a slow elaboration/expansion of the opening, in which the two hands become increasingly disconnected, moving from homophony to dissonant counterpoint (this is mirrored within each individual phrase). The process continues until bar 13; after two bars' rest there is a short recapitulation of the original (rhythmic) homophony.

Section <u>B</u> is a kind of exercise in three-part dissonant counterpoint; of the *concertante* only the voice, oboe and piano (the latter in octaves) are involved as

Example 3.28. Crawford: 'In Tall Grass'; bars 1–12* (*concertante* only)
© 1933 New Music Edition. Used by permission of the publisher Theodore Presser Company.

the percussion (with the exception of the bass drum – see later) is omitted. Then, in section C̲, we find the first developed example in Crawford's music of the new kind of heterophony mentioned earlier in connection with *Diaphonic Suites Nos. 2* and *3* (example 3.29). Seeger termed this kind of writing 'complete heter-

Example 3.29. Crawford: 'In Tall Grass'; bars 40–47* (*concertante* only)
© 1933 New Music Edition. Used by permission of the publisher Theodore Presser Company.

† Percussion: 1 Triangle
          2 Tambourine
          3 Cymbal
          4 Bass drum (plays with low wind/string ostinati)

ophony' and defined it as being 'a polyphony in which there is no relation between the parts except mere proximity in time-space, beginning and ending, within hearing of each other, at more or less the same time'.[38] Significantly, Seeger ends the paragraph thus: 'But from an artistic point of view, a high degree of organization is necessary (1) to assure perfect non-coincidence and (2) to make the undertaking as a whole worthwhile.' The implication is that to achieve complete heterophony (i.e. a totally diaphonic, or fully dissonant, texture) most or all of the musical parameters of each individual line must in some way be organised. In other words, there needed to be some equivalent to what was later termed integral serialism.

Here (example 3.29) the individual lines show varying degrees of organisation. The voice part (which simply declaims the text syllabically and inflexionally) is free. The percussion – after dwelling initially on variants of its phrase from section A – from bar 55 explores an unsystematic sequence of attacks and rests. The oboe plays a set of free variations on the phrase first announced in bars 40–44, while the piano part makes use of an isorhythmic technique very similar to that of the *Piano Study in Mixed Accents*, in which unrelated pitch and rhythmic sets are superimposed. The pitch material consists of an internally unstructured 74-pitch set which is played three and a half times between bars 40 and 63 (see example 3.29: the second appearance commences as marked in bar 47). Against this pitch material Crawford places an entirely separate rhythmic scheme, derived from a basic five-crotchet unit (though this later expands into larger units). Each unit is phrased in the score and begins with an accent (>). *Within* the unit each crotchet is subdivided into a number of equal attacks, the most usual arrangement being

quintuplet–sextuplet–septuplet–quintuplet–quadruplet

(see example 3.29). However, the third and seventh units are elongated (5–6–7–8–5–4 and 5–6–7–8–7–5–4 attacks per crotchet, respectively) while the eighth unit overlaps with the incomplete final ninth unit.

At the end of each unit the two hands drift out of unison, the number of non-unison pitches per unit increasing by arithmetical progression. Thus the first and second units conclude with five non-unisons (see example 3.29), the third and fourth with seven, fifth and sixth with ten,[39] seventh with eleven, eighth with twelve, and the incomplete ninth unit with thirteen non-unisons. Thus the process of breaking up the unison line gathers pace as it progresses. In this, as in her choice of pitches at the start of bar 40 (and thus of the repeating 74-pitch set) Crawford consciously refers us back to the piano writing in section A (c.f. example 3.28). Most of the non-unison writing consists of upward or downward moving chromatic lines in the left hand, in contrast to the more usual leaping line. A final detail lies in the overall rise of pitch level from extreme depth to extreme height: in this Crawford again invokes the *Piano Study in Mixed Accents*.

Having dissected section C's various lines it is worth noting that their diverse paths may possibly be a musical reflection of the action described in the text, as 'the bees go [out] honey hunting with yellow blur of wings'.

Section D is in complete contrast to this frantic heterophony. The pianist – presumably suffering from exhaustion – remains silent, while the percussion (after the first five bars) is limited to a series of triangle trills. The voice and oboe invoke the texture of section A̲, though here the central pitch (indeed, the alto's only pitch) is d'. The vocal line progressively slows and 'the bees come home and the bees sleep'.

As was mentioned earlier, the orchestral ostinati follow to a greater or lesser extent the four-section plan of the *concertante*. In this song alone they are divided into two groups:

1 high strings
2 winds (omitting the trumpet) plus low strings and bass drum (from *concertante* percussion)

Group 2 appear on only four occasions to play a low, dense chord whose dynamic shape is $ppp < pp > ppp$. The four appearances coincide with the major structural divisions of the song: the first covers the join between the instrumental opening and the vocal entry (bars 5–9) while the remaining three 'smear the edges' of the four sections (A̲–B̲: bars 18–22; B̲–C̲: bars 32–40; C̲–D̲: bars 62–73). The pitch content of this low chord is interesting: assuming that the double bass part is written at pitch, and that the horn sounds a fifth lower than written (neither of these points being clear in the score) then the chord consists of a pair of interlocking, intervallically and timbrally palindromic trichords, as shown in figure 3.6.

Figure 3.6. Possible structuring of low ostinati in Crawford's 'In Tall Grass' (*Three Songs*, iii)

wind	bass clarinet	D	
			M2↓
brass	horn	C	
			m3↓
string	double bass	A̲	
string	'celli	D♭	
			m3↑
brass	trombone	B♭̲	
			M2↑
wind	contrabassoon	A♭̲	

In contrast, the high strings play throughout the song. Their material also consists basically of clusters of pitches though this is confused by their alternation of moving and stable textures. The former features upward and downward glissandi (the upward often including the direction *il più alto possibile*); the latter is essentially static (example 3.30).

There are no rhythms as such in either texture. Rather, rhythmic patterns are created through a linking of dynamics and vibrato. The high strings, like the low ostinati, use a dynamic envelope shaped $ppp < pp > ppp$. At the opening Crawford includes the following direction:

sempre molto vibrato
con ciascuno crescendo, poco a poco più vibrato
con ciascuno diminuendo, poco a poco meno vibrato

Example 3.30. Crawford: 'In Tall Grass'; bars 38–41* (high string ostinati only)
© 1933 New Music Edition. Used by permission of the publisher Theodore Presser Company.

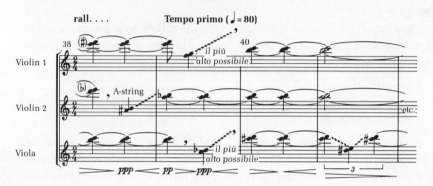

In other words, the dynamic envelope indicates not only the loudness of the pitch, but also the degree of vibrato associated with it. As can be seen from example 3.30 this envelope is shared by all of the high strings. Crawford is quite specific as to the reason for this – 'The rhythmic pattern made by the *crescendi* and *diminuendi*. . .must be distinguishable as unified pulsating masses of sound' – and controls her patterns very carefully indeed. One is reminded here not only of Seeger's comments regarding consonant and dissonant tone quality,[40] but also (once again) of the later work of Ligeti.

However, let us not forget the purely aural function of the ostinati here: the high and low clusters together form a kind of double horizon, or frame, for the pitch content of the piece, perhaps in response to the line 'And I ask no better a winding sheet (over the earth and under the sun).' At the same time they evoke quite brilliantly the drone of the bees of the text.

There is no place, however, for such Bartókian nature-painting in the middle song, 'Prayers of Steel', which was the last to be completed in November 1932. Instead, Crawford concentrates almost exclusively on the techniques of complete heterophony, though this in no sense suggests that the musical setting of the poem is abstract, as will be seen later. Again, we encounter here a dissonant overall structural relationship between the *concertante*, who play the same piece twice, and the ostinati, who have a separate scheme involving a quasi-retrogression (see figure 3.7).

Figure 3.7. Relationship between structures of *concertante* and ostinati in Crawford's 'Prayers of Steel' (*Three Songs*, ii)

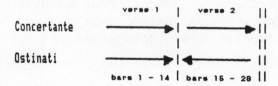

But before dissecting the song into its constituent horizontal lines, let us examine a vertical segment from the opening (example 3.31). Each line implies a different metre: the result of this polymetric confusion might be termed dissonant accents. Additionally, there is extreme rhythmic dissonance between the

Example 3.31. Crawford: 'Prayers of Steel'; bars 1–2*
© 1933 New Music Edition. Used by permission of the publisher Theodore Presser Company.

† Percussion: 1 Tamtam
          2 Bass drum
          3 Cymbal (padded drum stick)

lines. Each part proceeds on its own terms without any real reference to any of the others, the only exceptions to this being that

1 the voice and oboe fall into two-bar phrases, which themselves fit into the four-bar phrases of the piano and percussion;
2 the ostinati – who otherwise operate completely independently – have a pitch structure partly related to that of the oboe.

The vocal line – *f* throughout – is of necessity the least structured: the words dictate the rhythmic content, while the pitches consist of a series of chanting notes, deviated from towards the end of each phrase. After the narrow-ranged opening the tessitura slowly expands, and the chanting pitch moves successively higher. It eventually reaches c#″ (at bar 11) before returning to the original g#′ in bars 12–13.

The percussion gives three *mf* performances of a four-bar polymetric unit, plus final bar, while the piano (which shares the percussion's dynamic) plays in quadruple octaves throughout. It, too, has a basic four-bar phrase structure, but this makes use of two separate pitch/rhythm units. The first – which appears in bars 1, 2, 5, 6, 9, 10 and 13 – has free pitches and the rhythmic pattern

> quintuplet quavers–crotchet rest–quintuplet quavers

(c.f. example 3.31). The second – which appears in bars 3, 4, 7, 8, 11 and 12 (bar 14 is silent) – includes elements of pitch organisation and has the rhythmic pattern

> crotchet rest–quintuplet quavers–quintuplet quavers

The oboe, meanwhile, uses a seven-pitch permutation system (similar to those discussed previously) whose first five incomplete series of permutations each fit into a two-bar phrase (i.e. only 35 of the available $7^2 = 49$ pitches are used on each occasion). The accents within the two-bar phrases imply a metrical microstructure of five 'bars' of $\frac{7}{16}$, plus $\frac{5}{16}$ rest (c.f. example 3.31). The sixth and final phrase (bars 11–13) has a complete permutation (i.e. it uses all 49 available pitches) and implies seven 'bars' of $\frac{7}{16}$, plus $\frac{11}{16}$ rest. The permutation system itself is not rigidly adhered to: the basic set has five variants, and even within these variants some pitches are occasionally changed. Permutations are made on only the first six pitches of the original set (i.e. the system as a whole is incomplete) and there are additional minor alterations in the second verse.

The ostinati's overall structure is quite different from that of the *concertante*. Rather than playing the same piece twice they effectively play four versions of a 36-crotchet phrase whose rhythms and dynamics are totally organised. In Crawford's complex plan, the various parameters within each of these four phrases (length of basic unit, number of attacks per unit, 'straight' or retrograded rhythms, dynamic shape, etc.) are successively recombined to create different (consonant and dissonant) relationships within an overall acceleration/deceleration of the material, which reflects about the silent bar 14. The ostinati's pitches, however, are only partially organised, being derived initially from transposed versions of the oboe set but later becoming much freer.

As was seen earlier, the combination of the various *concertante* patterns with the accelerating and decelerating ostinati results in a completely heterophonous, polyrhythmic and polymetric, complex sound-world. However, these disparate means are used towards a single end – the accurate representation of a text concerned primarily with processes of construction and destruction:

> Lay me on an anvil, O God.
> Beat me and hammer me into a crowbar.
> Let me pry loose old walls.
> Let me lift and loosen old foundations. [etc.]

Thus, in her setting, Crawford introduces a number of constructed, quasi-mechanical musical processes: the apparent formalism of the song is actually, therefore, word-painting of the highest order.

Similar considerations predominate in the *Two Ricercari* of 1932–33. The vocal lines of both *Chinaman, Laundryman* and *Sacco, Vanzetti* are free, except in their use of recurrent musical phrases; they also often remain for long periods on single chanting pitches (c.f. 'Prayers of Steel'). But their piano parts are organised to a remarkably high degree: the accompaniment to *Chinaman, Laundryman* returns to the isorhythmic techniques of the *Piano Study in Mixed Accents* and the *Three Songs*, while that of *Sacco, Vanzetti* is even more complex. Once again, therefore, we can identify dissonant relationships between the implied structures of the individual parts in a work. But here, as elsewhere, the intention is merely to balance the heart and the mind, to control musical emotion through carefully planned musical structures. In *Chinaman, Laundryman* Crawford clearly distinguishes between the humanity of the Chinee who addresses us and the mechanical, monotonous work from which he scrapes a living.

In Crawford's compositions, therefore, we can see the most advanced of Seeger's theories being turned into actual musical substance. Indeed, it would be tempting to describe Crawford's music of 1930 to 1933 as being the transcription of someone else's ideas. However, such a supposition would be dangerously simplistic. The reality is of Crawford's very personal response to a set of theoretical concepts: a response as individual as those of Carl Ruggles, Henry Cowell and Seeger himself. The theory of dissonant counterpoint, like Schoenberg's 'method of composing with twelve notes related only to each other', was a tool to be used by the composer, not an autocratic system which dictated to him (or her). The proof of this lies in the wide variety of means to which the theory was put, and the even wider variety of ends which were the result.

4 New Musical Resources

Radical innovation in the music of Henry Cowell (1897–1965)

I want to live in the *whole world* of music.
Henry Cowell

According to Charles Seeger, Henry Cowell was his first brilliant student. Certainly, by the time that Harry Cowell took his seventeen-year-old son along to meet Seeger at Berkeley – probably in the autumn of 1914 – Henry had composed his Opus 108.[1] Seeger was duly impressed.

The circumstances of Cowell's life and education in the years prior to this meeting had been unusual, to say the least.[2] His formal schooling had lasted for only a few months, while his informal teaching had consisted of endless conversations with his mother, and profuse reading. As the family's sole income-earner he had worked as a janitor, gardener, and collector of wild flowers. The music produced during these early years – increasing greatly in quantity following the purchase of an upright piano in 1912 – shows a corresponding freedom from academic constraint. To Cowell, anything was valid source material for a new composition, and this is reflected in many of his titles: *The Night Sound* (10), *Waltz, Rippling Waters* (15), *Polish Dance* (31), *Savage Suite* (40) and *Mist Music* (65 and 66) (all of which date from 1910–13) are typical. A few pieces point towards the future: the third movement of *Adventures in Harmony* (59) (Jun. 1913) employs primitive tone-clusters; in *Sounds from the Conservatory* (60) (Jun. 1913) two tonally different pieces are performed simultaneously. And in *Anger Dance* (104/6) (May 1914) the composer's frustration with an unsympathetic doctor is translated into the multi-repetition of short musical phrases in an early premonition of the minimalist processes which over fifty years later produced Philip Glass' *Music in Similar Motion*. The experience of these years is best summarised in *Resumé in Ten Movements* (120) (Sep. 1914), whose movements both chart a chronological path through musical history and provide emphatic evidence of Cowell's innate eclecticism. Among the items are a *Classic Sonate*, Norwegian, English, Irish and Oriental *Folk Music*, and a *Romantic* sonata. The *Futurist* coda-cadenza includes the use of piano harmonics: the silently-held pitches are notated in a manner (using diamond-shaped noteheads) now familiar, but which must have been rather uncommon in California in 1914.

Once Cowell had started his studies at Berkeley, Seeger convinced him of the importance of two separate – and yet linked – points: that Cowell needed to examine systematically his own use of new and experimental compositional techniques; and, conversely, that he should compose a repertory of works which would further explore these innovations. The theoretical half of this equation was met by a remarkable book, *New Musical Resources*, written between 1916 and 1919 though revised before its original publication in 1930. The practical half, however, was only partially realised: some of the ideas contained in *New Musical Resources* – for instance the ordering of tempi through the use of ratios derived from the harmonic series (see pages 90–98) and the suggestion of a notated 'scale' of tone-quality (see pages 32–35) – were seemingly never used by Cowell himself.[3] In other cases, well developed ideas found only limited practical expression: fully fledged examples of polyharmony (see pages 24–32) – which is discussed below – are found in only a few works, including the song *Where She Lies* (400) (1924) and the first movement of the Concerto for Piano and Orchestra (440) (Mar. 1928). The use of sliding tones (pages 19–21) is, again, encountered only rarely, for instance in the third movements of *A Composition* (406) (1925) and the *Mosaic Quartet* (518) (1935), and in the string piano piece *The Banshee* (405) (1925).

Of the more often encountered techniques explored in *New Musical Resources*, the most familiar is dissonant counterpoint, discussed between pages 35 and 42. As was mentioned earlier, Seeger's teaching of this discipline at Berkeley was connected with the arrival there of Cowell. In later years, Seeger recalled that Cowell had made much more of the technique than had any other student, particularly quantitively. Having apparently filled several notebooks with exercises,[4] he produced the String Quartet No. 1 (197) (Apr. 1916). Here, the dissonance is melodic and harmonic, rather than rhythmic (c.f. Seeger's *Psalm 137* and the works by Ruggles discussed in chapter 3) and of its three movements only the first two are contrapuntal. The opening *Andante sostenuto* clearly shows the extent to which the techniques of dissonant counterpoint had been developed at this point (example 4.1). The level of horizontal intervallic dissonance is quite high in all parts, major dissonances such as the semitone predominating. But pitches are often repeated in close proximity, thus rather negating the later principle of non-repetition of tones. Rhythmically, the work is

Example 4.1. Cowell: String Quartet No. 1 (197), i; bars 1–5

very consonant; but harmonically the four lines produce a high level of vertical dissonance. This *Andante* proceeds musically by quite traditional means: two motifs (marked x and y in example 4.1) constantly recur in new guises, within an overall three-part structure. The joins between sub-sections are clearly marked by the breaks in texture (A, bars 1–13; B, 14–28; C, 28–43). The music builds to an impressive climax before a pizzicato eleven-pitch chord heralds the arrival of the second – *Allegro non troppo* – movement. (Ruth Crawford was to use a similar gesture to mark the opening of the second movement of her String Quartet – see example 3.22). Here the music is arranged as a fairly strict canon, the initial set of entries being viola (bar 44)–'cello (45)–violin 2 (46)–violin 1 (bar 47, but delayed by a quaver). The viola subsequently presents a series of contrasting points of imitation (at bars 54, 61 and 66) before the final, freer section commences at bar 78. Here, the undulating lines conceal the reinstatement of harmony over counterpoint as Cowell's primary consideration.

In the short third movement – marked *Andante* – there is only really harmony; melody, counterpoint and even rhythm seem hardly to exist (example 4.2). Perhaps the most important feature of this movement is the way in which

Example 4.2. Cowell: String Quartet No. 1 (197), iii; bars 1–8

much of the harmony is constructed: a consonant triad is dissonated by the addition of one or more pitches. This technique was mentioned by Seeger in 'On Dissonant Counterpoint', and was previously discussed in chapter 3 in connection with Harrison's *Saraband*. In Cowell's music it assumes major importance.

A second interesting facet of this movement is its seeming (and very early) exemplification of the principle of phrase balancing, discussed previously in relation to Seeger's *The Letter* and Crawford's *Diaphonic Suite No. 1*.[5] The music is structured as shown in figure 4.1, with the phrase markings, harmonic movement, texture and dynamics all contributing to the overall shape.

The kind of dissonant writing found in the String Quartet No. 1 recurs in many later works from this period, both small-scale and large-scale. Among the

Figure 4.1. Structure of Cowell's String Quartet No. 1 (197), iii

section	A		Ai		B	
phrase	a	b	ai	bi	c	d
bars	1-4	5-8	10-13	14-17	19-21	22-25
dynamics	pp		ff		*nf⟨sff⟩p* ⟨ ⟩ *pp*	

G.P.　　　　　　G.P.

former can be included the *Seven Paragraphs* for string trio (408) (1925) and the second piano *Woof* (451/2) of 1928; among the latter are the *Movement for String Quartet* (450) (1928), the chamber orchestra work *Polyphonica* (458) (1930) and the string quintet *Ensemble* (380) (1924). The *Movement for String Quartet* has an overall quasi-sonata-form shape, while *Polyphonica* is a multi-section single movement, whose music is primarily melodic and contrapuntal in nature. *Ensemble*, on the other hand, is in four movements of variable instrumentation and type. Although the 1956 revision of the work is for strings only, the original 1925 version also calls for three Southwestern American Indian instruments called thundersticks: one accompanies the 'cello solo of the third movement, while all three play in the opening *Larghetto*. The instrument apparently produces a soft whirring sound whose volume and pitch are directly related to the speed at which it is swung around the player's head. Cowell notates only the first eleven bars of the thundersticks' music in the first movement, and only the first and last two bars in the third movement. During the remaining bars of these movements the players improvise their parts. Additionally, the notation which *does* appear consists merely of a graphed indication of *crescendi* and *diminuendi* (equalling the rise and fall of pitch): see example 4.3.

Example 4.3. Cowell: *Ensemble* (380); thunderstick notation

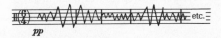

pp

We thus find in *Ensemble* a very early example of improvised music being combined with determined music, and of the use of (relatively) non-specific graphed notation as an initial guide to that improvisation (c.f. Ives' *Halloween* (W11), etc.).

The strings' music in the first movement falls basically into two large sections, the second of which (starting at bar 64) is a much varied repeat of the first. Generally speaking, in each half there is a gradual shift of emphasis from harmonically biased writing (e.g. bars 5–9) to polyphonically biased writing which may include the use of some free imitation (e.g. bars 39–46), though the movement contains a full range of dissonant textures, from monody (e.g. bars 24–27) through harmony (e.g. bars 18–23) to counterpoint.

The second movement is a *Prestissimo* Scherzo and Trio, in $\frac{3}{4}$ throughout; rhythmic variety is provided by frequent syncopation and cross-accent. The form is articulated by means of both variable phrase lengths and contrasts of texture, as is shown by an examination of the first Scherzo (figure 4.2). The a

Figure 4.2. Structure of the first Scherzo of Cowell's *Ensemble* (380), ii

```
sub-section      |      a      :           b              :      ai      |
                 |             :                          :              |
phrase lengths   | 7 + 7 + 7 + 7 : 4 + 4 + 4 + 4 + 4 + 4 + 4 + 6 : 6 + 6 + 6 + 6 |
(no. of ³/₄ bars)|             :                          :              |
```

music is conceived polyphonically and is very much in four independent parts (example 4.4). The melody seen here in the 'cello is passed around from voice to voice during the course of the sub-section. The harmony produced by this polyphony is freely dissonant and there are relatively few occasions where we find triads being dissonated.

Example 4.4. Cowell: *Ensemble* (380), ii; Scherzo, bars 1–7

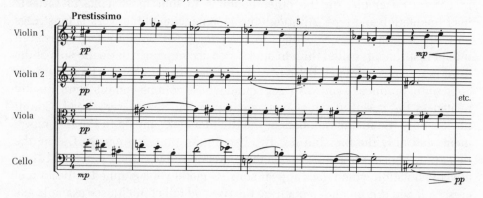

The b music is conceived quite differently, as melody plus chordal accompaniment (example 4.5). Approximately half of these four-pitch chords are dissonated triads, and the accompaniment becomes increasingly syncopated during each new phrase.

When the ai music appears, the shortened main melody is otherwise much as before, but the accompaniment has been substantially rewritten. Texturally, it is now partly homophonic and partly polyphonic; and in the hemiola rhythm of its first two bars it imitates the main melody.

In the opening section of the Trio, the syncopated melody plus chordal accompaniment suggested by b is taken a stage further: the melody here is much more syncopated and the harmony is generally bitonal. The syncopation is then applied to all four voices in the movement's first completely homophonic section (Trio, bars 17–35) whose harmony – like that of the succeeding music – generally consists of dissonated triads. All of the above textures, with the exception of b, are subsequently varied in the remainder of the Trio, and second Scherzo.

Example 4.5. Cowell: *Ensemble* (380), ii; Scherzo, bars 29–40

Throughout the Scherzo and Trio, individual lines show a reasonably high degree of intervallic dissonance. This is also a feature of the third movement, an extended monody for solo 'cello and thunderstick. Here, though, Cowell additionally holds tightly to the principle of non-repetition of tones (very few pitches recur before six or more other pitches have intervened); and although there is relatively little rhythmic dissonance, the dangers of rhythmic regularity are partially counteracted through the use of syncopation, tied notes and irregular phrasings. The very Rugglesian character of the resulting melody is perhaps an indication of Cowell's knowledge of and interest in the work of the older composer.

In the final *Allegro* – whose form is very similar to that of the first movement – we find the principles of dissonant counterpoint being applied rather more strictly than elsewhere in the work. Apart from the general considerations of dissonant melody and harmony – which abound here – there is considerably more rhythmic dissonance. Cowell relies heavily on freely imitative counterpoint, initially in two parts with harmonic accompaniment (e.g. bars 1–5) but later in three to five parts (example 4.6). Note particularly the quasi-retrogressions of violin 2 and the successive rhythmic dissonance of the imitative point. The movement also contains – in the link between the two main sections, at bars 37–41 – a hint of polymetre (or metric dissonance).

Other works of this period – for instance *What's This?* (213/2) (Nov. 1917), *Time Table* (213/6) (Dec. 1917), a number of the *Ings* (353) (mainly 1917–22) and partic-

Example 4.6. Cowell: *Ensemble* (380), iv; bars 22–28

ularly *Vestiges* (305) (Jul. 1920) – also show in different ways Cowell's grounding in and indebtedness to the disciplines of dissonant counterpoint. However, their complexities pale by comparison with those of the two *Rhythm-Harmony Quartets*: the *Quartet Romantic* (223) (Sep. 1917), for two flutes, violin and viola, and the *Quartet Euphometric* (283) (Sep. 1919), for string quartet. For according to Seeger, once Cowell had been through the class in dissonant counterpoint, he 'went off on a tangent to a system of his own which differed radically from mine'.[6] This system was based on the identification by Cowell of a physical relationship between rhythm and harmony:

I entered the University of California in the fall of 1914 and was faced for the first time with an actual textbook in music theory – the famous *Foote & Spalding*. I was already exploring the possibilities inherent in counter-rhythms – 2 against 3, 3 against 4, and others much more complex – and on first opening *Foote & Spalding*, I was struck with the fact that the lower reaches of the overtone series were expressed by the same ratios I had been using to describe counter-rhythms. Could they be somehow the same?[7]

Experiments with two sirens confirmed Cowell's suspicions: he made many written examples showing relationships between rhythm, metre and pitch, which culminated in the composition of the *Rhythm-Harmony Quartets*. Some years later, in a further development of his ideas, Cowell collaborated with the scientist Leon Theremin in the production of a keyboard electronic instrument – the rhythmicon – which could produce up to sixteen simultaneous rhythms. Each rhythm was inextricably linked to its corresponding harmonic in the overtone series, though the fundamental to which these harmonics related could be altered; additionally, the keyboard's seventeenth key produced syncopation. For this instrument Cowell composed a Concerto for Rhythmicon and Orchestra (481) (1931 – though not performed until 1971) and the lost *Music for Violin and Rhythmicon* (485) (?1932). Seeger, incidentally, held that the principle underlying the rhythmicon and its music was first demonstrated by him at Berkeley, using a phonograph disc with increasing numbers of clicks (1–16) in the concentric circles radiating out from its centre. Through this, he and his students learned to articulate rhythms of 2:3, 3:2, etc., up to 5:6.[8] However, Seeger's description seems to be only of counter-rhythms and not of the relationship between harmony and rhythm which was explored by Cowell in the *Rhythm-Harmony Quartets*, etc.

The principles underlying the first movement of the *Quartet Romantic*[9] are described in *New Musical Resources* (pages 49–66). Cowell derives the rhythmic content of the movement from the harmonic ratios of a pre-composed harmonic theme. Taking C as fundamental (equalling a rhythm of 1), a simple treble clef triad, whose harmonic ratios to the fundamental are 4, 5 and 6, produces the rhythms shown in example 4.7.

Example 4.7. Translating harmony into rhythm (1)

The rhythmic value of pitches outside the overtone series of any given fundamental has initially to be expressed as a vibration ratio: f′ is two octaves and a perfect fourth above C; the vibration ratio for this interval is $^{16}/_3$ and the consequent rhythmic value is $5^{1}/_3$ beats per $^4_4$ bar (example 4.8).

Example 4.8. Translating harmony into rhythm (2)

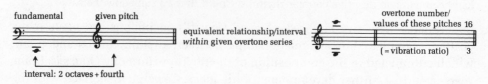

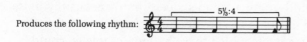

There are potentially enormous problems involved in the notation of such rhythms as these. Indeed, Cowell stated that the writing down of both *Rhythm-Harmony Quartets* was delayed for two years simply for this reason.[10] His solution was to devise a complicated series of geometrically based note-head shapes (example 4.9) which make unnecessary more traditional figurations. Cowell never fully exploited this system: it makes limited, and useful, appearances in the *Rhythm-Harmony Quartets*, and is used extensively in the piano piece *Fabric* (307) (Sep. 1920) with which it was originally published in 1922. In other works, however – for instance *Vestiges* and the much later *Rhythmicana* (557) (1938) – Cowell abandoned the system in favour of traditional solutions.

Example 4.9. Cowell's system for the notation of complex rhythms

Whole-note series
Oval-shaped notes
Whole-note: ○ half-note: ♩ quarter-note: ♩ 8th-note: ♪ 16th-note: ♬ 32nd-note: ♬

Third-note series
Triangular-shaped notes
2-3rds-note: △ 3rd-note: ♩ 6th-note: ♩ 12th-note: ♪ 24th-note: ♬ 48th-note: ♬

Fifth-note series
Square notes
4-5ths-note: ▫ 2-5ths-note: ♩ 5th-note: ♩ 10th-note: ♪ 20th-note: ♬ 40th-note: ♬

Seventh-note series
Diamond-shaped notes
4-7ths-note: ◇ 2-7ths-note: ♩ 7th-note: ♩ 14th-note: ♪ 28th-note: ♬ 56th-note: ♬

Ninth-note series.
Oblong notes
8-9ths-note: ▭ 4-9ths-note: ♩ 2-9ths-note: ♩ 9th-note: ♪ 18th-note: ♬ 36th-note: ♬

Eleventh-note series
Oval notes with stroke
8-11ths-note: ◖ 4-11ths-note: ♩ 2-11ths-note: ♩ 11th-note: ♪ 22nd-note: ♬ 44th-note: ♬

Thirteenth-note series
Triangular notes with stroke
8-13ths-note: △ 4-13ths-note: ♩ 2-13ths-note: ♩ 13th-note: ♪ 26th-note: ♬ 52nd-note: ♬

Fifteenth-note series
Square notes with stroke
8-15ths-note: ▪ 4-15ths-note: ♩ 2-15ths-note: ♩ 15th-note: ♪ 30th-note: ♬ 60th-note: ♬

Returning to the *Quartet Romantic*, it should be clear that a simple harmonic theme can provide the rhythmic material for a lengthy composition. The problem lies in the choice of pitches to be added to this rhythmic material. In a work like the Concerto for Rhythmicon and Orchestra, harmony and rhythm are truly linked in the sense that only one pitch (that of the overtone in question) is applied to each derived rhythm. In this system, one bar of a simple harmonic theme (actually the first bar of the *Quartet Romantic*'s first harmonic theme)

Example 4.10. Sample bar from a harmonic theme

would provide the following music:

Example 4.11.

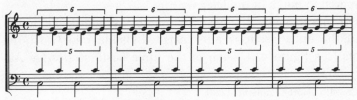

Another answer would be to apply free pitches to the given rhythms

Example 4.12.

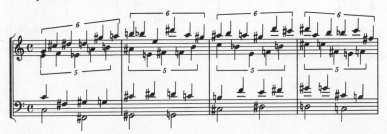

though then the basic relationship between harmony and rhythm has been lost: one cannot 'hear' the fundamental harmonic theme in this music. What Cowell does in the *Quartet Romantic* is to swing between these two poles (see example 4.13). Of the seventeen attacks in each bar, the number whose pitches belong to the underlying chord of C major are as follows:

bar	1	2	3	4
no. of pitches	7	7	4	4

Looking at individual lines, the viola seems clearly to outline a minor, the violin C major, flute 2 D major, and flute 1 a mixture of C major and c minor. On balance, therefore, it could be argued that Cowell here subtly suggests the

Example 4.13. Cowell: *Quartet Romantic* (223), i; bars 1–4
© 1974 by C.F. Peters Corporation, New York, USA. Reproduced by permission of Peters Edition Limited, London.

underlying C major of the harmonic theme. However, this passage is relatively diatonic when compared to much of the later writing.

The overall form of this movement is ternary, though the middle section is relatively short and the outer sections are clearly divisible into two quite separate components (see figure 4.3). Each of the three basic sections – Aa,

Figure 4.3. Structure of Cowell's *Quartet Romantic* (223), i

section	A		B	A	repeated	Coda
sub-section	a	b		a	b	
bars	1 - 56	57 - 129	130 - 167	1 - 56	57 - 125	168 - 175
tempo	crotchet=100	(crotchet=75);Presto,rit.	crotchet=100→			Presto
		canon			canon	
harmonic theme	1	2	3	1	2	2a

Ab and B – is derived from a separate harmonic theme. Those pre-composed by Cowell for Aa and Ab are reproduced in the published score (though the second, especially, contains a number of inaccuracies; harmonic theme 3 has apparently not survived – if it ever existed – but can be reconstructed from the music of the actual Quartet).

On a few occasions the pitches used in the Quartet resemble those of the underlying harmonic theme; generally such passages occur at structurally important moments. The end of the Aa section (bars 53–56; see example 4.14) is marked by a chromatically altered chord of G major while the end of Ab (bars 126–129) is marked even more clearly by a 4–3 suspension over a G major chord,

Example 4.14. Cowell: *Quartet Romantic* (223), i; bars 53–56
© 1974 by C.F. Peters Corporation, New York, USA. Reproduced by permission of Peters Edition Limited, London.

an exact duplication of the corresponding moments of harmonic theme 2. The end of the whole movement (coda, bars 168–175) is marked in both harmonic theme 2 and the actual music by octave Gs, while the octave F♯s of bars 162–163 and the rhythmic regularity which follows them (though not corresponding to any pitches in harmonic theme 3) suggest that the end of section B is imminent (example 4.15). In this example (and, indeed, in the whole passage from bars

Example 4.15. Cowell: *Quartet Romantic* (223), i; bars 162–167
© 1974 by C.F. Peters Corporation, New York, USA. Reproduced by permission of Peters Edition Limited, London.

Example 4.15. (cont.)

158 to 167) the ratios derived from the harmonic theme are inverted in the parts of the Quartet: flute 1 has the slowest moving rhythms (derived from the lowest pitches of the harmonic theme) and the viola the fastest moving rhythms (derived from the highest pitches of the harmonic theme) etc. This possibility is described in *New Musical Resources* on pages 52 and 53. But at no point in the Quartet are two other possibilities exploited: that of shifting ratios from one voice to another *within* a given bar, or of the subdivision of notes of any given ratio-length. The latter is, however, approached in the joining together of two bars of a given ratio, so as to produce more equal rhythmic durations than those indicated simply by the ratio (e.g. flute 1, bars 5–6, where two bars of $6\frac{2}{3}$ are ironed out to one two-bar unit of $13\frac{1}{3}$).

In addition to the exceptions demonstrated above, Cowell also makes some re-use of pitch materials. Perhaps the most important of these is the recapitulation of the opening pitches of the work near the beginning of section B̲. While the pitches in bars 132 + are unaltered, the rhythms to which they are linked are derived from a different harmonic theme. The opening four bars of the work (see example 4.13) when 'recapitulated' appear as shown in example 4.16. As in a kaleidoscope, the same materials come to be seen (or rather heard) in a new and different alignment to each other: like Ives before him and Crawford after him, Cowell is happy to treat the various parameters of a musical idea with complete independence.

A second re-use of materials is associated with much of section A̲b: the music, like its harmonic theme, is arranged as a canon. The canon in harmonic theme 2 is tonal, rhythmically regular, and uses pairs of entries a fifth apart. The canon in the Quartet, however, shows no melodic or rhythmic trace of this

Example 4.16. Cowell: *Quartet Romantic* (223), i; bars 132–137
© 1974 by C.F. Peters Corporation, New York, USA. Reproduced by permission of Peters Edition
Limited, London

underlying harmonic theme. All four entries use the *same* pitches, taken from a
complete set of 67; but to compensate for this the second pair of entries has new
rhythms, as a consequence of the different pitches of the harmonic theme. The
canonic subject also makes an appearance in section B: following flute 1's
recapitulation of its bars 1–12 as bars 132–139 (see above), a one-bar link leads to
a reiteration – between bars 141 and 149 – of the pitches originally played by
flute 2 in bars 57–72. Of course, the new harmonic theme 3 which underlies this
passage ensures that the pitches are associated with yet another set of rhythms.

Cowell may never have written down the harmonic theme 3 which underlies section $\underline{B}$: the harmonic themes of sections $\underline{Aa}$ and $\underline{Ab}$ are properly composed in four real parts, and are stylistically satisfactory. By comparison, that of $\underline{B}$ seems improvised – it contains some unfortunate false relations, and its very stodgy arpeggiated harmony bears little comparison to that of harmonic themes 1 and 2. It is quite possible that Cowell, by now having a 'feel' for his system, may have improvised harmonic theme 3 as he composed.[11]

In its overall sound the *Quartet Romantic* is quite unlike anything else in music. As with some of Ruth Crawford's later pieces one is simply unaware of traditional values of synchrony between parts: rather, one hears only the complete heterophony of four independent lines co-existing in musical space. Given Cowell's original intention here – to show an alchemical link between harmony and rhythm – this is rather paradoxical. Certainly, no unprepared listener would be aware of the harmonic themes underlying the work, let alone their link to the actual music being heard. Cowell also intended, however, that the music should be 'flowing and lyrical, not severe or harsh, or ejaculatory'[12] and stated that it was 'conceived as something human that would sound warm and rich and somewhat *rubato*'. In performance this, at least, is found to be true.

Perhaps the main problem with the system Cowell employed in the *Quartet Romantic* was that he was left with relatively little to compose: rhythm, metre and form were all in effect pre-determined. It simply remained for him to add the pitches – a kind of musical equivalent to colouring by numbers. This is certainly not true of the much shorter, one-movement *Quartet Euphometric*, whose pre-compositional procedures are described in *New Musical Resources* between pages 66 and 81. Whereas in the previous system it is the rhythms which are generated by the underlying harmonic theme, here it is the metrical structure. Thus the C major triad of example 4.10 produces a polymetric unit of $\frac{4:5:6}{4:4:4}$, rather than a polyrhythmic unit of 4:5:6 (example 4.17). In theory, the three metres will not coincide until a cycle of 60 crotchet beats is completed.

Example 4.17. Translating harmony into metre

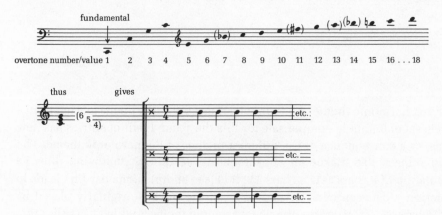

Thus a potential problem here is that a simple chord can generate a vast metrical framework. Cowell overcomes this, however, by cheating: in the *Quartet Euphometric* he invariably moves to a new set of polymetres before the existing cycle has been completed, a procedure suggested on page 75 of *New Musical Resources*. Indeed, Cowell's whole approach in this piece is much more casual than that in the *Quartet Romantic*: at the simplest level, this is shown by the work's framing between an introduction and conclusion unrelated to the metrical structure (see figure 4.4).

Figure 4.4. Structure of Cowell's *Quartet Euphometric* (283)

section	Intro^n		a	b	c	d	e	f	; Conc^n
length in crotchets	17		30	16	15	15	16	28	+ 12
tempo	Largo (crotchet=66)		Allegro (crotchet=108)	rit	a tempo		accel	Largo (crotchet=66)	;

A ‖ ———————— B ———————— ‖ Ai

The harmonic theme on which sections a–f are built is surprisingly short – see example 4.18. Taking C (=1) as fundamental, each chord produces the metres depicted in figure 4.5. The work is thus polymetrically complex, and potentially of epic length. However, taking section a (30 crotchets in length) as the equivalent of a minim in the original harmonic theme, Cowell proportions sections b–f accordingly. To achieve this he simply alters – or cuts short – one or more metrical patterns (e.g. violin 1, end of c).

Example 4.18. Cowell: *Quartet Euphometric* (283); harmonic theme

Where the harmonic theme provides only three metric voices, the fourth in the actual Quartet doubles one of the extant lines (e.g. violin 2/viola in c). Two additional freedoms allowed here are the exchanging of metres between voices (e.g. the $\frac{3}{4}/\frac{5}{4}$ exchange between violins 1 and 2 near the start of a) and the introduction of free voices not generated by the harmonic theme (e.g. viola at the start of d).

The music which fills this metrical framework is quite unlike that of the *Quartet Romantic*. It avoids entirely the pitches implied by the harmonic theme

Figure 4.5. Relationship between harmony and metre in Cowell's *Quartet Euphometric* (283)

section	a			b			c			d			e				f			
chord	1			2			3			4			5				6			
pitch	e'	g	c	c'	a	f	c'	g	e	f'	a	d	f'	b	g	d	e'	c'	g	c
vibration ratio	5	3 2		4	$3^1/_3$	$2^2/_3$	4	3	$2^1/_2$	$5^1/_3$	$3^1/_3$	$2^1/_4$	$5^1/_3$	$3^3/_4$	3	$2^1/_4$	5	4	3	2
resulting metre	$\frac{5}{4}$	$\frac{3}{4}$ $\frac{2}{4}$		$\frac{4}{4}$	$\frac{5}{6}$	$\frac{4}{6}$	$\frac{4}{4}$	$\frac{3}{4}$	$\frac{5}{8}$	$\frac{8}{6}$	$\frac{5}{6}$	$\frac{9}{16}$	$\frac{8}{6}$	$\frac{15}{16}$	$\frac{3}{4}$	$\frac{9}{16}$	$\frac{5}{4}$	$\frac{4}{4}$	$\frac{3}{4}$	$\frac{2}{4}$
theoretical length of cycle (in crotchets)	30			40			60			720			2160				60			
actual length (in crotchets)	30			16			15			15			16				28 + Conc			

(N.B. Metres resulting from complex vibration ratios [e.g. $2^1/_4$] are calculated as follows :
$2^1/_4 \rightarrow 2^1/_4/4 = {}^9/_4/4 = {}^9/_{16}$.)

(thus again negating the concept of harmony and rhythm being linked) and instead reminds us of the early quartet music of Schoenberg, Berg and Webern (see example 4.19).

The polymetres of the introduction are freely conceived and seem to be based on the musical phrasings of the four voices; conversely, the musical phrasings of sections a–f often contradict the pre-determined metrical structure. The use of imitation (seen in example 4.19, and marked as such) continues in section b while in c the instruments pair off, as in the String Quartet No. 1. Again using imitative gestures, the music builds through section e to an impressive climax in f, just before the return of the original slow tempo. Here, the melody first heard in a is presented on the solo 'cello; as the other instruments re-enter, they drift back into metrical unison before the quasi-recapitulation of the opening texture (final three bars).

The harmony of the *Quartet Euphometric* generally results from the superimposition of the four melodic voices; but a number of vertically conceived chords are dissonated triads. Despite this more familiar sound world, however, the unprepared listener will again be unaware of the processes underlying the music he is hearing.

Cowell never again employed the pre-compositional systems described above. Indeed, virtually all of his later music eschews anything like the degree of rhythmic and metric complexity found in the *Rhythm-Harmony Quartets*.

Example 4.19. Cowell: *Quartet Euphometric* (283); introduction and opening of section a
© 1974 by C.F. Peters Corporation, New York, USA. Reproduced by permission of Peters Edition
Limited, London.

There are, however, some exceptions to this, most notably the piano pieces
Fabric (307) (Sep. 1920) and the three-movement *Rhythmicana* (557) (1938). In
both *Fabric* and *Rhythmicana*'s second (*Andante*) movement, Cowell's rhythmic
writing is extremely dissonant (indeed, *Fabric* makes use of the notational
system shown in example 4.9). Yet both pieces feel tonal: this is because the
initial bass pitches of each bar provide a strong harmonic root for the other
pitches (c.f. Ives' use of bass pedal pitches). Additionally, these pitches may
well be followed by others forming triads or other harmonic groupings. The
progression from bar to bar of these harmonic roots and groupings is also
fundamentally tonal, thus suggesting a relatively simple harmonic skeleton for
each piece.

Formally, *Rhythmicana*'s second movement has a ternary structure, shown in
figure 4.6. Section A̲i consists of a reordering of the bars of A̲, as follows:

A̲   1 2 3 4   5 6 7 8   9 10 11 12   13 14 15 16
A̲i   1 2 4 3   6 5 8 7   10 12 11   14 13 15 16

(There is no equivalent in A̲i to the original bar 9.)

Figure 4.6. Structure of Cowell's *Rhythmicana* (557), ii

section	A	B	Ai + Coda	
	alto melody	soprano melody	alto melody	
bars	1 - 16	17 - 24	25-39 40-42	

Thus in <u>Ai</u>, both the harmony and the melody formed from it are 'new' and yet entirely integrated with the existing material. This reordering of given units – reminiscent of techniques often used by Ives – is similar to that found in the *Mosaic Quartet* (518) (1935) and the 'Ritournelle' from the incidental music to *Les Mariés de la Tour Eiffel* (563/2) (1939). In this *Andante*, though, it is Cowell rather than the performer(s) who reorders the units. The effect of this procedure can be seen if bars 1–4 are compared with their later *alter ego* (bars 25–28) (example 4.20).

Example 4.20. Cowell: *Rhythmicana* (557), ii; bars 1–4, 25–28

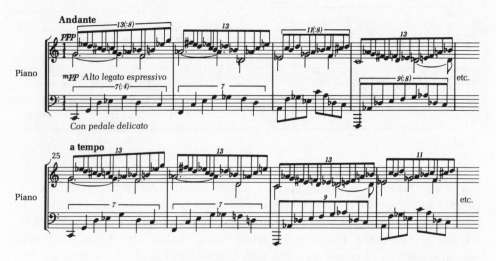

There seems to be some underlying rhythmic structuring present in this movement, as recognisable ostinato patterns occur in both hands. Whether this was intended by Cowell is unknown: but certainly the rhythmic patterning is like that found in his own String Quartet No. 4: *United Quartet* (522) (1936) and *Ostinato Pianissimo* (505) (1934), as well as in the earlier works of Ruth Crawford.

The outer movements of *Rhythmicana* are tonal; yet complex rhythmic and metric structures appear in both. The first movement – marked 'Impetuously' (crotchet = c.100) – is again arranged in ternary form: the <u>B</u> section occupies bars 17–29, and the exactly repeated second <u>A</u>, bars 30–45. There is a final four-bar coda. The melody and harmony relate to a modal b minor, and both hands make use of limited 'interior' clusters, similar to those found in *Maestoso* (429) (1926). The clusters here decorate both the right-hand melody and the left-hand accompaniment, the cluster pitches generally being drawn from either the 'b minor' scale or a transposition of it (example 4.21).

Example 4.21. Cowell: *Rhythmicana* (557), i; bars 1–4

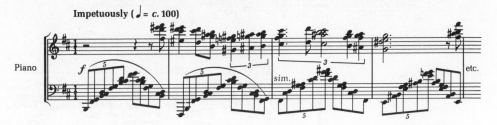

Within the overall ternary structure, the music is constructed in a series of three-bar rhythmic units. The left hand plays a simple rhythmic ostinato pattern, one bar long, which is altered (by a process of deceleration) only in the final bars. Against this the right hand plays polyrhythmically: in each three-bar phrase a new rhythmic idea, in dissonant relationship to the left hand, is introduced. The degree of dissonance created by this superimposition of different rhythmic units increases through sections A and B, and then through the second A to the coda. The rhythmic similarities between this music and the outer movements of Crawford's *Diaphonic Suite No. 3* (which Cowell may well have known) are hard to miss.

Just as the polyrhythms of the first two movements of *Rhythmicana* can be traced back to the *Quartet Romantic* and *New Musical Resources*, so the polymetres of the third and final movement can be traced back to the *Quartet Euphometric*. This *Allegro Vivace* is again arranged as a ternary structure whose proportions (in crotchets) are 70:60:70. Throughout each section the two hands operate independently: each has its own metric framework, built from melodic, harmonic and/or rhythmic ostinato patterns. The overall F major diatonicism of these ensures that harmonic dissonance does not occur where patterns overlap. In the outer sections the melodic right hand is in $\frac{3}{4}$, and the accompanying left hand in $\frac{5}{4}$. The right-hand melody is in two-part counterpoint and arranged into six three-bar phrases. These have an overall A–B–Ai shape – defined by the harmonic areas they occupy – which mirrors that of the whole movement. The left hand, meanwhile, has a one-bar rhythmic ostinato; harmonically, this is arranged into seven two-bar phrases (the first is introductory) having an overall A–B–Bi shape. Thus when the right hand recapitulates its A material, it does so over a harmonically different left hand (example 4.22). The quasi-ostinati of the two hands are set in a different perspective to each other: new harmonies are created not through re-invention, but rather through the realignment of existing elements. The effect is again kaleidoscopic.

The middle section of the movement is similarly arranged, though here the melodic right hand is in $\frac{5}{4}$, and the accompanying left hand in $\frac{3}{4}$. The right hand

Example 4.22. Cowell: *Rhythmicana* (557), iii; opening of first section and close of first section

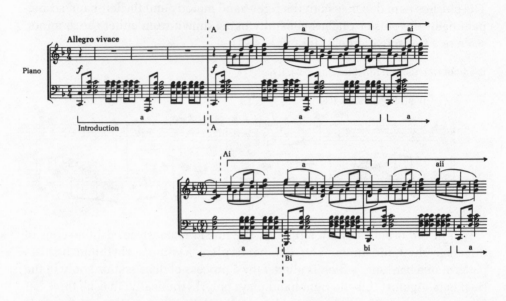

is written in two- to three-part counterpoint. Each of its bars contains the five-beat rhythmic ostinato associated with the left hand in the A sections; there are three four-bar phrases. The left hand plays five versions of a four-bar harmonic ostinato, rather chaconne-like in character. As in the A sections, the two hands together create new harmonic and rhythmic patterns through their constant realignment. A further refinement here is that the patterns of the two hands reflect each other arithmetically:

$$
\left.
\begin{array}{lccccc}
\text{right hand} & 3 & \times & 4 & \times & 5 \\
& \text{phrases} & & \text{bars} & & \text{beats} \\
\text{left hand} & 5 & \times & 4 & \times & 3
\end{array}
\right\} = 60 \text{ crotchet beats}
$$

The techniques used in this third movement of *Rhythmicana* are an obvious precursor of those of more recent minimalist or process music; yet they themselves may reflect the influence on Cowell of non-Western rhythmic systems, for instance those of India or South-East Asia. However, before we examine some of the later works in which Cowell further explores rhythmic structuring, it is necessary to turn our attention to his innovations in the fields of sonority and harmony.

Much of the preceding discussion relates to the large middle section – 'Rhythm' – of *New Musical Resources*. The outer sections of the book are entitled 'Tone Combinations' and 'Chord Formation', and occupy pages 3–42 and 111–139 respectively. With the exception of the passages on tone-quality and dissonant counterpoint, these sections deal with the theory and practice of new harmonic techniques. We need not concern ourselves here with Cowell's acoustically based justification of his ideas, but rather turn our attention to their use in his works. The two most important techniques discussed and employed by him are polyharmony and tone-clusters.

Polyharmony consists of the succession of polychords, which might themselves be defined as being harmonic complexes built from the overtones of a given fundamental and, occasionally, the overtones of *those* overtones. Thus, both common triads and more chromatic formations can be included in this categorisation (example 4.23). Usually, polychords appear in simple triadic

Example 4.23. Polychords

fundamental overtones   simple polychord   complex polychord†

† See Cowell: *New Musical Resources*, page 25.

forms, additional chromaticisms being provided by their combination and/or juxtaposition with other (polychordal) material. This is demonstrated at possibly its simplest level in the first *Woof* (451/1) (1928) where the left-hand melody generates a right-hand accompaniment of distantly related triadic polychords. A more believable polychordal passage occurs in bars 13–18 of the song *Where She Lies* (400) (1924), which also includes the use of dissonant counterpoint and a wide variety of clusters. If one accepts the principle of undertones,[13] then the final chords of *Maestoso* (429) (1926) also make polychordal sense, as do some passages in the orchestral work *Synchrony* (464) (1930).

Mention of the use of tone-clusters by Charles Ives and, more briefly, Ruth Crawford, has already been made in chapters 2 and 3. Neither of these composers employs clusters systematically; rather, clusters appear in their works either as the result of local organisation, or in purely pictorial contexts. Cowell, however, conducted a particularly thorough and long-term investigation of their musical possibilities: unlike polychords and polyharmony, therefore, tone-clusters are frequently found in his works, especially those for, or involving, the piano.

Tone-clusters are essentially chords built from major and minor seconds. At the simplest level, a C major triad with added second, sixth and seventh could be said to consist of two tone-clusters, as could a pentatonic, black-note or white-note, chord. More usually, though, the tone-cluster will consist of a larger number of adjacent pitches, either diatonic (white-note), pentatonic (black-note), or chromatic (white *and* black notes).

Cowell devised a special notation to indicate the use of clusters. Further refinements include anatomical indications ('Play with flat of hand'; 'Play with both forearms together'), the use of a specific notation (× or +) to indicate the use of the fist, and the appearance of silently held clusters (see example 4.24).

Example 4.24. Cowell: notation for tone-clusters

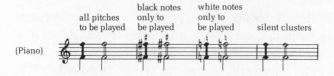

Cowell frequently used tone-clusters in diatonic works: probably the most famous of these is the piano piece *The Tides of Manaunaun* (291/1) (Jul.– Aug. 1917) in which a right-hand folk-like melody is accompanied by left-hand/arm clusters, evoking the Irish god Manaunaun's 'tremendous tides, which swept to and fro through the universe'.[14] Most of the clusters are chromatic, and either one or two octaves wide; at the climax, however, Cowell introduces both black- and white-note clusters whose top notes form a counter-melody, plus very wide, arpeggiated chromatic clusters (example 4.25).

Example 4.25. Cowell: *The Tides of Manaunaun* (291/1); bars 22–24

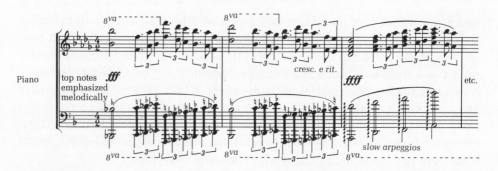

Cowell obviously felt tone-clusters to be appropriate to mythological contexts, as they appear in other works of this type. The song *Manaunaun's Birthing* (387) (1924) initially uses chromatic bass clusters as a kind of super-emphasised chordal root (e.g. bars 1–7). Later, wide diatonic clusters perform a similar function, though their 'whiteness' collides with the c minor/A♭ major of melody and accompaniment (e.g. bars 32–37). *The Voice of Lir* (354/3) (20 Nov. 1920) starts similarly to *The Tides of Manaunaun*, but later includes the two-arm chromatic punctuation of a chordal melody (e.g. bars 21–22). More difficult to perform are its 'interior' clusters – the staccato infilling of held bass octaves – and the arm-cluster shadowing of a melody played one octave higher by the fingers of the same limb (e.g. bars 17–20). And in *The Hero Sun* (354/2) (1922) pitches are systematically subtracted from pentatonic semi-clusters (e.g. bars 1–3), an effect similar to that described on pages 134–136 of *New Musical Resources*.

But in almost all of the above instances, Cowell's employment of tone-clusters is essentially decorative, and adds nothing of real importance to the musical substance. In a number of other more dissonantly conceived works, however, tone-clusters are more fully integrated into the tonal fabric. This is apparent in even a relatively consonant piece like *Maestoso* (429) (1926), where the importance of the clusters increases as the piece progresses. Two-pitch clusters (e.g. bars 1–4) are succeeded by three-pitch clusters (e.g. bars 33–35); these in turn are succeeded by three-pitch clusters which hold a rhythmically dissonant relationship to the surrounding music (e.g. bars 52–54). They are therefore conceived as an integral, rather than decorative, texture within the context of the overall musical argument. Similar instances of the structurally important use of clusters are found in *What's This?* (213/2) (Nov. 1917), *Time Table* (213/6) (Dec. 1917) and the song *Where She Lies* (400) (1924).

What's This? is a short piece in two distinct sections. The first – marked *Allegro* – consists of three dissonant monodic phrases (bars 1–2; 2–5; 5–6), the first two of which are closed by clusters. The third phrase leads directly into the main *Presto* section. This contains four phrases, the first and third of which use fist clusters, and the second hand clusters. In *Time Table*, a rhythmic canon of clusters underlies much of the middle section. Silent clusters frame the entire piece, while the quiet forearm clusters at bar 7 neatly divide the opening section into its constituent halves, before leading into the canon.

Where She Lies introduces a variety of cluster techniques, all of which are structurally important. The song opens with subtraction clusters (where the pitches of a cluster are either successively removed, leaving a single pitch, or selectively retained, leaving a chord. Its middle section is introduced and accompanied by diatonic subtraction and addition clusters. (These techniques are described in *New Musical Resources*, pages 126–136.) At bar 11, there is a silent cluster, against which a triad is sounded to produce sympathetic resonance.

In marked contrast to the gentleness of the tone-clusters in *Where She Lies* are those found in a group of violent pieces. The earliest of these is *Dynamic Motion* (213/1) (Nov. 1916), a work inspired – like Ives' contemporary *Tone Roads No. 3* (V38/iii) – by the New York subway system.

Antinomy (213/5) (Dec. 1917) opens with a *pp* < *fff* tremolo passage of alternating black-note and white-note forearm clusters, which move up the keyboard through almost three octaves. Following some high fist clusters, a very high tremolo leads to a rapid leaping descent, using full double-forearm clusters. These pyrotechnics serve merely to introduce a large-scale theme and variations. The structure of the piece is shown in figure 4.7.

Of interest in the twice-stated theme are the diatonic clusters which underpin it and the 'spread' clusters in the bass which accompany it (see example 4.26). Note also the expanding cluster of bar 23.

Variation 1 resembles the theme only skeletally but variations 2–4 adopt more of its melodic characteristics. Variation 4a leads naturally into the recapitulation of the theme, now accompanied by mainly white-note clusters.

Of particular note are the bass patterns which accompany the variations. Those of variations 1–3 consist of repeated three-quaver-length units, while that of variation 4 presents three variants of a three-quaver-length unit. Thus in variations 1–4, a polymetric relationship is established between the right hand

Figure 4.7. Structure of Cowell's *Antinomy* (213/5)

section	Introduction	Theme (x2)		Variations			
				1	2	3	4
bars	1 - 15	16-23	24-31	32 - 35	36 - 39	40 - 43	44 - 47
tempo	Moderato maestoso Più mosso	Presto		Moderato			
'key'		modal c		eb	r.h:d l.h:6b	r.h:b l.h:d	r.h:g l.h:0b
dynamic	pp < fff	ff dim		ppp	mp	f	ff dim

section	Variations							Theme + Variation	Coda
	3	2	1	2	3	4	4a		
bars	48 - 51	52 - 55	56 - 59	60 - 63	64 - 67	68 - 71	72 - 75	76 - 85	86-89
tempo			a s	b e f o r e					
'key'							r.h:g l.h:-	modal c	
dynamic	mp	pp	pp	mp	mp	ff	cresc.	fff	ffff➤

Example 4.26. Cowell: *Antinomy* (213/5); bars 16–19

('in' $\frac{2}{4}$) and the left hand ('in' $\frac{3}{8}$); and in each successive variation the relative power of the left-hand pattern is increased. In the final variation and coda, Cowell reverts to using full double-forearm clusters: the presentation of the rhythmic outline of the theme is followed by almost Chaikovskyan cadential gestures.

Similarly understated is *Tiger* (463/2) (1929), conceived as a large ternary form whose outer sections conceal a set of double variations. Cowell employs many types of tone-cluster in this piece, ranging in size from two or three pitches to around fifty – the *Presto* section of the coda (bars 89–98) opens with a *ffff* reappearance of the double-forearm cluster first encountered in bars 5–6. White-note, black-note and fully chromatic varieties freely intermingle and combine with dissonant chords and melodies. Also of importance are the silently-depressed clusters and chords, sometimes used to 'catch' pitches which have already been played (as in bar 6), or else to provide sympathetic resonance when other pitches are sounded. The degree of violence encountered in the roaring tone-clusters of *Tiger* is exceptional but by no means unique: similar effects also appear in *It Isn't It* (355) (1922) and *Advertisement* (213/4) (Nov. 1917). In these works, like *Where She Lies*, *Time Table* and *Dynamic Motion*, the tone-clusters are an integral part of the musical fabric. Cowell was working here with a quite new timbre, the dense accumulation of adjacent pitches, which in its most extreme forms (as Cage has noted) 'pointed towards noise and a continuum of timbre'.[15] It also, in Cowell's own music, pointed towards a development quite unforeseen in *New Musical Resources* – the direct manipulation of the strings of the piano to produce an even wider variety of available sounds.

Cowell coined the term string piano to describe an ordinary grand piano whose strings – as well as keyboard – are performed on. The use of the instrument is shown at its simplest in *The Fairy Bells* (447) (1928), where various hand-sized keyboard clusters accompany a simple melody plucked directly on the strings by the pianist's right hand. More developed examples of the integration of keyboard and non-keyboard elements are found in *Piece for Piano with Strings* (389/1) (1923) and *A Composition* (406) (1925). *Piece for Piano with Strings* makes consistent use of a small number of motifs, though its overall form is rhapsodic; it reads like 'a virtual catalogue of Cowell's new piano sonorities'.[16] The first two-thirds of the work (bars 1–51) are given over to the kind of 'conventional' keyboard writing already encountered in *Dynamic Motion* and *Tiger*. There then follows the first of two sections in which attention is focussed on the piano's strings (bars 51–55). Two basic techniques are used:

1 damping the strings while playing at the keyboard;
2 playing directly on the strings:
   a playing glissandi with the pads of the fingers;
   b playing glissandi with the fingertips;
   c gently striking the strings with the palm;
   d plucking strings with the pad of the finger.

After a return to the earlier keyboard writing (bars 56–74) the work closes with more playing on the strings; added to the above repertory of effects is the playing of a string glissando against a silently held keyboard cluster (bars 75–84).

In the first movement of *A Composition*, the new sounds of the solo string piano are superimposed on the conventional sounds of the *ripieno* winds and strings. The movement is in two roughly equal halves. In the first, the strings play a rhythmically regular, neo-baroque sequence of harmonies, around which the string piano moves in three distinct strata (example 4.27):

Example 4.27. Cowell: *A Composition* (406), i; bars 1–4
© by C.F. Peters Corporation, New York, USA. Reproduced by permission of Peters Edition Limited, London.

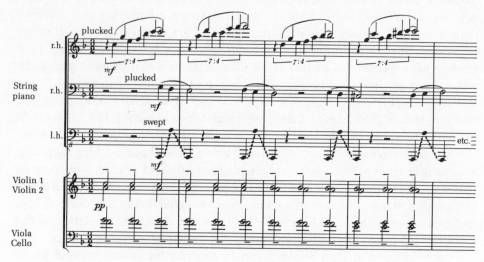

1 a plucked bass line which supports the strings' harmony;
2 a 'dominant pedal' of swept bass strings;
3 a rhythmically dissonant plucked melodic decoration of the harmony. Initially this decoration restricts itself to pitches close to the strings' chords, but as the section progresses, the pitches become increasingly dissonant.

The second half of the movement begins at bar 21. Here, the string piano retains only its plucked right-hand melody: the swept 'dominant pedal' is lost, while the plucked bass line is taken over by the bassoon. An oboe and a clarinet weave additional melodic lines imitating the bassoon, while the string piano performs a quasi-cadenza until bar 26. During the remainder of the movement the strings and winds continue along these lines. The string piano, meanwhile, retains its rhythmically dissonant countermelody; but in a reversal of the process found earlier, the pitches it plays become increasingly consonant.

The second movement is written for violin and string piano only – the violin carries the (rhythmically dissonant) melody, while the string piano provides a neo-baroque cluster-harmony accompaniment (example 4.28). (The accom-

Example 4.28. Cowell: *A Composition* (406), ii; bars 1–9
© by C.F. Peters Corporation, New York, USA. Reproduced by permission of Peters Edition Limited, London.

① Sweep strings (quickly) on 2nd & 4th beats of every measure.
② Notes in lower staff throughout are to be pressed down without striking, allowing the tones to sound when strings are swept.
③ Plucked.
④ Pluck first note always, in each measure.

panimental techniques used here are those of *The Aeolian Harp* (370) (?1923) – see below.) This string piano rhythmic pattern is adhered to rigidly throughout the movement, but the violin melody becomes much more fluid around the middle section.

The final movement of *A Composition* – for string piano and string quartet – is in distinct contrast to its predecessors. Marked *Presto*, it is constructed as a large ternary form with short coda. The opening A̲ section (bars 1–30) features for the string quartet the kind of dissonant counterpoint seen earlier – indeed, this music is quite similar to that of *Ensemble*'s second and fourth movements, in its harmonic use of dissonated triads. The micro-structure of this section is interesting both for its re-use of material in transposition, and for its overall shaping, which mirrors that of the entire movement. These features recur in the Ai section (bars 71–92).

Against the dissonant counterpoint of A, the string piano performs a variety of glissando effects which involve the alteration via the strings of pitches being sounded at the keyboard:

1 bars 1–4: a metal object is used to 'bend' a reiterated c′;
2 bars 5–8/9–12; 23–26/27–30: the fingers are slid up, then down, two strings (c′ and db′; d#′ and e′) allowing successive harmonics to sound;
3 bars 13–22: in each bar the player slides his fingers down the string to the pitch being sounded.

In section Ai the repertory of effects is altered: initially, the player performs two elongated versions of 3 above. After this, however, both hands move inside the body of the piano and two new effects are employed:

4 bars 79–90: right-hand fingernails flick quickly along a given string; the string one octave below is hit with the metal object;
5 bars 91–92: both hands flick along strings, on alternating crotchet beats, in a descending sequence.

In the middle section, the music of both string piano and accompanying quartet is composed almost entirely of glissandi. This passage would seem to be a practical illustration of the ideas postulated on pages 19–20 of *New Musical Resources*:

Sliding tones. . .are sometimes used in music. . .there is no clearly defined method of notating them. Natural sounds. . .all make use of sliding tones. . .such tones may be made the foundation of an art of composition by some composer who would. . .build perhaps abstract music. . .not with the idea of trying to imitate nature, but as a new tonal foundation.

Cowell's mention of notational problems is apt: in the present instance he generally relies on graphic notation. However, the degree of exactness of this notation varies from the relative precision of the strings in bars 31–32, to the rather less precise corresponding bars in the string piano part (example 4.29). Although the first and last pitches of the string piano's glissando are given here, the pitch of the apex of the curve is not: as with *Ensemble*'s thundersticks, we find what is effectively semi-improvised music. The performer does not merely have to play the notes; he has also to decide which notes to play.

Unlike the outer sections, the music written here for the string piano does not fall into the same micro-structural units as that for the quartet. However, both soloist and *ripieni* show a general progression from small-scale to large-scale glissandi. Around bar 50 we find contrapuntal glissandi on the string piano,

Example 4.29. Cowell: *A Composition* (406), iii; bars 31–32
© by C.F. Peters Corporation, New York, USA. Reproduced by permission of Peters Edition Limited, London.

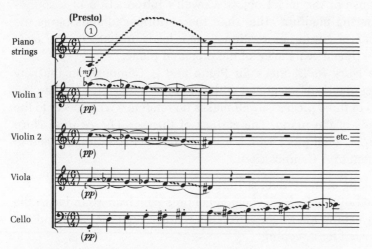

① Slide up [strings?] with fingers, following curve.

violin 2 and viola playing as a pair, and violin 1 imitating the 'cello at one bar's distance; by the end of the section all five instruments are performing wide and continuous glissandi.

In the short coda (bars 93–96; example 4.30) Cowell reintroduces glissandi, as

Example 4.30. Cowell: *A Composition* (406), iii; bars 93–96
© by C.F. Peters Corporation, New York, USA. Reproduced by permission of Peters Edition Limited, London.

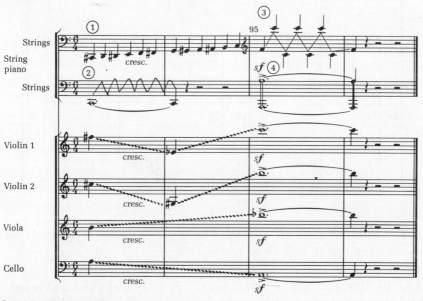

① Flicked along string.
② Flick back and forth with fingernail [on one string?].
③ Sweep back and forth with fingernail [over many strings].
④ Hit with metal object.

well as a number of other ideas. Note here the fingernail's flicking back and forth along a single string, an effect central to *The Banshee* (405) (1925). Also of importance is the use of the metal object: Cowell's introduction of a sound-inducing/sound-altering medium other than the performer's hands paves the way for all manner of future innovations[17] and leads ultimately to Cage's development, some fifteen years later, of the prepared piano.

Whereas in *The Fairy Bells, Piece for Piano* and *A Composition* the new sounds of the string piano are integrated with existing timbres, in a further and more radical group of three pieces Cowell makes no reference whatsoever to the conventional sounds of the piano. The earliest of these is *The Aeolian Harp* (370) (?1923), a simple, tonal piece which uses two basic effects already seen in the second movement of *A Composition*:

1 the plucking of individual strings;
2 the silent holding at the keyboard of chords which are sounded by the player sweeping his finger across the strings. Both the flesh and the nail are used for sweeping.

In fact these two effects have structural significance, as the piece consists simply of four varied statements of a modal, chordal pattern, each of which ends with a plucked arpeggio.[18]

Sinister Resonance (462) (1930) consists of a series of monodic variations, with simple harmonic accompaniment, arranged as in figure 4.8. Additionally,

Figure 4.8. Structure of Cowell's *Sinister Resonance* (462)

section	I					II					III	
sub-section/phrase	i	ii	iii	iv	v	i	ii	iii	iv	v	i	ii+
bars	1-5	6-10	11-14	15-19	20-22	23-27	28-32	33-36	37-41	42-44	45-49	50-56
timbre (see text)	3a	1a				3b	1a			1b	2	1b
harmonic accompt		f+c		ab+eb		f+c			ab+eb		f+c	

the various melodic phrases are subjected to small chromatic alterations on successive appearances, though those in Cowell's recorded performance sometimes differ from those in the published score. The real variation, however, is provided by the different timbres Cowell uses. The notes are played on the keyboard throughout, but three basic techniques of timbral modification are employed, for each of which the composer draws an analogy with conventional stringed instrument techniques:

1 Muting
   a Each string is muted at the bridge (c.f. muting violin strings, etc.). Octave transpositions are provided for if the desired register is impractical. (E.g. bars 6–23; 28–42.)
   b Each string is muted near the dampers – gives a drier tone than 1a (c.f. muting violin strings, etc.). (E.g. bars 42–50; 55–56.)
2 Production of natural harmonics
The note one octave below that notated in the score is played; the corresponding string is pressed gently at its centre (c.f. natural harmonics of violin or harp). (E.g. bars 51–54.)
3 Production of 'artificial harmonics'
   a The lowest string of the piano is pressed firmly at various points to produce a number of different pitches (c.f. artificial harmonics on violin). (E.g. bars 1–5; 46–49.)
   b The f string is pressed firmly at various points to produce a number of different pitches (c.f. artificial harmonics on violin). (E.g. bars 24–27.)

Even more complicated is *The Banshee* (405) (1925), which requires an assistant (or a wedge) to depress the sustaining pedal throughout (the performer stands in the crook of the instrument). The form of the piece is again simple, consisting of three timbral phrases each of which ends with a plucked motif, followed by a link or conclusion. As in *Sinister Resonance*, three basic techniques are used here, two being modified in various ways. All the music, however, is produced directly on the strings of the piano – the keyboard is not touched.

1 Sweeping chromatically across a large number of strings
   a With the flesh of the finger
      i From A (8va↓) to a given pitch (letter A in score) (e.g. bar 1).
      ii Up and back from A (8va↓) to b♭ (letter C in score) (e.g. bar 7).
      iii Sweeping back and forth from A (8va↓) to b♭, but in both directions simultaneously crossing the sweeps in the middle (letter H in score) (e.g. bar 20).
   b With the flat of the hand, producing a cluster (letter L in score) (e.g. bars 32–33).
2 Sweeping along one or more individual strings
   a With the flesh of the finger
      i Sweeping along one string (letter B in score) (e.g. bar 1).
      ii Sweeping along three strings, generally arranged as a diminished chord (e.g. bars 9–12; 34–37) or as a cluster (e.g. bars 38–40) (letter E in score).
      iii Sweeping along five strings, generally arranged as a cluster (letter I in score) (e.g. bars 21–24).
   b With the fingernails
      i Sweeping along one string (letter F in score) (e.g. bar 13).

    ii Sweeping along five strings (letter J in score) (e.g. bar 25).

    iii Sweeping along a chromatic cluster of strings (letter K in score) (e.g. bars 26–31).

  c With the flesh of one finger and the nail of another along one string; partly damped by combining the two actions when the nail is halfway along the string (letter G in score) (e.g. bars 14–19).

3 Plucking

With flesh of finger (letter D in score) (e.g. bars 8, 20, 33).

The problem with this piece, and to a greater or lesser extent all of the other works for string piano discussed previously, is that their notation is inadequate. At the simplest level, even *The Fairy Bells* requires a footnote explaining that the left hand plays at the keyboard while the right hand plays directly on the strings. Its notation does, however, give both an accurate series of instructions to the performer and a reasonably accurate picture of the sounds to the reader/listener. This is also true of *The Aeolian Harp*, and the first two movements of *A Composition*. In other pieces – for instance *Piece for Piano* and the outer sections of *A Composition*'s finale – conventional notation suffices both for performance instructions and as an aural guide, so long as adequate explanatory footnotes are included. In *Sinister Resonance*, however, Cowell chooses to provide an aural guide at the expense of succinct performance instructions: the pitches he writes are those which sound, not necessarily those which the performer plays (examples of this occur in bars 1–5, 24–27, 46–49, and 51–54, where the note played is different to that notated in the score). A large number of (potentially confusing) explanatory instructions are needed.

The reverse is true in *The Banshee* and the finale of *A Composition*, where the performance instructions are relatively clear but the aural picture difficult to imagine. Thus the score of *The Banshee*, once explained, makes good sense to the performer as a series of actions to be made, but virtually no sense to the reader or listener. In such pieces the traditional relationships between notation, execution and perception are fundamentally changed – the score becomes at least partly indeterminate of its performance. This is especially true in *The Banshee* and the middle section of *A Composition*'s finale, where graphic approximations of pitch and rhythm replace accurate conventional notation. As with the thunderstick parts in *Ensemble*, we find a situation in which the traditional performer-interpreter becomes a performer-creator making fundamental decisions concerning the music's public appearance. An extreme instance of this occurs with *Sinister Resonance*, whose Directions for Performance concede that

While on most standard makes and models [of grand piano] it is practical to perform Sinister Resonance just as written, there are to be found makes and models on which it is impractical, in which case it is always permissible to make such adjustments in the work as may be necessary.

Problems of notation, execution and perception similar to these recur in the percussion and prepared piano works of Cage (see chapter 5).

In his later work of this period, Cowell (like Ives in *Halloween* (W11) and *Over the Pavements* (V20)) makes some innovations in the realm of variable form, anticipating more recent developments. Such a move was already implicit in the early *Anger Dance* (104/6) (May 1914), whose published score gives specific instructions regarding the number of repetitions each musical fragment should be subjected to. Cowell, in his recorded performance, generally follows these.[19] But in the booklet accompanying the record, we read that 'each phrase may be repeated many times, depending on how angry the player is able to feel', a sentiment seemingly borne out by Cowell's 'improvised' extension of bars 25–26 and 27–28.

Later pieces, including the *Mosaic Quartet* (518) (1935) and the *Amerind Suite* (564) (1939), also encourage the performers to take creative decisions. The former has five movements which may be played in any order. In the *Amerind Suite* – intended as educational music – each of the three movements is in five versions of increasing difficulty; but the score also allows for the simultaneous performance on two or three pianos of different versions of the same movement. Perhaps Cowell's most radical innovation in this area – paradoxically brought about for purely pragmatic reasons – is elastic form: an example is the Ritournelle from the incidental music to *Les Mariés de la Tour Eiffel* (563/2) (1939). The intention with elastic form was to provide choreographers and dancers with music whose length could be 'stretched' according to their needs. (It also meant that dancers and choreographers could collaborate with composers without actually meeting them.) Thus the Ritournelle consists of 24 bars of music, any of which can theoretically be combined with any number of others to provide differing lengths of music; there is also an eight-bar Trio to which the same considerations apply. In practice, Cowell provides suggestions as to which bars should be combined to produce music of various lengths, though he does concede that 'Other elastic constructions may be made, rather than those suggested here. There are many other ways in which different measures may be fitted together plausibly.' Some of the suggested combinations, however, are less successful than others, this being a result of the melodic and tonal basis of the music. When shorter elastic constructions are used, the implied voice-leading and harmonic direction of the 'full' original are broken, for instance in the suggested five- and eleven-bar versions. Some years later, Cowell compared the process used in Cage's *Music of Changes* (1951) to that found in Mozart's *Musikalisches Würfelspiel*: 'Mozart eliminated many of the hazards accepted by Cage, for he composed and set down all the measures that might be called for by the dice.'[20] The same words might apply to Cowell's own elastic musics, excepting that choreographers' choice is substituted for the throwing of dice. But despite both Mozart and Cowell predetermining the musical content of each individual bar, neither composer (and especially the latter) can be entirely sure that the final results of chance or choice will be totally aesthetically acceptable.

Paradoxically, during the same years he was allowing performers to play an active part in determining the structure of his music, Cowell was also writing pieces with rigidly mathematical, predetermined structures. Three such works

– *Ostinato Pianissimo* (505) (1934), the String Quartet No. 4: *United Quartet* (522) (1936), and *Pulse* (565) (1939) – are particularly worthy of note.

Ostinato Pianissimo is one of the earliest pieces written for percussion band. The major Western precedent for such a work is Varèse's *Ionisation* of 1931, with which Cowell had been associated as promoter, performer, conductor and publisher. However, the musical style of Varèse's piece is fundamentally different from that of Cowell's. More likely influences are some of the other Western percussion music Cowell had been in contact with (for instance that of William Russell (b. 1905)), and particularly the non-Western musics he had been studying and teaching since at least 1931. This is especially apparent in the instrumentation and the form of *Ostinato Pianissimo*.[21] The work is written for eight players, each of whom performs an ostinato pitch-pattern of fixed length (shown in figure 4.9). The three sets of instruments marked with an asterisk (players 5, 7 and 8) form a kind of continuo which is present throughout the piece. Their patterns, when combined, produce a larger cycle which repeats itself every twenty bars.

Figure 4.9. Ostinati in Cowell's *Ostinato Pianissimo* (505)

Player	Instrument(s)	Length of ostinato	No. of presentations, and starting point	Ending ('coda')
1	string piano 1	13 bars = 52 crotchets	6, starting at bar 1	8 free bars
2	string piano 2	11 bars = 44 crotchets	5, starting at bar 27	5 free bars
3	8 rice bowls	15 bars = 60 crotchets	4, starting at bar 13, +1 incomplete (bars 73–83)	3 free bars
4	xylophone	9 bars = 36 crotchets	5, starting at bar 40	2 free bars
5*	2 woodblocks, tambourine, guiro	10 bars = 40 crotchets	8, starting at bar 1	6 free bars
6	2 bongos	6 bars = 24 crotchets	5, starting at bar 53	4 free bars
7*	3 drums	4 bars = 16 crotchets	21, starting at bar 1	2 free bars
8*	3 gongs	5 bars = 20 crotchets	16, starting at bar 1	6 free bars

* Continuo: see text.

Over this continuo, the other five players join in one by one. Each of their ostinati, however (together with that of player 5) is subsequently varied through the superimposition of a variety of accentual patterns: Cowell effectively subjects each line to constant, individual, implied polymetric reorganisation. The result of this, when combined with the cumulative form and its cyclical component parts, is an aural progression from vertical monometre and monoaccent (i.e. rhythmic consonance) at the opening, to complex polymetre and polyaccent (i.e. rhythmic dissonance) at the close. *Ostinato Pianissimo* is both an admirable witness to Cowell's knowledge of the rhythmic structures of Asian music, and a worthy successor to the rhythmic intricacies of the quite differently organised *Quartet Euphometric*.

Rhythmic structuring is taken a stage further in the *United Quartet*, which in retrospect can be considered a prototype of the square-root form developed and used by Cage from 1939 onwards (see chapter 5). However, the sophisticated patterning found here is allied to pseudo-ethnic music of almost startling banality. Cowell went to some ends to explain this situation:

The United Quartet is an attempt toward a more universal music style. Although it is unique in form, style and content, it is easy to understand because of its use of fundamental elements as a basis, because of repetitions which enable the auditor to become accustomed to these elements, because of the clarity and simplicity of its form, and because of the unity of form, rhythm and melody.

There are in it elements suggested from many places and periods. For example, the classical feeling is represented not by the employment of a familiar classic form, but in building up a new form, carefully planned. . .Primitive music is represented. . .by using a three-tone scale, and exhausting all the different ways the three tones can appear, which is a procedure of some primitive music. . .The Oriental is represented by modes which are constructed as Oriental modes are constructed. . .The modern is represented by the use of unresolved discords, by free intervals in two-part counterpoint and by the fact that the whole result is something new – and all that is new is modern![22]

Thus the piece can be seen both as a product of Cowell's studies of ethnic musics, and as an attempt by him to de-mythologise contemporary music, an intention shared during the 1930s and 1940s by a number of other American composers, including Crawford and Copland.

The rhythmic structuring is shown at its best in the first movement – an *Allegro* – which is dominated at all levels by a simple pattern of relative stresses:

      v   v   –   v   –

This five-stress pattern is found in each bar, and in the dynamics of each five-bar phrase (see example 4.31). It also dominates the relative dynamics,

Example 4.31. Cowell: *United Quartet* (522), i; bars 1–5 (= 76–80)
© 1966 by C.F. Peters Corporation, New York, USA. Reproduced by permission of Peters Edition Limited, London.

musical material and pitch-centres of the movement's five main sections (see figure 4.10). Further variety within the various sections is provided as follows: each A section, after the initial five-bar phrase, contains a 'cello melody of five four-bar phrases, which takes no account of the dynamic shadings and stresses

Figure 4.10. Structure of Cowell's *United Quartet* (522), i

section	A :	Ai	B	A	B	Coda
bars	1 – 25 :	26 – 50	51 – 75	76 – 100	101 – 125	126 – 130
phrases (no.of bars)	5 x 5 :	5 x 5	5 x 5	5 x 5	5 x 5	1 x 5
dynamic range	ff→f :	ff→f	p→pp	ff→f	p→pp	ff→f
base pitch	c'' :	A	G	c''	G	c''

of the accompaniment. In Ai there is a corresponding violin 1 melody, arranged similarly, though here the dynamic levels of the five four-bar phrases *do* reflect the basic stress pattern. In the B sections, a viola melody is arranged in four five-bar phrases which share the dynamics of the accompanying instruments, while the short five-bar coda recalls the music of the A sections.

The second movement – marked *Andante con moto* – is constructed along similar lines to the first, but here the stress pattern is

v   v   –

as is shown in the first nine bars of the A section (example 4.32). This simple pattern again appears at all musical levels, including dynamics of phrases, dynamics within phrases, harmony of accompanying parts and rhythmic

Example 4.32. Cowell: *United Quartet* (522), ii; bars 4–12

Example 4.32. (*cont.*)

stresses within bars. It also dominates the overall structure of the movement, though it should be noted that the repeated A section has four, rather than the expected three, sub-sections. Like the four-bar melodic phrases of the first movement, this seems to be a deliberate attempt by Cowell to destroy the symmetry he has created. Interestingly, such an act is reminiscent of the deliberate imperfections created in their work by some American Indian tribes, a point made by Sidney Cowell in a footnote to Hitchcock's discussion of *Ostinato Pianissimo*.[23]

The third movement – an *Andante* – is slightly more complex, as in addition to a basic stress pattern of

v   v   –

there is also a basic rhythmic ratio of 2:3 present, both vertically and horizontally (see example 4.33). Thus the violins' music falls into two large sections (A, B, each subdivided threefold) and the lower strings' music into three large sections (C, Ci, D, each also subdivided threefold).

Example 4.33. Cowell: *United Quartet* (522), iii; opening
© 1966 by C.F. Peters Corporation, New York, USA. Reproduced by permission of Peters Edition Limited, London.

Example 4.33. (*cont.*)

Selected examples of the 'v v –' stress pattern are:

1 the dynamics of the three large sections of the viola/'cello music;
2 the dynamics of the subdivisions of each of the large sections;
3 the base pitches of the two pairs of instruments, both within sections and overall (e.g. g′, g′, d′).

Selected examples of the 2:3 ratio are:

1 the time signatures of the two pairs of instruments;
2 the total number of $\frac{3}{4}$ bars (36) in the violins' music, in relation to the total number of $\frac{2}{4}$ bars (54) in the lower strings' music;
3 the number of sub-sections in the violins' music (6), in relation to the number of sub-sections in the lower strings' music (9);
4 the implied hemiola rhythm of the violins in example 4.33;
5 the triplets of the viola and 'cello.

The melodic material of this third movement is all derived from a single scale: g′–a′–b′–c♯″–d″–e″–f♯″–g″. This ensures that when the four polymetric, polyrhythmic and polyphrased instrumental lines are brought together, no dissonance results; unfortunately it also means that the music – even more so than in the other movements – is completely lacking in direction. Once again we are reminded of the floating, non-developmental, nature of much recent minimal music.

The final two movements of the *United Quartet* are more freely structured. The *Allegretto* fourth movement makes use of many interlocking, but seemingly unrelated, patterns, the rhythms and accents of the melody and accompaniments tending to contradict both the implied phrase-structure and each other. Of note here are the derivation of the pitched material from three-note scales (c.f. Cowell's introduction to the work); and the use throughout of two of the instruments in a percussive accompaniment, the players being instructed to 'Tap back of instrument with padded drum stick – not hard enough to injure, or with back of bow.'

The finale – marked *Tempo di marcia* – is a kind of developing ternary structure in which the materials are compressed on successive appearances. But the
form is also cumulative, like that of *Ostinato Pianissimo*: each section is shorter
and louder than its predecessor, and contains more material. Thus the hesitant
opening is transformed into a much shorter, triumphant conclusion. This movement feels like a giant upbeat: the reason becomes apparent if the work as a
whole is examined. The five movements are actually arranged as a large-scale
representation of the original five-stress pattern (shown in figure 4.11). Thus it is
natural that the last movement, as the final unit in a cyclic pattern, should seem
to be directed beyond its own conclusion (example 4.34).

Figure 4.11. Overall structure of Cowell's *United Quartet* (522)

movement	1	2	3	4	5
(tempo)	(Allegro	Andante con moto	Andante	Allegretto	Tempo di marcia)
dynamic range	loud	loud	soft	loud	soft
base 'pitch'	C	C	G	C	G
resulting stress	v	v	–	v	–

Example 4.34. Cowell: *United Quartet* (522), v; bars 72–77
© 1966 by C.F. Peters Corporation, New York, USA. Reproduced by permission of Peters Edition Limited,
London.

Many of the points discussed in relation to *Ostinato Pianissimo* and the
United Quartet are also of importance to the percussion work *Pulse*, which was
written for, and first performed by, Cage's percussion group. Indeed, its instrumentation reflects the wide range of resources available within this group,
as well as Cowell's own knowledge of percussion instruments of the world:
included are pipe-lengths and brake-drums, alongside Korean dragon's mouths,
Chinese tom-toms, Japanese temple gongs, and rice bowls. The piece is struc-

tured similarly to the first movement of the *United Quartet*, though here no pattern of stresses is used. Excluding a small number of 'decorative' bars, the total number of bars is $5 \times 5 \times 5 = 125$. This is again an imperfect example of square-root form, though the macrocosmic proportions of the work (5:5:4:5:6) are not matched microcosmically.[24] Cowell articulates the structure in a number of ways, of which the most obvious is the contrast of dynamics between successive sections. Large formal units are distinguished by the type of rhythmic material they contain and by their instrumentation. Subdivisions within these units, though possessing similar rhythmic repertories, are differently instrumented. Subsequent appearances of sub-units are distinguished from their predecessors by the reworking of the 'pitch' patterns superimposed on their (identical) rhythmic materials. This kind of rhythmic structuring, similar to that of the *United Quartet*, must surely – like the instrumentation and methods of articulation found in both *Pulse* and *Ostinato Pianissimo* – have influenced Cowell's pupil and protégé Cage. This point will be discussed further in the next chapter.

As well as considering Henry Cowell to have been his first brilliant student, Charles Seeger felt that he had been a good autodidact.[25] This becomes very apparent when one considers the quite different reactions of Cowell and Ruth Crawford to Seeger's ideas on dissonant counterpoint: Crawford followed the implications of the system through to their logical conclusion – complete heterophony. Cowell, however, as was pointed out earlier, 'went off on a tangent to a system of his own which differed radically from mine',[26] a system linking harmony and rhythm which produced the *Quartet Romantic* and *Quartet Euphometric*. Despite the similar aural end-products of the two approaches, Cowell in his *Rhythm-Harmony Quartets* was trying to cultivate a 'sounding together' fundamentally different from the deliberate 'sounding apart' of 'Prayers of Steel' and the *Two Ricercari*.

There is a certain irony in Seeger recalling in later years the young Cowell's statement that for him, music came from the head rather than the heart, and that he wanted to write music which was without feeling.[27] For in spite of the cerebral complexities of the *Rhythm-Harmony Quartets*, *Rhythmicana*, the *United Quartet*, and so on, the quality which most clearly characterises Cowell's work is that 'it was conceived as something human that would sound warm and rich and somewhat *rubato*. . .its composer hopes that it need not sound icy in tone nor rigid in rhythm.'[28]

The norm in Cowell's music during the period under discussion is actually of systematic experimentation and an excitement for all things new, being tempered by an almost naïve delight in sound for sound's sake. As is shown by the synthesis of the *United Quartet*, and the very wide range of styles employed elsewhere in his output, Cowell did indeed live in the whole world of music.

5 'The Future of Music: Credo'

The development of a philosophy of experimentation in the early works of John Cage (born 1912)

I found that I liked noises even more than I liked intervals.
John Cage, 'Lecture on Nothing'

Having graduated from Los Angeles High School with the best academic record in the school's history, great things were expected of the young John Cage. He subsequently entered Pomona College in Claremont, California, but stayed there for only a year: the remainder of his early education took place as he travelled around Europe.[1] He returned to California in the autumn of 1931, having already started to compose; but none of his pre-1933 music is extant. Cage himself has explained the reason for this:

Well, every time I moved, I used to look through my papers, letters, music, and so forth, and I threw away whatever I thought I could just to lighten the travel. That way I threw away all my earliest work. There used to be, for instance, some settings to choruses from *The Persians* by Aeschylos and an *Allemande*. But before that there were some short, very short, pieces composed by means of mathematical formulae.[2]

It is interesting to find that on his own admission Cage's earliest works used extra-musical structuring, for this is a trait found – to a greater or lesser extent – in all of his subsequent pieces. Even in the motivic writing employed in the unpublished *Three Stein Songs* of 1933, it is possible to discern the beginnings of Cage's later serial technique, as well as an anticipation of the modality of the *Five Songs* of 1938. Cage had known Gertrude Stein's work since his Pomona College days, and had even written college essays in her style. The time he spent in Paris around 1930 would have provided ample opportunity for further discovery of her writing, as well as that of two composers of equally sparse and humorous music – Erik Satie (1866–1925) and Virgil Thomson (born 1896). Certainly the style of the *Three Stein Songs* is similar to that of both Satie's *Descriptions automatiques* of 1913, and portions of Thomson's *Four Saints in Three Acts*, etc. But neither relies so exclusively on a small repertory of purely melodic motifs as does Cage in his songs which, indeed, employ no harmony as such, let alone the repeated harmonic clichés which characterise so much of the work of Satie and Thomson. An equally likely influence is the Stravinsky of *Five Easy Pieces*, etc., for Cage had certainly encountered music by him, as well as by Hindemith and Skryabin, while in Paris.

The *Three Stein Songs* probably pre-date Cage's period of study with the pianist Richard Buhlig, which seems to have taken place during 1933. Cage's method of composition at this time was to 'improvise at the Piano and then try to write [the pieces] down quickly before they got away. Buhlig showed him that these [pieces] were not really composed at all, since they lacked any sort of structural relationship.'[3]

Cage had originally approached Buhlig for information on Schoenberg and his music (Buhlig had given the first performance of the *Three Piano Pieces*, Op. 11), and through him was eventually introduced to serialism. The outer movements of Cage's earliest published work – the Sonata for Clarinet of September 1933 – are freely chromatic, the *Vivace* finale being an exact pitch retrograde of the first movement. The second movement, however – marked *Lento* – stands apart from its companions in its independence of pitch and rhythmic content, and in its completely contrasting mood. Rhythmically, it seldom strays far from the gently irregular motion of the opening bars (example 5.1). The pitch

Example 5.1. Cage: Sonata for Clarinet, ii; bars 1–9* (written, not sounding, pitch)
© 1963 by Henmar Press, New York, USA. Reproduced by permission of Peters Edition Limited, London.

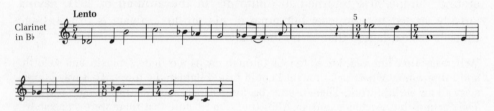

* An asterisk following the caption indicates that accidentals apply only to those pitches they immediately precede.

content of this *Lento* is almost conventionally serial. The first two phrases consist of a set and its inversion, sharing one pitch (the written e♭" of bar 5). The next two phrases – a kind of middle section – are constructed from the incomplete retrograde, a 'mixed' original/retrograde, and an interversion of the inversion; the final 'recapitulation' phrase (bars 20–24) is the retrograde inversion of the original.

What this movement shares with the others is a complete lack of dynamics, phrasings and accentuations. Thus, in his earliest published work, Cage shows a desire for freedom of expression and an unwillingness to commit himself to complete control over all parameters. This becomes increasingly typical in his later – and present – work.

The Sonata for Clarinet also brought Cage to the attention of Henry Cowell – some time after its completion, Buhlig persuaded Cage to send it and some other pieces for publication in *New Music*.[4] Cowell suggested that the Sonata be performed at a New Music Society of California workshop in San Francisco. Having hitch-hiked up from Los Angeles, Cage discovered that the clarinettist could not perform the piece, and so was obliged to play it himself, on the piano.

The appearance of 'strict' dodecaphony in the second movement of the Sonata for Clarinet may be attributable to Buhlig's influence, but Cage's later uses of serialism all tend to take a characteristically oblique view of the technique. His next three works – the Sonata for Two Voices (Nov. 1933), *Composition for Three Voices* (1934) and *Solo. . .and Six Short Inventions* (1933–34) – all make use of a newly-invented 25-pitch non-repetitive version of serialism. This technique is shown at its simplest in the fugal second movement of the Sonata for Two Voices (example 5.2). Each of the two (instrumental) voices is restricted within its own 25-note pitch area:

> Voice 1: $c' \to c'''$
> Voice 2: $c \to c''$.

The two voices share the octave $c' \to c''$.

Example 5.2. Cage: Sonata for Two Voices, ii; bars 1–11*
© by Henmar Press, New York, USA. Reproduced by permission of Peters Edition Limited, London.

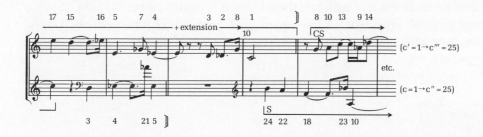

The basis of the technique is that each voice goes through its set of 25 pitches in any order – no pitch can be repeated until all 25 have appeared. The voices are rhythmically free, but as a general principle their sets tend to be completed at approximately the same point in the composition – the completion of a set of 25 pitches is normally designated in the score by a double bar-line. Another general (though by no means rigid) principle is that octaves, and especially unisons, tend to be avoided between the parts; so too are the 'repetitions' that could occur between pitches in the shared octave (although Cage sometimes positively exploits these possibilities).

Each of the voices in example 5.2 presents its 25 pitches in no particular order;

nor, after the double bar, does any group of pitches reappear. Instead, groups of pitches are gathered to form a subject and a countersubject (the latter itself a rhythmically altered inversion of the subject). These, together with free parts, form the total melodic content of the piece; but their appearances are invariably contained within altered rhythmic and intervallic gestures. While their general shapes are retained on the page, they are not necessarily recognisable to the ear.

One of the disadvantages of this technique – shown by the extended or free material in example 5.2 – is that once the majority of pitches in any set of 25 have been used imitatively, a small group of unrelated pitches may remain. Theoretically, they must be used, but their deployment may cause difficulties. In the first movement of the Sonata for Two Voices – an *Allegro* misleadingly titled 'Sonata' – Cage quite often fails to use the full complement of each 25-pitch set. The piece is constructed as a quasi-palindrome, in which the first eleven bars of voice 2's music are repeated an octave higher and in almost exact pitch and rhythmic retrogression by voice 1 in bars 13–23. (A 'free' central bar – 12 – acts as a pivot.) The first two presentations of the 25-pitch set by voice 2 (bars 1–8) are perfect (i.e. all 25 pitches are used on both occasions). But the third presentation contains some 'errors' which are only partly corrected in the reflection by voice 1.

The accompanying voices in both halves of the reflection are quite free. But while voice 1, in bars 1–8, makes two perfect and one very imperfect presentations of its set, voice 2's three presentations (bars 13–23) are all perfect. The central pivot bar stands quite outside the system which otherwise operates, and consists instead of a quasi-twelve-note row (containing two Es and no A).

The rhythmically nervous style of the Sonata is continued in the one-movement *Composition for Three Voices*. Formally, the *Composition* consists of twelve sections, each of which is three $\frac{4}{4}$ bars (i.e. twelve crotchets) long. Thus it is an isolated precursor of the square-root form which characterises Cage's work from 1939 onwards. Within each section, each of the three voices – whose ranges are

> 1: d′ → d‴
> 2: a → a″
> 3: d → d″

– presents one of three rhythmic motifs (marked I, II, III in section A̲ of the published score) according to the plan given in figure 5.1. The pattern of sections A̲–F̲ is repeated in sections G̲–L̲. Thus within each half of the piece, every possible ordering of the motifs appears; and there is an additional refinement in that within each triple-section (A̲–B̲–C̲, D̲–E̲–F̲, etc.) each voice plays all three motifs. The motifs are flexible (i.e. they are varied rhythmically, are not generally associated with particular intervallic groupings, and can start at any pitch). Furthermore, the remainder of each voice-line within each section is rhythmically free (i.e. new counterpoints are constantly being created); these 'free' rhythmic parts may well cut across sectional divisions, as happens in voice 1 between B̲ and C̲.

Figure 5.1. Deployment of motifs in Cage's *Composition for Three Voices*

section	A	B	C	D	E	F	:	G	H	I	J	K	L
Voice 1	II	I	III	III	II	I	:	II	I	III	III	II	I
Voice 2	III	II	I	II	I	III	:	III	II	I	II	I	III
Voice 3	I	III	II	I	III	II	:	I	III	II	I	III	II

In contrast to this rhythmic structuring, much of the pitch material is freely arranged against the rhythms. However, in the second half of the piece there are a number of occasions when the intervallic material allotted to a particular motif is a quasi-inversion of the intervallic material allotted to the corresponding motif in the first half (e.g. compare voice 3's presentations of motif I at the beginnings of sections A and G in example 5.3). And, of course, there is the further constraint of each voice being restricted to only one presentation of its 25-pitch set per section.

The pedantically-titled *Solo with Obbligato Accompaniment of Two Voices in Canon, and Six Short Inventions on the Subjects of the Solo* is a much freer piece, both structurally and in its use of the 25-pitch sets. It is also much more inventive, more varied in its materials, and – despite a number of factors which will be discussed later – more musical than the two works which directly pre-

Example 5.3. Cage: *Composition for Three Voices*; sections A (bars 1–3) and G (bars 19–21)*
© 1974 by Henmar Press, New York, USA. Reproduced by permission of Peters Edition Limited, London.

↑— this gb' is 'borrowed' from section B

Example 5.3. (*cont.*)

cede it. In the opening *Solo* (marked *Grave Adagio*) the upper[5] two voices are those in canon, and the lower voice is the solo.

The two canonic voices each perform twelve 'perfect' presentations of the 25-pitch set; but the solo voice has fifteen presentations of its set, three of which – the tenth, eleventh and twelfth – are jumbled together. The initial difficulties, in bar 82, arise from the supposed arrival on unison pitches of the solo and accompaniments; substitute pitches are therefore used in the solo, 'borrowed' from the next presentation of its set. Also, it is during this part of the movement (bars 79–84) that the canonic material assumes prominence within the texture. The solo in effect becomes the uniformly-quaver accompaniment to the two-part harmony of the canon, and its pitches are therefore somewhat affected by a desire to avoid unisons, etc., between it and the two-part harmony (example 5.4). Overall, the structure is similar to that of many fugal movements, the appearances of the various subjects being separated by freer episodes and links.

The musical material of this work is varied in type and content, and its formal structure much less rigid than that of Cage's earlier works. This relative accessibility is continued in the much shorter *Six Inventions*; in all of these the lowest, third, voice carries the initial presentation of the subject. In general, the *Inventions* are freely imitative pieces in which there is much use of unrelated materials. (The fourth is particularly free, there apparently being only two references to the subject.) In *Invention 2*, though, the material is almost exclusively derived from the subject; *Invention 3* is semi-fugal, while the first shows how free pitch (but not rhythmic) imitation can become (example 5.5).

Example 5.4. Cage: *Solo. . .and Six Inventions; Solo*, bars 79–84*
© 1963 by Henmar Press, New York, USA. Reproduced by permission of Peters Edition Limited, London.

PRESENTATIONS 10–12 (jumbled together)

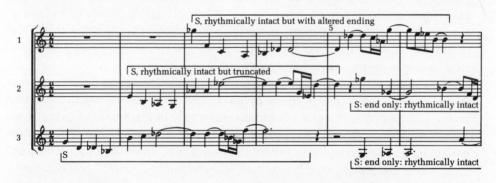

† Notes marked with a dagger in the 'solo' voice 3 occur 'out of order' – i.e. before the remainder of the set has been presented.

Example 5.5. Cage: *Solo. . .and Six Inventions; Invention 1*, bars 1–12*
© 1963 by Henmar Press, New York, USA. Reproduced by permission of Peters Edition Limited, London.

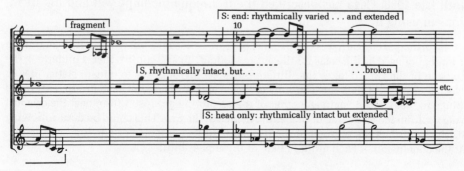

But the *Inventions*, like the *Solo* (and, indeed, the *Composition for Three Voices* and Sonata for Two Voices) lack two important things. The first is a sense of (Western) harmony, as was later noted by Schoenberg. Only occasionally – for instance during bars 79–84 of the *Solo* – is there any relief from the otherwise incessant dissonant melody and counterpoint. Harmony is certainly considered; but it is never afforded any prominence. The resulting lack of vertical interest makes these pieces two-, rather than three-dimensional. Also missing here is a sense of reality. None of Cage's works up to this time includes dynamics, accents, phrasings or (with the exception of the Sonata for Clarinet) specific instrumentation. Perhaps Cage's intention was to involve the performers in decisions concerning the works' nature. What is clear is that they seem to be mere abstracts, waiting to be realised. In this context it is interesting to note that once instrumentation, dynamics, etc., have been added – as they were to the *Six Inventions* by Cage and David Tudor in 1958 – these works do become satisfying aurally as well as visually.

Around the time of the completion of the *Solo. . .and Six Inventions*, Cage may have studied dissonant counterpoint and composition with Cowell in California, for a season.[6] Certainly it was at Cowell's instigation that he moved to New York during 1934, principally to study with Adolph Weiss, though he also attended classes (including Cowell's) at the New School for Social Research. The lessons Cage received were intended to prepare him for study with Weiss' own teacher, Schoenberg, recently arrived on the East Coast of America, and teaching in Boston and New York. Ironically, within six months of Cage's arrival in New York, a number of factors forced Schoenberg to move to California. Cage followed him back there in 1935, but by then the seeds of experimentalism had been sown in his mind alongside those of serialism, through his studies with Cowell and at the New School. During the whole of the remaining period discussed here, these polarised influences jostled for attention in Cage's young, excited and susceptible mind.

Any work produced by Cage between the completion of the *Solo. . .and Six Inventions* and the commencement of his studies with Schoenberg in California in the summer of 1935 seem not to have survived. In the music of 1933–34 we have already encountered the use of a surprisingly advanced form of alternative serialism. Cage's surrender to twelve-tone serialism, albeit in a rather unusual form, came about soon after his studies with Schoenberg began, and continued until late 1938. Cage has described the technique he employed and his intentions in using it:

. . .my principal concern was not to make the row noticeable, but to mask it, even though it was being used as the basis for the entire method. To accomplish that, I undertook the division of the twelve tones into little groups; each group was to remain static, that is, was not to vary. . .I took those groups of tones, and at the end of each group, I arranged things so that I could begin any other of the remaining groups. . .(or repeat the one just used). . .from the following or preceding degree of the row. This could be done following either the form of the original or the inversion, or its retrograde or retrograde inversion. At the conclusion of each group, I had all these possibilities.[7]

As a practical example of the technique, let us examine the *Two Pieces for Piano*. Here, Cage does not succeed in masking the row, for it is fairly easily deducible:

e″–a′–f″–b′–bb′–g′–d″–eb″–db″–ab′–gb′–c″

From this row, Cage extracts a number of intervallic units (e.g. 5↓–m6↑; Π↓; 5↑; 4↓; m2↓ = M7↑ = m9↓; etc.); these are rhythmicised, and then combined in various ways to produce the groups of tones to which he refers (see example 5.6). The

Example 5.6. Cage: *Two Pieces for Piano*, i; 'groups of tones'*

groups of tones are then arranged in two separate lines – left hand and right hand (l.h., r.h.) – whose bar-lines (which delineate the groups of tones) seldom coincide.

In the first system of the first piece (example 5.7) the final pitch of l.h.

Example 5.7. Cage: *Two Pieces for Piano*, i; first system*
© 1970 by Henmar Press, New York, USA. Reproduced by permission of Peters Edition Limited, London.

bar/group 1 is g; referring to the row, we find that g′ is preceded by bb′ and followed by d″. Thus any of these pitches (bb′, g′, d″) can be used (in any octave transposition) as the first pitch of the next l.h. bar/group. Cage picks d′, which then becomes the first pitch of whichever group of tones he chooses to appear as l.h. bar/group 2. Additionally, as the intervallic content of the group of tones is fixed,[8] it also determines the exact pitches which follow. The group of tones Cage chooses is a pair of interlocking fourths, whose final pitch is thus eb. From the row, we can see that this gives the choices as the starting pitch for l.h. bar/group 3 of d″, eb″ and db″ . . . and so on. The choice of groups of tones for the right hand operates quite independently, though Cage obviously takes some account of contrapuntal and 'harmonic' relationships between the two lines. The realignment of fixed units found here is thus similar to that found in the *Three Stein Songs* and – less clearly – some of Cowell's later works (see chapter 4).

There are only a very few places in the *Two Pieces for Piano* where Cage deviates from this simplest application of his system. In the first movement, he twice retains a final pitch as the first pitch of a new group of tones, and on one of these occasions ties the two pitches together (see r.h. bars/groups 3–4 and l.h. bars/groups 9–10). In the second movement there is one occasion where Cage opts for the previous pitch from the row (r.h. bars/groups 22–23) and another where the system apparently breaks down owing, perhaps, to some confusion over the number of leger lines (l.h. bars/groups 35–36). Occasionally Cage builds ostinato patterns, as in the first piece, fourth system, l.h. But however ingenious the system (and the present one is quite unlike any other twelve-note method of its time) what matters are results. Here, at least, their quality is open to question. As with the earlier 'exercises', the *Two Pieces for Piano* contain no dynamics, phrasings or accentuations. The bald two-part counterpoint is almost pointillistic (especially in the second movement) and again there is no harmonic relief, in either sense of that word.

Two other pieces from 1935 which follow this system fare a little better. For one thing, Cage does at least succeed in masking the original row – that is, his skill in using the system has passed beyond the employment of only its simplest possibilities. The short piano piece *Quest* contains a surprisingly high percentage of harmonic material, which is juxtaposed against a chromatic, leaping melody and an ostinato sevenths pattern. Dynamics here make their welcome first appearance in a work by Cage, a direct result of the piece being written not as an exercise, but rather for a specific purpose. (Cage's involvement with dance, as accompanist and composer, started at around this time.) Dynamics and phrasings also appear in the second and third of the *Three Pieces for Flute Duet*. There are some superficial resemblances, though, to the *Two Pieces for Piano*, notably in the lack of phrasings and dynamics in the first movement, and the non-alignment of measures in the second. The writing throughout is very chromatic and contrapuntal (only in the austere third piece are there hints of harmonic thinking, in the rhythmic unisons between the parts), but the range of materials employed is much wider than in *Quest* and the *Two Pieces for Piano*. Additionally, Schoenberg's influence is strongly felt in the much more elaborate manipulation of the materials. Comparative rhythmic freedom and spontaneity are achieved through Cage choosing not to assign particular intervallic groups to specific rhythmic ideas: there is surprisingly little use of ostinati here. But this rhythmic flexibility does not entirely compensate for the lack of formal structure of these pieces.

After completing the *Three Pieces for Flute Duet*, Cage suddenly dismissed the developments of the previous two years, temporarily abandoned intervals, and turned instead to writing percussion music. There are a number of factors which contributed to this. As early as the summer of 1933, at the Hollywood Bowl, Cage had been tremendously impressed by Varèse's all-percussion piece *Ionisation*; while in New York he had attended Cowell's classes in ethnic musics and (apparently) percussion. He may already have seen Cowell's recent *Ostinato Pianissimo*; and he certainly credits Cowell – along with Varèse – for having 'very greatly contributed to getting us used to the idea of a limitless tonal universe'.[9] On the negative side, Schoenberg's criticism of Cage's lack of feeling for (Western) harmony[10] virtually ensured that he would search for methods of structuring other than those based on tonality (and instruments other than those with a tonal/harmonic bias).

The final piece in the jigsaw was probably contributed by the abstract film-maker Oscar Fischinger whom Cage believes he met in 1935 or (less likely) 1936:

. . .he began to talk with me about the spirit which is inside each of the objects of this world. So, he told me, all we need to do to liberate that spirit is to brush past the object, and to draw forth its sound. That's the idea which led me to percussion. In all the many years which followed up to the war, I never stopped touching things, making them sound and resound, to discover what sounds they could produce. Wherever I went, I always listened to objects.[11]

It was this catholicity of taste, combined with impecuniosity, which led to the creation in 1935 of the twenty-minute, four-movement *Quartet*, for unspecified percussion. It would seem to be the *Quartet* (as well as the later *Living Room Music* of 1940) to which Cage refers in the following statement:

I gathered together a group of friends, and we began to play some pieces I had written without instrumental indications, simply to explore instrumental possibilities not yet catalogued, the infinite number of sound sources from a trash heap or a junk yard, a living room or a kitchen. . .We tried all the furniture we could think of.[12]

As well as the complete lack of instrumental specification, dynamics appear only in the fourth movement; the tempi are only relative ('Slow', 'Fast', etc.) and – in a gesture similar to that made by Cowell in his *Mosaic Quartet* (518) of the same year – Cage directs that either of the two slow movements may be omitted at the wish of the performers. The notation (example 5.8) both reverts to that of earlier pieces in its non-alignment of bars – effectively creating polymetre – and points far into the future with its semi-graphic appearance (c.f. the work of Morton Feldman in the 1950s).

But however bold the move forward into new territory, something of the past had to remain:

In all my pieces coming between 1935 and 1940, I had Schoenberg's lessons in mind; since he had taught me that variation was in fact a repetition, I hardly saw the usefulness of variation, and I accumulated repetitions. All of my works for percussion, and also my compositions for piano, contain systematically repeated groups of sounds or durations.[13]

Example 5.8. Cage: *Quartet*, i; bars 1–51
© by Henmar Press, New York, USA. Reproduced by permission of Peters Edition Limited, London.

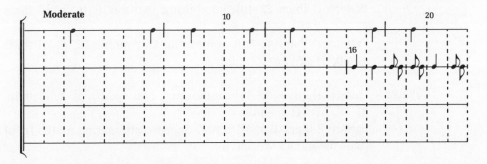

Example 5.8. (*cont.*)

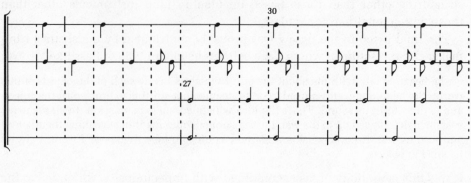

Thus in the *Quartet* we find the rhythmic equivalent of Cage's row technique: in each movement matrices or repertories of rhythmic motifs are created, which are repeated, rather than varied, in various ways. The 'Moderate' first movement is based on a particularly large repertory of rhythmic motifs, many of which share similar characteristics. The motifs can be used by themselves, either singly or in multiples (to form ostinati); and in combination with other motifs, either singly or in multiples. For instance, the opening page (see example 5.8) contains the following patterns:

       Player 1 Pattern A (bars 1–83), containing two alternating motifs (bars 1–6; 7–11, etc.);

       Player 2 Pattern B (bars 16–26), containing two motifs (bars 16–21; 22–26);
                 Pattern C (bars 27–46), combining two motifs (a, a, b) (bars 27–28; 29–30; 31–36, etc.);
                 Pattern F (bars 47–83), combining two motifs (c, d, d) (bars 47–50; 51–55; 56–60, etc.);

       Player 3 Pattern D (bars 27–38), combining two motifs (e, f, e) (bars 27–30; 31–34; 35–38);
                 Pattern E (bars 39–58), containing two alternating motifs (g, c) (bars 39–42; 43–46, etc.);

> Player 4 Pattern E (bars 36–47) (as for player 3 above) (bars 36–39; 40–43; 44–47);
> Pattern C (bars 48–57) (as for player 2 above) (bars 48–49; 50–51; 52–57).

When the same pattern appears in two separate parts, these are non-aligned (e.g. player 4 begins pattern E at bar 36, player 3 at bar 39) to produce rhythmic counterpoints.

From an examination of the types of ostinato used, and the overall density of writing, the movement would seem to fall into a three-part form, shown in figure 5.2.

Figure 5.2. Structure of Cage's *Quartet*, i

1 Accretion	bars 1–233	Texture slowly builds in density Two 'climaxes of action' around bars 165 and 206
2 Erosion	bars 234–377	Texture slowly decays in density
3 Recapitulation/ conclusion	bars 378–531	Maximum activity throughout Re-use of patterns from opening, though use of regular patterns deteriorates towards end

Both the 'Very slow' second movement – which features the juxtaposition and superimposition of very long and very short notes – and the third 'Slow' movement are constructed along similar lines, though this latter (titled 'Axial Asymmetry') uses only four basic motifs. Three of these are combined in various ways to produce textures both simple and complex. But it is only towards the end of the movement (from bar 365) that the long sustained notes of the fourth motif are introduced by player 4. Against these, players 1–3 perform the opening motif, either in rhythmic unison (e.g. bars 398–404), or with the notes shared between them (e.g. bars 372–378). Unlike the preceding movements, the finale (marked 'Fast') contains quite precise dynamic markings, which may indicate that it was intended for, or used in, performance. Its musical material falls into three distinct groups – short notes, long notes, and *crescendi* – and its structure seems to be derived from the interplay between these types of material.

The percussion *Trio*, of 1936, stands in complete contrast to the *Quartet* – its three movements are short, and its tempi, instrumentation and dynamics precisely notated. It also possesses a more varied rhythmic repertory. The processes Cage uses in the first (*Allegro*) movement are similar to those encountered previously. A small number of rhythmic motifs (seven) appear both by themselves and in combination with others. Given that the instrumentation and dynamic level (*f*) are constant throughout, the movement's machine-like qualities are hard to miss (example 5.9).

Example 5.9. Cage: *Trio*, i; bars 1–8

The second movement – a March – is cast in ternary form. This is defined not only by the motifs used but also by the timbres associated with them: a distinct polarity is set up between the rhythms of the wood blocks, bass drum and tom-toms, and those of the bass drum and bamboo sticks. After the widely varying dynamic levels and instrumental sounds heard here, the final Waltz comes as something of a surprise: the dynamic never rises above *piano*, and the only instruments used are the wood blocks (in this, the Waltz clearly complements the opening *Allegro*). There are but two motifs, formed by combining existing motifs (see example 5.10), which are deployed in a manner reminiscent of the

Example 5.10. Cage: *Trio*, iii; motifs

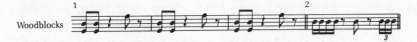

Quartet's third movement, creating a three-part form shown in figure 5.3. The effect, again, is almost machine-like – this is certainly not a waltz to dance to.

We have already noted Cage's remarks regarding the influence Schoenberg's teaching had on his work; elsewhere, he speaks in extremely positive terms of his feelings towards the older man: 'I worshipped him!. . .Everything he said, I believed.'[14] Yet a work like the *Trio* shows just how wide a gap there was between them. This distancing is confirmed by the story of Schoenberg's reaction to Cage's invitation to a percussion concert: he would not be free to attend

Figure 5.3. Structure of Cage's *Trio*, iii

section	1	2	3
bars	1 - 12	13 - 22	22¹/₂ - 33
dynamic	constant *p*	constant *p*	*pp (>) ppp >*
remarks	slow accumulation of material motif 2 little used	faster accumulation of material; motif 2 used more	rhythmically complex throughout; motif 2 used substantially, but then eliminated

on that night or any other night.[15] Nor do we find in the rhythmic inflexibility and limited timbres of the *Quartet* and *Trio* any real evidence of Varèse's influence either. Rather, one is again reminded of Cowell's *Ostinato Pianissimo*, and more particularly of the work of William Russell (born 1905), which often exploits repetitive and accumulative textures. It is perhaps not coincidental that Russell's *Three Dance Movements* (Waltz, March, Foxtrot) had appeared in *New Music's* all-percussion issue of early 1936.[16]

In Cage's music of 1933–36 we can identify what are effectively five different compositional systems, each of which in a sense reflects his current interests and/or teachers. Like Cowell in 1914, Cage in 1936 lacked a coherent theoretical base from which he could work and develop consistently. But whereas Cowell's solution – in *New Musical Resources* – was to produce a compendium of actual or possible compositional practice, Cage's solution was to adopt a radical philosophical and aesthetic stance. His lecture-manifesto 'The Future of Music: Credo' was written for, and delivered to, an arts society in Seattle, Washington, in 1937. Although it was not published until 1958[17] it has achieved some distinction, or perhaps notoriety, as being in many ways prophetic of the subsequent developments in Cage's life's work. For while retrospect imbues most aspects of life with layers of added significance, this lecture seems remarkably oracular in detailing a number of issues which have subsequently obsessed Cage. Broadly speaking these are:

1 the desire to use all available sounds in musical composition (with the implication that sounds should be allowed to be themselves – to paraphrase Cage) (lines 1–15; 46–48) and the citation of percussion music as an intermediate stage in this process (lines 68–71);
2 the anticipation of, and search for, electronic instruments and music (lines 16–45; 84–89);
3 the establishment of new methods of organising sounds (lines 49–52; 58–67; 72–83; 90–91) and – thereby by implication – the need for new notational systems to contain these methods (lines 53–57).

When, however, the 'Credo' is examined more closely, and is compared with two other texts extant at the time, it begins to lose some of its originality. In the List No. 2,[18] compiled in 1960–61 while he was a Fellow of Wesleyan University, Cage itemises the ten books which had most influenced his thought. Among these we find:

Luigi Russolo *The Art of Noise*
  Put this with *New Musical Resources*, by Henry Cowell, and the early book by Carlos Chavez and you get (circa 1935) a sense of music renaissance, the possibility of invention.

(The work by Chavez is *Toward a New Music*, of which chapter 5 is of particular interest and relevance.)

Of these three texts, *New Musical Resources* seems to have had no specific influence on Cage's lecture, except in the sense that it inspired and sustained Cage's own search for such resources. Some of the issues raised in the book did, though, have an effect on Cage's work. For instance, Cowell's thoughts on the use of sliding tones (discussed earlier) may have influenced Cage's use of frequency recordings with variable-speed turntables in *Imaginary Landscape No. 1* of 1939 (see below); and – less plausibly – of the lion's roar in the *Third Construction* (1941) and the water gong in the *First Construction (in Metal)* (1939) and *Second Construction* (1940). It should be noted in this context that Varèse's use of sirens (e.g. in *Ionisation*) would also have been of interest to Cage.

If, however, the 'Credo' is compared with the works by Russolo and Chavez, some distinct similarities begin to emerge. Of these, the most obvious is the almost identical style of typography used by Cage and Russolo, in which important remarks are rendered in capital letters. Indeed, this kind of typography is typical of Futurist documents: see, for instance, Pratella's 'Manifesto of Futurist Musicians'.[19] It should be noted, however, that Cage differs from Russolo and Pratella in having the upper-case sections of his text form a continuous line of thought. Beyond this, there are some more specific correspondences of ideology and even phraseology:

Cage	Russolo
lines 2–3:	line 143:
Wherever we are, what we hear is mostly noise	Every manifestation of our life is accompanied by noise.
lines 5–6:	lines 126–127:
We want to capture and control these sounds, to use them not as sound effects but as musical instruments.	WE WANT TO ATTUNE AND REGULATE THIS TREMENDOUS VARIETY OF NOISES HARMONICALLY AND RHYTHMICALLY.
lines 31–34:	lines 193–197:
The special function of electrical instruments will be to provide complete control of the overtone	The new orchestra will achieve the most complex and novel aural emotions. . .by manipulating

structure of tones (as opposed to noises) and to make these tones available in any frequency, amplitude, and duration.

fascinating juxtapositions of these varied tones and rhythms. Therefore an instrument will have to offer the possibility of tone changes and varying degrees of amplification.

In Chavez's book, and particularly its chapter 5 on music and the film, there were more recent ideas to help stimulate Cage's mind and form his prose. Pages 100–102 of the Chavez, where he speaks, among other things, of 'sirens, klaxons and machines for imitating wind, thunder, rain, the roaring of the sea, raging mobs, etc.' and 'all kinds of sounds, of nature, industry, and city especially recorded. . .on a sound track or disc. . .[forming] the so-called libraries of sound' are clearly related to lines 4–11 of the 'Credo':

The sound of a truck at fifty miles per hour. Static between the stations. Rain. . .

Every film studio has a library of 'sound effects' recorded on film. . .

Given four film phonographs, we can compose and perform a quartet for explosive motor, wind, heartbeat, and landslide.

Also directly comparable are the two composers' comments on Theremin's instruments (Chavez: page 165; Cage: lines 19–30); and while not relevant to a discussion of the 'Credo', the following passage from page 17 of Chavez's book, with emphasis in original – 'if we study an isolated sound. . .we see that it possesses physical qualities: *intensity, duration, timbre, pitch*' – has been taken up by Cage on a number of occasions.[20]

Oddly enough, what appear to be the most obvious borrowings in 'The Future of Music: Credo' – the use of the Varèsian terms 'organization of sound' (line 15) for music, and 'organizer of sound' (line 53) for composer – may be nothing of the kind. It has been impossible to trace any published use of these terms in Varèse's writings before 1940, and it is unlikely that Cage and Varèse met before 1938. Given, however, the closeness of the American avant-garde during the 1920s and 1930s, it is always possible that the terms were transmitted to Cage through a third party (perhaps Cowell?).

Thus, in 'The Future of Music: Credo', we see Cage taking stock of, and responding to, a series of intellectual stimulae, in much the same way that he had responded to the teaching of Buhlig, Weiss, Schoenberg and Cowell. Despite this, the results of his adoption of such an uncompromisingly radical philosophical and aesthetic stance were not immediately noticeable in his music. The three works Cage produced during 1938 – *Metamorphosis*, the *Five Songs*, and the *Music for Wind Instruments* – were all written for acoustic/interval rather than electric/noise instruments; and although they return to the twelve-note method developed in 1935, they are by far the most approachable and superficially conventional of Cage's pieces from this early period. However, the appearance of mathematical structurings in the *Music for Wind Instruments* and some movements of *Metamorphosis* and the *Five Songs* may well be due to a desire, as expressed in lines 68–73 of the 'Credo', to find a durational structuring which could by implication encompass both sound and silence, and be 'FREE FROM THE CONCEPT OF A FUNDAMENTAL TONE' (lines 77–78).

The five-movement piano work *Metamorphosis* was completed in May 1938. It is a substantial piece which exploits a wide variety of textures in a decidedly musical way; and yet at the same time its basic language is no different from that of the *Two Pieces* of 1935. What has changed is Cage's fecundity in using that language. The first movement is based on only four motivic ideas:

A̲ a five-crotchet motif, generally with the intervallic shape M2↑–5↑–m2↓–M2↓;

B̲ a three-pitch motif (minim–dotted minim–crotchet), derived from A̲, generally with the intervallic shape m7↑–m9↓;

C̲ a variety of semibreve, two-pitch and four-pitch chords, all based on one or more of the following intervals:
   m2, M2, m3, M3, 4;

D̲ a two-pitch motif (dotted minim–dotted minim) plus crotchet rest, derived from B̲, generally with the intervallic shape M2↑ or M9↑.

These motifs are subjected to a wider and more skilled range of variation techniques than in any earlier work: metric dislocations, dynamic shaping and particularly octave transpositions of individual pitches are all superimposed on the basic materials to create a developing yet integrated texture (see example 5.11). The different sounds of these various textures hint aurally at the presence of some underlying formal principle. In fact, this movement has a form derived from the kind of rigid mathematical structure encountered earlier in Cowell's *United Quartet* (522) (1936).

The structure (see figure 5.4) consists of the 25-fold repetition of a basic 26-crotchet unit, these units being gathered into a series of larger groupings. (These are defined by motivic areas, changes of metre and density of texture. Although not shown here, dynamics also play a part in this definition.) Perhaps

Example 5.11. Cage: *Metamorphosis*, i; bars 10–19; 24–33; 50–59
© 1961 by Henmar Press, New York, USA. Reproduced by permission of Peters Edition Limited, London.

Example 5.11. (cont.)

Figure 5.4. Structure of Cage's *Metamorphosis*, i

26-crotchet unit	1 2 3	4 5 6	7 8 9 10	11 12 13 14	15 16 17 18 19 20	21 22	23 24 25
motif(s)	A→	A+B→B	C→	Ci+D→Ci+D+D	D+D+D→D+D→D	D+A A	A+B→
no. of 'voices'	1	2	4	2 3	3 2 1	2 1	
metre	5/4 3/4	6/4	8/4	4/4	7/4 2/4	5/4 2/4	6/4
no. of 26-crotchet units	3	3	4	4	6	2	3
length (in crotchets)	78	78	104	104	156	52	78

the figures 25 and 26 refer to the fact that at the time of *Metamorphosis'* completion, Cage was aged 25 and in his 26th year. But the first movement of Cowell's *United Quartet* (see chapter 4) also consists essentially of 25 × 25-crotchet units, plus short coda. Given the close teacher–pupil relationship between Cowell and Cage, as well as the *United Quartet's* publication in *New Music* in 1936, it is thus quite possible that this, and similar, schemes show Cage's knowledge of Cowell's use of ethnically inspired rhythmic structures.

The second movement seems to have no numerical or metrical structuring. Rather, it has the appearance of an elaborate contrapuntal exercise based on five motivic ideas: A, B and D, as above, plus two new motifs:

E long held pitches;
F an eight-quaver pattern, usually repeated, generally having the intervallic shape
m2↓–m2↑–repeated pitch–m2↓–m2↑–repeated pitch–m2↓.

These ideas are superimposed and juxtaposed in a variety of ways (see example 5.12).

Example 5.12. Cage: *Metamorphosis*, ii; bars 11–18
© 1961 by Henmar Press, New York, USA. Reproduced by permission of Peters Edition Limited, London.

The second movement's two-part structure resembles that of a simple sonata:

$$
\left\{ : \left. \begin{array}{l} 29 \ \text{bars} \\ 154 \ \text{crotchets} \end{array} \right\} : \left. \begin{array}{l} 44 \ \text{bars} \\ 220 \ \text{crotchets} \end{array} \right. \right\}
$$

(c.f. many of the *Sonatas and Interludes* of 1946–48) but the diversity of the materials and their manner of treatment contradict this.

The third movement, constructed as a Passacaglia-cum-Canon, is based almost exclusively on a new motif:

G eleven crotchets long (crotchet–minim–minim–crotchet–minim–minim–
crotchet) plus optional extension, generally having the intervallic
shape
repeated pitch–Π↓–m2↑–repeated pitch–m3↓–Π↑.

Successive entries of this main motif become increasingly close, reaching
rhythmic unison at the approximate mid-point (bars 25–26; see example 5.13).

Example 5.13. Cage: *Metamorphosis*, iii; bars 1–3; 16–17; 23–26
© 1961 by Henmar Press, New York, USA. Reproduced by permission of Peters Edition Limited, London.

This process has twice been interrupted (e.g. at bar 15) by the interpolation of
a motif derived from F:

Fi an eight-quaver pattern, generally having the intervallic shape
m9↓–m9↑–8↓–M7↑–M7↓–8↑–m9↓.

In the second half of this movement – which starts with the intention of repeating the process found in the first half – these interpolations (four of F or Fi,
three of B and one of D) gradually come to dominate the texture and destroy the
process (example 5.14).

Extremes of dynamics and register are used here. In the latter case the
predominantly low-register writing is occasionally counterbalanced by very
high pitches. Also, there is extensive use of (multi-) octave transposition to vary

Example 5.14. Cage: *Metamorphosis*, iii; bars 36–39
© 1961 by Henmar Press, New York, USA. Reproduced by permission of Peters Edition Limited, London.

the motifs, this sometimes making G̲ virtually unrecognisable, as, for example, at bars 45–47:

D♭–D♭–g‴–A♭–A♭–F–b‴

A number of features of the *perpetuum mobile* fourth movement – including its speed (crotchet = 208), mathematical structuring, use of octaves, and extreme chromaticism – make it reminiscent of both Lou Harrison's *Prelude for Grandpiano* and, especially, Ruth Crawford's *Piano Study in Mixed Accents*.[21] Cage's piece is arranged in twelve × 46-quaver units – delineated by bar lines – which alternate two ideas. The first of these (x), occupying units 1, 3, 5, 7, 9 and 11, consists simply of motif H̲ – a pair of quavers a tone apart – which appears either singly or in multiple combination (example 5.15). The number of combi-

Example 5.15. Cage: *Metamorphosis*, iv; unit 1 (i.e. opening)
© 1961 by Henmar Press, New York, USA. Reproduced by permission of Peters Edition Limited, London.

nations (or rhythmic groupings) and the total number of pitches and rests per 46-quaver unit are controlled, as is shown in figure 5.5a. Thus both the number of rhythmic groups per unit and the number of pitches/rests per unit increase/ decrease arithmetically. The rests (see example 5.15) are arranged in such a way that each x-unit begins and ends with a quaver rest, and its constituent rhyth-

Figure 5.5a. Arrangement of odd-numbered units in Cage's *Metamorphosis*, iv

46-quaver unit number	1	3	5	7	9	11
no. of rhythmic groups	6	7	5	8	4	9
total no. of pitches	34	32	36	30	38	29*
total no. of rests	12	14	10	16	8	17*

* +1 in unit 12

mic groups are always separated by two quaver rests. Thus the number of quaver rests per unit is double that of the number of rhythmic groups; and the number of pitches per unit increases/decreases in inverse proportion to the number of rhythmic groups.

Example 5.16. Cage: *Metamorphosis*, iv; unit 2 (follows on directly from example 5.15)
© 1961 by Henmar Press, New York, USA. Reproduced by permission of Peters Edition Limited, London.

† Note that in the printed score these notes are mistakenly prefaced by a ♮.

Figure 5.5b. Arrangement of even-numbered units in Cage's *Metamorphosis*, iv

46-quaver unit number	2	4	6	8	10	12
motif quoted	F̱	F̱ × 2	Ḇ	Ḇ × 2	G̱	G̱ × 2
length of quotation (in quavers)	8	16	12	24	22	44
length of rhythmic group of H̱ (in quavers)	36	28	32	20	22	0
no. of rests	2	2	2	2	2	2

The second idea (y) – occupying the even-numbered 46-quaver units – consists of the quoting of a motif other than H̱, followed by a large multiple combination of H̱ itself (i.e. there are only two – large – rhythmic groupings of pitches per unit) (example 5.16). The quotations are of motif F̱ (units 2, 4), Ḇ (units 6, 8) and G̱ (units 10, 12). As in the odd-numbered units, there is an underlying process here; it is shown in figure 5.5b. Therefore:

1 each appearance of idea y includes only two quaver rests, the first between the quotation and the multiple combination of H̱, and the second after this multiple combination (see example 5.16);

2 on their second appearance (i.e. in units 4, 8, 12) the quoted motifs are repeated: consequently, the lengths of the quotations in these units are twice those of the quotations in units 2, 6, 10;

3 the actual length of each quoted motif in its simplest form is greater than that of its predecessor (i.e. F̱ is eight quavers long, Ḇ twelve quavers, and G̱ 22 quavers);

4 as a direct consequence of 1–3 above, the multiple combinations of H̱ eventually evaporate;

5 an additional detail consists in the treatment of quoted motifs Ḇ and G̱: on each occasion Cage mixes two simultaneous vertical presentations of the motif, creating new melodic configurations.

The only deviation from this rigid structuring occurs at the end of unit 11, where the final rhythmic grouping of H spills over the bar-line to requisition the first quaver of unit 12; consequently, there is no final quaver rest in unit 12.

The dynamics lie totally outside these processes – they are applied freely to shape the material – while the pitch and interval aspects of the movement are controlled by the rules governing Cage's twelve-note method. The musical result of all this structuring is that the listener is made aware of the alternation of increasingly long and increasingly short groups of regular quaver pitches, which are interspersed with variants of previously heard motifs.

In contrast, the fifth and final movement sounds like a set of variations – or perhaps a Passacaglia – on a new motif:

> I a three-pitch motif (dotted crotchet–quaver–dotted minim) generally
> with the intervallic shape m3↑–M2↓.

Once again, however, an elaborate mathematical structure – this time based on the number 22 – is the framework upon which these variations are built. There are seventeen repetitions of a 22-crotchet unit. These are arranged into three large groups of five repetitions, separated by single repetitions (numbers 6 and 12) giving an overall rondoesque shape to the movement, shown in figure 5.6.

Figure 5.6. Structure of Cage's *Metamorphosis*, v

crotchet = 120

22-crotchet units	1; 2 ;3;4; 5	6	7 ;8 ; 9 ;10;11	12	13 ;14 ;15 ;16 ; 17
metre	5 x 22 / 4	varied (see text)	5 x 22 / 4	varied (see text)	5 x 22 / 4
motifs used	I x (22) H;(I);H;H;(I)	I	I x (22) (I);H ;(I);H ;H	I	I x (22) H ;H ;(I);(I);H/(I)
resulting texture	a; b ;c;c; b	d	b ;ci;bi ;ai;c	d	cii/c;aii; b ;bii;b+ciii ⌊___↑___⌋ actually 21+23; see text
bars	1 – 22	23 – 30	31 – 52	53 – 60	61 – 82

What distinguishes the two dividing sections from the others is their contrapuntal nature (evident both visually and aurally) and their irregular metres (each has the pattern $\frac{3}{4}, \frac{2}{4}, \frac{3}{4}, \frac{2}{4}, \frac{2}{4}, \frac{2}{4}, \frac{3}{4}, \frac{5}{4}$, as opposed to the regular $\frac{5}{4}$ of the larger sections). Each of these dividing sections contains ten appearances of I (example 5.17).

Each of the three larger sections is divided metrically into 22 regular $\frac{5}{4}$ bars (note the complementary arithmetic relationship here between metre/number of

Example 5.17. Cage: *Metamorphosis*, v; bars 23–30
© 1961 by Henmar Press, New York, USA. Reproduced by permission of Peters Edition Limited, London.

units (5), and number of bars/length of units (22), reminiscent of that found in the final movement of Cowell's contemporary *Rhythmicana* (557) (1938) – see chapter 4). Each bar contains one appearance of I̲ in its simplest (i.e. non-contrapuntal) form, though occasionally the final note of I̲ is extended by five crotchets to fill the next bar (e.g. at bar 37), or otherwise metrically altered (e.g. in bars 81–82).

There are two levels of variation in this movement. Melodically, I̲ is subjected to a multitude of free, interior, octave transpositions; this – in combination with the controlled bar-by-bar transpositions of I̲ resulting from Cage's application of his twelve-note method – ensures that there is a constant flow of melodic variation.

To ensure textural variation, Cage invents a new accompaniment for each of the fifteen 22-crotchet units, most of these being based either on H̲, or on I̲ itself. These accompaniments include:

1 regular quaver movement (either ascending, descending or static) (e.g. bars 12–14; 36–37) which may be doubled at the third (e.g. bar 61);
2 patterned quaver movement (e.g. bars 1–2; 66–67);
3 I̲ itself treated as a monody (e.g. bars 40–41), homophonically in two to six parts (e.g. bars 6–9; 31–34) or canonically (e.g. bars 74–76).

The final (coda) unit combines a chordal, homophonic version of I̲ with a chordal version of H̲ (example 5.18).

An interesting result of the simultaneous two-fold variation techniques which appear in the three larger sections is that textures often overlap. For instance, in bar 35 texture b̲ (from unit 7) is extended into unit 8 to preserve its continuity,

Example 5.18. Cage: *Metamorphosis*, v; bars 79–82

and thus overlaps briefly with texture c_i; elsewhere, Cage uses rests to cover the dividing line between units. The strict division into 22-crotchet units breaks down only once: texture c_{ii}/c (unit 13; from bar 61) commences on the final beat of unit 12, and thus lasts only 21 crotchets into unit 13. The subsequent texture (a$_{ii}$) also commences 'one beat early' but is allowed to continue until the end of unit 14 (i.e. it has a total of 23 crotchets). Throughout all these variations, dynamics and accents are used to colour the material, rather than playing an integral part in the structural patterns.

The virtuosity of technique and rich textural palette employed by Cage in *Metamorphosis* are found also in the *Five Songs* on texts by E.E. Cummings, though here the mathematical structures found necessary in more abstract works are generally superseded by text-derived forms. The texts[22] – with their child-like imagery – also determine the approachable (and at times almost tonal) music. The generally simple rhythms of the vocal line (and therefore, by implication, of the accompaniment) are a direct result of the syllabic setting of the words – though the accents and stresses of the vocal line often contradict those implied by the metrical layout, and the rhythms Cage uses are at least partly subservient to the rules governing his twelve-note method. Consequently there is comparatively little word painting. The writing is in general contrapuntal rather than harmonic; also – and perhaps surprisingly – Cage includes no dynamics or phrasings in the score.

The first song – 'little four paws' – employs a repertory of only four motifs, shared by voice and piano, three of which are linked by their common use of stepwise, secundal movement. The vocal line – which generally proceeds in nimble, regular quavers – relies exclusively on these four motifs, in various transpositions (derived from the fundamental row) and combinations. There are no extensions or adaptations to fit the words; rather, the words are made to fit the motifs (example 5.19).

The piano often decorates the motifs in a quasi-harmonic fashion; as in parts of *Metamorphosis* the harmonies are created by the superimposition of a number of transpositions of the same motif, which may then be subjected to interior octave transposition and displacement (see, for instance, bars 13–14 of example 5.19, where two presentations of motif 2, a fifth apart, are superimposed). These

Example 5.19. Cage: *Five Songs*, i; bars 13–18 (motifs marked in voice part)
© by Henmar Press, New York, USA. Reproduced by permission of Peters Edition Limited, London.

harmonisations are sometimes quite dense; although their formation could be attributed to a verticalisation of the secundal nature of the melodic lines, it seems more likely that here – as in the closing bars of *Metamorphosis* – we are seeing the influence of Cowell's tone-clusters (see bars 15–16 of example 5.19, noting additionally that Cage rhythmically expands the basic motif 1: each of the first three pitches is presented twice as many times as expected, while the fourth pitch is placed off-beat following a rest). Overall, this song often feels metreless, the metrical displacement of the vocal line being complemented by that of the accompaniment.

Harmonic considerations are almost entirely avoided in the more extended second song – 'little Christmas tree' – though there are some examples of both types of chord formation so far encountered. Most of the writing, however, is contrapuntal and consists of the intricate interweaving of a number of short motifs (example 5.20). Sometimes – and partly as a result of word painting – ostinato patterns are built up, as in bars 29–32, and particularly bars 59–65.

In contrast to this song, the next – 'in Just' – might almost be described as minimalist. It also anticipates *The Wonderful Widow of Eighteen Springs* of 1942, for in both songs the chanted vocal line consists of only three pitches. In 'in Just' two of these – a and c′ – are reserved for the beginning and the end. Furthermore, in both songs the piano merely provides rhythmic punctuation between statements of lines of text, though 'in Just' does use specific pitches

Example 5.20. Cage: *Five Songs*, ii; bars 1–5
© by Henmar Press, New York, USA. Reproduced by permission of Peters Edition Limited, London.

rather than the 'drumming' of *The Wonderful Widow*. In reality, the holding throughout of the sustaining pedal ensures that the piano is never silent. Its material consists of a combination of rhythmicised static chords (see example 5.21) with rhythmicised unisons, these latter occurring mainly in the middle section (e.g. bars 27–31; 33–36; 40–42). The rhythms of both types of accompaniment are shared in common with the voice. As elsewhere, the inflexible application of these rhythmic motifs ensures that the vocal line often contradicts the metrical pattern as, indeed, do the changes of 'harmony' in the piano part.

A closer examination of the metrical structure (see figure 5.7) of the song indicates that the lengths of both the vocal lines and the piano punctuations are

Example 5.21. Cage: *Five Songs*, iii; bars 1–8
© by Henmar Press, New York, USA. Reproduced by permission of Peters Edition Limited, London.

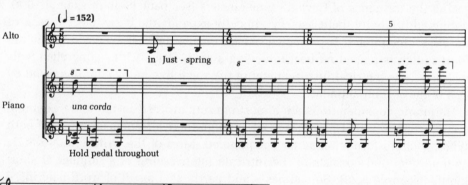

Figure 5.7. Structure of Cage's 'in Just' (*Five Songs*, iii)

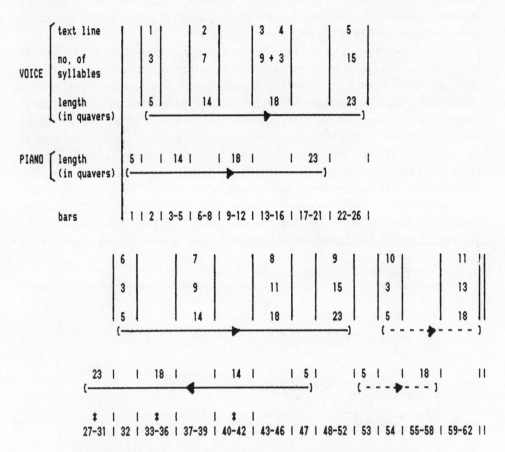

‡ denotes bars of rhythmicised unison accompaniment. Bar 30 is silent.

mathematically structured. Cage counteracts the potentially tedious nature of this repetitive phrase structuring by reversing the piano's second main presentation of the pattern (bars 27–47) and by introducing new accompanimental material at this point. Within each section, the metrical structure consists of freely arranged combinations of $\frac{4}{8}$ and $\frac{5}{8}$ bars (see example 5.21).

The fourth song – 'hist whist' – is similar to the second in its predominantly contrapuntal writing, though this is balanced by the use of motivic two- and three-part chords. These, in combination with a melodic motif (M2↑–m2↑–M2↑–M2↑) possessing definite tonal implications, imbue the song with a distinct feeling of polytonality. The child-like qualities of the verse are thus matched by a musical simplicity similar to that found in parts of such later works as *In a Landscape* (1948), the *Suite for Toy Piano* (1948) and the concluding Quodlibet of the *String Quartet in Four Parts* (1950). In the very short final song, 'another comes', the melodic vocal line is accompanied by variants of the opening motif (dotted crotchet–quaver at same pitch–crotchet a semitone lower), a number of which are 'harmonised' through multiple superimposition (see the discussion of 'little four paws', above).

The musical delicacy of the *Five Songs* is partially continued in the middle movement of the *Music for Wind Instruments*, a Duet for oboe and horn, whose dynamic level never rises above *mf*. It thus stands as a haven of comparative peace and tranquillity wedged between two outer movements whose brutality is emphasised in Cage's introductory remarks to the score: 'The 1st and 3rd pieces are to be played as percussively as possible: the isolated notes to be treated as punctuations.' For while the *Music for Wind Instruments* is the last piece from this period in which Cage uses intervals rather than noises, the intervallic content here is almost irrelevant (as, indeed, is the concept of instrumentation). The opening Trio and concluding Quintet, with their generally high dynamic levels and 'framing' silences, treat the instruments as little more than sound-producing media (example 5.22). Unusually, there is virtually no counterpoint

Example 5.22. Cage: *Music for Wind Instruments*, iii; bars 1–4
© 1961 by Henmar Press, New York, USA. Reproduced by permission of Peters Edition Limited, London.

present here and thus the combination of two or more percussive instrumental lines produces neither polyphony nor harmony. Cage's attention has turned away from intervals to new timbres – or noises. It is in this sense that the implications of 'The Future of Music: Credo', and the influence of Cowell and Varèse (rather than Schoenberg), come to the fore in this work, rather than in the more overtly experimental *Imaginary Landscape No. 1* of spring 1939. Indeed, all that distinguishes the *Music for Wind Instruments* from the *Imaginary Landscape* is that instead of trying to conjure percussive timbres from melodic instruments, Cage instead employs unconventional forces to produce startlingly new timbres. In all other aspects of form and construction the two works show a remarkable consistency. Structurally, the *Imaginary Landscape* consists of four large sections, each of fifteen $\frac{6}{4}$ bars, separated and ended by four shorter sections which grow in arithmetic progression. This seventy-bar form is delineated in the score by rehearsal letters. Thus, as in a number of earlier works, the metrical structure is precomposed and the music made to fit it (see figure 5.8).

Figure 5.8. Structure of Cage's *Imaginary Landscape No. 1*

```
rehearsal letter |  A B | C | D E F | G | H I J | K | L M N : O ||
                                                           :
no. of 6 bars    | 5 5 5 |   | 5 5 5 |   | 5 5 5 |   | 5 5 5 :
         4       |       | 1 |       | 2 |       | 3 |     : 4
                                                           :
section          |   x   | z |   x   | z |   y   | z | xi + : z ||
```

The musical material still consists of a number of fragmentary ideas which are combined in various ways: the difference lies in the instruments Cage chooses to produce these materials with.[23] Of the four players, 1 and 2 are equipped with gramophone turntables and records of constant and changing frequency tones. By altering the turntable speed (between $33\frac{1}{3}$ and 78 r.p.m.) different pitches, as well as the siren-like glissando between those pitches, can be obtained from each record. Indeed, these glissandi are by far the most unusual sound to emanate from the score of *Imaginary Landscape No. 1*: their other-worldly swoopings quite transcend the music of Varèse, Crawford and Cowell which may have influenced them. (Varèse had used sirens in *Ameriques, Hyperprism* and *Ionisation*; '. . .the sliding tones of Ruth Crawford' – probably a reference to either the strings' writing in 'In Tall Grass', or the vocal writing in the *Two Ricercari* – are mentioned by Cage in *Silence*, on page 73.)

Player 3 has a large suspended Chinese cymbal, and player 4 a string piano, this being the first occasion on which Cage makes use of his teacher's invention. Here a gong beater is used to sweep the bass strings of the instrument (c.f. Cowell's *Synchrony* (464) (1930)). Additionally, three muted pitches (b, c', d♭') are played in various rhythmic patterns, an effect reminiscent of Cowell's *Ostinato Pianissimo* (505) (1934). The muting – as in a number of works by Cowell and William Russell – is achieved by placing the palm of the hand on the strings, and then playing at the keyboard as normal.

The various sound sources described above are arranged to produce three types of texture (x, y and z) which define the musical form (see figure 5.8). The first two x sections are almost identical: their texture consists of held tones, glissandi and occasional staccati from the frequency recordings, punctuated by trilled cymbal tones and swept bass piano strings. In the second x section the string piano also plays a repeated triplet pattern. The y material features different glissandi and a five-bar rhythmic pattern from the frequency recordings. The cymbal is silent, while the string piano sports the swept bass string sound, with a 'middle section' (between letters I and J) in which two rhythmic ideas for the muted pitches (triplet and quadruplet) are subjected to an elaborate ordering system, based first on substitution, and then alternation, of types. During the interrupting z̲ sections (at letters C̲, G̲ and K̲) the frequency recordings are silenced: the material consists solely of single strokes (of various durations) on the cymbal, and the three muted pitches of the string piano. In the final section the original x̲ material returns; but from letter N̲ onwards, the cymbal and string piano substitute their z̲ materials, thus ending the piece with a combination of the two main ideas.

Unfortunately the extended form of this work (which lasts approximately seven minutes) is hardly justified by the meagre materials with which Cage attempts to fill it. Whereas previously the hypnotic (and normally quite fast) rhythmic ostinati can sustain the listener's interest over long time spans, the almost complete lack of rhythm here leads to monotony, once the novelty of the sounds has worn off. Although *Imaginary Landscape No. 1* can be seen as a direct response to certain aspects of 'The Future of Music: Credo' (for instance the use of phonographs, frequency recordings, and a tempo of crotchet = 60 (c.f. lines 54–56 of the 'Credo')), it is debatable whether Cage's vision of 'the entire field of sound' and the 'all-sound music of the future' is realised in the work.

From the music Cage produced between 1933 and 1939 – which culminates in the *Imaginary Landscape No. 1* – it is possible to isolate a number of inter-dependent traits and obsessions. Of these, the most important are Cage's interest in using all available sounds and his search for new sounds, these partially combined with the employment of percussion instruments; the use of extra-musical – often mathematical – systems to determine musical parameters (especially pitch); and the quest for a structure other than Western harmony/tonality with which to build form.

All these lines of thought coalesced in November 1939 to produce a work which can be considered Cage's earliest masterpiece – the *First Construction (in Metal)*. As with some previous pieces, the *First Construction* is based on a number – in this case 16. The difference here is that this number dominates not only the structure but also the number of sounds used and the regularity of their appearance. In fact this plan is imperfectly realised, as will be demonstrated.

In theory, each of the six percussionists has 16 separate sounds:

1 16 orchestral bells, played with metal and hard rubber beaters; thundersheet.

2 String piano, effectively requiring the alteration of 14 tones; additionally, the bass strings are swept with a gong beater. (Player 2 has an assistant who applies a metal rod to the strings, producing various effects including a glissando of harmonics. This technique was first used by Cowell in the third movement of *A Composition* (406) (1925) – see chapter 4.)

3 12 oxen bells, played with metal and rubber beaters; sleigh bells; thundersheet.

4 Four brake drums; 8 cowbells, some occasionally damped (+); three Japanese temple gongs, two of which are trilled together; thundersheet.

5 Four Turkish cymbals, open and stopped; eight anvils; four Chinese cymbals, open and stopped; thundersheet.

6 Four muted gongs (hard and soft beaters); water gong (played in four ways); tamtam (played in two ways); thundersheet.

As Cage himself realised, the number 16 is not rigidly adhered to:[24] the thundersheets (employed as background noise) were never included in the original totals; the use of different types of beaters (players 1, 3 and 6) and of muting (players 4, 5) doubles the intended number of sounds, and so on. Interestingly, one of Cage's own criticisms – that there were only three Japanese temple gongs available for player 4 – is redundant, as two of these instruments are trilled together, producing a fourth sound.

There are also supposed to be 16 different rhythmic motifs (c.f. Cage's earlier motivic serialism and percussion works) though this figure is arrived at only if long held notes and *gruppetti* (triplets, etc.) are discounted. These sounds and rhythms are contained within a beautifully and simply shaped structure which has much in common with the forms of Cowell's *United Quartet* (522) (1936) and *Pulse* (565) (1939). (Cage and his percussion group had first performed the latter work in May 1939, some six months before the completion of the *First Construction*.) The construction of the title refers to Cage's use of square-root form, whereby a rhythmic unit of length x bars is repeated x times: thus the whole work will be x^2 bars long. In addition, the x-bar units are arranged both microcosmically and macrocosmically according to a common series of durational proportions.

In the *First Construction*, each unit is 16 $\frac{4}{4}$ bars long (giving a supposed total length of $16^2 = 256$ $\frac{4}{4}$ bars) and the common series of durational proportions is 4:3:2:3:4. The structure, in $\frac{4}{4}$ throughout, is shown in figure 5.9. The macrocos-

Figure 5.9. Structure of Cage's *First Construction (in Metal)*

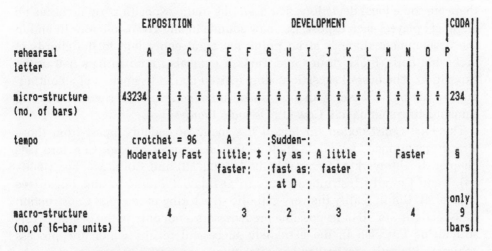

‡ = Slowing down very much   § = Slowing down very much to the end

mic proportions are emphasised by changes of tempo. However, the symmetry and proportions of the plan are compromised somewhat by the addition of the nine-bar coda. The microcosmic proportions are emphasised by changes in timbre and dynamics (c.f. Cowell's *Pulse*; see example 5.23).

Example 5.23. Cage: *First Construction (in Metal)*; bars 17–21
© by Henmar Press, New York, USA. Reproduced by permission of Peters Edition Limited, London.

Theoretically, in each of the exposition's four 16-bar units four of the rhythmic motifs are used, while each player introduces four new sounds. Thus each of the four 16-bar units possesses its own repertory of sounds and rhythms. These four repertories then become the basic material for each of the four large sections of the development. In general this theory is converted to practice, though there are some local deviations. For example, in the exposition, on no occasion do all six players each expose four new sounds in any given 16-bar unit; and in the development there is at no point any aural equivalent to the chords of orchestral bells, brake drums and Turkish cymbals found in bars 8–9 of the exposition. The overall sensation, as perceived by the listener, is of a continuously evolving, and ever widening, spectrum of contrapuntal rhythms and tintinnabulating sounds (c.f. Cowell's *Ostinato Pianissimo*).

The *First Construction (in Metal)* has many precedents: apart from those already mentioned, we might include the later pieces of Ruth Crawford (see chapter 3), the work of George Antheil (1900–59) and Colin McPhee (1900–64),[25] and Cowell's instrumentations in *Ostinato Pianissimo* and *Pulse* (see chapter 4). But in reality the very catholic structuring of the *First Construction* transcends any or all of its possible predecessors – not only in the degree of this structuring but also in the extremely successful results which the process achieves. Beneath the excitement of rhythmic ostinati and new sounds displayed here lies a framework which – for Cage at least – could replace harmony and tonality, and encompass instead both pitched material and unpitched material, as well as the silence between them.

Having devised in the *First Construction* an elaborate repertory of systems and procedures from which an overall and more detailed structure could be shaped, Cage went on to ignore at least some of these systems and procedures in each subsequent work in which he used them. Thus in the *Second Construction* – which is again 16^2 bars long – the supposed micro- and macrocosmic structural proportions are 4:3:4:5. However, the effective macro-structure is actually 4:3:3:6, with the 6 section being a rhythmic fugue. The four macro-sections are quite differentiated in timbre. The second 3 section, for instance (starting at number 7 in example 5.24) has a startlingly direct opening, whose slowly moving lines are quite unlike the busyness found elsewhere. The final fugue also has an obvious start (see example 5.25). This subject is in fact based on the

Example 5.24. Cage: *Second Construction*; bars 109–116
© 1978 by Henmar Press, New York, USA. Reproduced by permission of Peters Edition Limited, London.

Example 5.25. Cage: *Second Construction*; bars 161–164 ('fugue' subject)
© 1978 by Henmar Press, New York, USA. Reproduced by permission of Peters Edition Limited, London.

sleigh bell solo which opens the work, while the final 16-bar unit (commencing at number 15) serves as both coda and recapitulation by being substantially based on this material for sleigh bells and tomtoms.

The majority of the 16 micro-sections adhere to the interior proportioning of 4:3:4:5 $\frac{4}{4}$ bars: the structure is articulated (as it was in the *First Construction*, and in Cowell's *Pulse*) by changes in instrumentation or rhythmic content (example 5.26). In a few 16-bar units, however, the micro-structure is altered

Example 5.26. Cage: *Second Construction*; opening 16-bar unit
© 1978 by Henmar Press, New York, USA. Reproduced by permission of Peters Edition Limited, London.

slightly, so that for instance in the fourth unit (commencing at number 3) the proportions appear to be 4:3:5:4, and in the ninth unit (commencing at number 8) 4:3:4½:4½. In the second, third and fourth units of the fugue (numbers 11–13) the micro-structure effectively breaks down completely, owing to the increasingly close entries of the subject; it is restored at number 14.

Unlike the *First Construction*, there is no apparent attempt here to structure either the number of sounds or rhythms, or the order or number of their appearance per section. The instrumentation relies more on wood-derived sounds than the *First Construction*, the resources assigned to each of the four players being:

1 Seven sleigh bells; wind glass; Indian rattle; two small maracas.
2 Snare drum (wire brush and snare stick); five tomtoms; three (large Japanese) temple gongs; two small maracas; two large maracas.
3 Tamtam (played at centre and edge); five muted gongs; water gong; thundersheet.
4 String piano.

The string piano re-employs a number of effects used in the *Imaginary Landscape No. 1* and *First Construction*, notably the sweeping of the bass strings with a gong beater, and the production of siren-like tremolandi through the use of a metal cylinder, placed on the strings. It also mutes a number of pitches: E and F are occasionally muted by the player's fingers. But Cage also uses two permanent mutes: a screw is placed between the two strings of pitch c, and a piece of cardboard is used to mute the pitches from a' to eb". Thus the string piano found in the *Second Construction* is in all but name a prepared piano – the screw and the cardboard are permanent mutes and the piano, therefore, has to be prepared beforehand.

The first official appearance of the prepared piano, as a solo instrument, is in *Bacchanale* (Mar. 1940); here, twelve pitches are prepared, using several items – see figure 5.10.

Figure 5.10. List of preparations used in Cage's *Bacchanale*

pitch	A	Bb	B	c	db	d	eb	g	ab	bb	c'	f'
preparation material	weather stripping *	"	"	"	"	"	"	"	"	screw with nuts weather stripping *	weather stripping *	small bolt
string (l. to r.)	1 - 2	"	"	"	"	"	"	"	"	2 - 3 1 - 2	1 - 2	2 - 3
distance from damper	**	"	"	"	"	"	"	"	"	"	"	c, 3"

```
     * fibrous
    ** determine position and size of mutes by experiment
```

Given, however, Cage's by this time intimate knowledge of string piano techniques, his own recollections of the genesis of *Bacchanale* (in 'How the Piano Came to be Prepared'[26]) are a little surprising. For while he describes in detail some of the effects used by Cowell in *The Banshee* (405) (1925) and elsewhere (which are of particular relevance to *Imaginary Landscape No. 1* and the *First* and *Second Constructions*), Cage mentions neither his own earlier experience of using a muting screw in the *Second Construction*, nor the fibrous weather stripping (c.f. the use of cardboard in the *Second Construction*) which provides the majority of the preparation material for the *Bacchanale*. (Interestingly, though, given his description of the fruitless search for an African twelve-note row, Cage employs twelve pitches here. Only ten of these, however, are different, as Bb and c are duplicated at the octave.)

The consequences of the invention (or, rather, evolution, by Cowell and Cage) of the prepared piano are several. Firstly, preparation makes available to the composer an infinitely variable keyboard percussion instrument. Secondly, Cage inadvertently came to use the piano (rather than true percussion instruments) as the medium through which he effected the 'contemporary transition from keyboard-influenced music to the all-sound music of the future'.[27] For while he continued to write percussion music after *Bacchanale*, from 1942 until about 1951 the prepared piano came to dominate his output. Thirdly, as with both Cowell's and Cage's percussion pieces, the relationship between notation and actual sound is fundamentally changed. Music for the prepared piano is written as a conventional piano score; but because of the preparation, the sounds that emanate from the instrument bear virtually no resemblance to either those of a normal keyboard or those (pitches) implied by the notation. And owing to the differences of piano construction, even the most precise instructions for preparation cannot guarantee the production of the actual sound intended by the composer. Thus here, and in percussion music, the link between notation and sound becomes even more tenuous, both in performances of a work given by different performers, and performances of a work given using different instruments. The performer's rôle in the creation, and selection, of suitable instruments and prepared sounds therefore becomes vitally important. (This, again, had been anticipated in a number of earlier works by Cowell – see chapter 4.) Consequently, it becomes difficult to describe in conventional terms the thuds and plonks of *Bacchanale* and other prepared piano/percussion works; all that can really be done is to discuss form and rhythm.

Unlike the other works which postdate *Imaginary Landscape No. 1*, *Bacchanale* was not conceived within the framework of an overall rhythmic structuring:

In the specific case of *Bacchanale*, I simply followed the structure of the dance. . .I took a metronome and a chronometer, and I asked Syvilla Fort for the measures of the dance; having taken its measurements, I was able to write the music. . .based on the structure of the dance. The music composers for Hollywood films proceed no differently.[28]

If we consider first this, and then Cage's statement that 'I wrote the *Bacchanal* [sic] quickly and with the excitement continual discovery provided',[29] much of the substance of the score becomes clear.

The work has a basic A–B–Ai (Fast–Slow–Fast) shape, though there is comparatively little real repetition: some musical elements recur in varied form (especially towards the very end) but there are at least 25 different ostinato bass and melodic fragments used. One of the few ostinati to achieve any degree of long-term prominence appears in the left hand at the beginning, and on many subsequent occasions (example 5.27).

An analysis of the lengths of the work's constituent sub-sections reveals that there is some number structuring present. For instance, the lengths (in crotchets) of the constituent parts of the first A section (delineated by double bar-lines and changes of tempo) are:

30   20   30   20   30   10   30   30   43.

But this structuring is almost certainly derived from the counts of the dance, as are the metric patterns from which these sections are built.

Perhaps the most striking feature of *Bacchanale* is its ethnic sound. Surprisingly, though, the derivation seems to be Asian rather than African: *Bacchanale*'s Balinese sound could well have been influenced both by the music and writings of Colin McPhee, and by the enthusiasm, music and teaching of

Example 5.27. Cage: *Bacchanale*; bars 1–5; 34–37; 87–91
© 1960 by Henmar Press, New York, USA. Reproduced by permission of Peters Edition Limited, London.

Cowell. (While in New York, Cage had attended a series of lectures on world musics, given by Cowell at the New School.)

In the remaining works of this period – *Living Room Music* (1940), the *Third Construction* (1941) and *Double Music* (Apr. 1941) – Cage returned to the use of rhythmic structuring on a micro- and macrocosmic scale, and to flexibility in instrumentation and performance. The instruction in the score of the four-movement *Living Room Music* that 'Any household objects or architectural elements may be used as instruments' is reminiscent of the statement quoted earlier in connection with the *Quartet*: '. . .the infinite number of sound sources from a trash heap or a junk yard, a living room or a kitchen. . .'.[30] And in the *Third Construction*, we find a wide array of instruments both trashy and exotic, ranging from tin cans and cricket callers to quijadas and teponaxtle.

The 1935 *Quartet* is also recalled – as is Cowell's *Mosaic Quartet* of the same year – in Cage's instruction that the third movement of *Living Room Music* (titled 'Melody') may be omitted. Here, players 1–3 use their household objects to accompany player 4's tune, which – the score instructs – 'may be played on any suitable instrument: wind, string or keyboard, prepared or not'.

In the second movement – 'Story' – the household percussion is set aside and replaced by a setting for speech quartet of a text by Gertrude Stein: 'Once upon a time the world was round and you could go on it around and around.' The manner and gestures used here are very similar to those found in the well known *Geographical Fugue* (1930) by Ernst Toch (1887–1964).[31]

The rhythmic structures of *Living Room Music* are often difficult to detect. This is also true of the *Third Construction* which, at $24^2 \frac{2}{2}$ bars, is by far Cage's largest work of the period. The macro-structure, based on an examination of changes of tempo and timbre, and dynamic shapes, would appear to be 5:3:2; 5:4:5 (or, alternatively, 10:14). But the distinguishing of either of these sets of proportions at a microcosmic level is more difficult to justify: while some 24-bar units divide exactly into these proportions, others ignore them completely. Elsewhere, in any given section some lines will pay greater attention to the proportions than others. It would seem that Cage, having devised a system through which he can structure form according to purely durational (or rhythmic) considerations, and having experimented with that system in more or less strict fashion, now feels able to use his structured forms with whatever degree of freedom he wishes (rather than letting the structures dictate to him).

This is certainly the case in *Double Music*, for four percussionists. As seeming proof of the flexibility of his system – and perhaps in part realising his ambition to create 'the means. . .for group improvisations of unwritten but culturally important music'[32] – Cage here writes only one (horizontal) half of the piece (i.e. the parts for players 1 and 3). Parts 2 and 4 were written by his fellow percussionist and composer Lou Harrison. The diversity of instruments chosen is no greater than in many of Cage's solo efforts:

> Player 1 Six graduated water buffalo bells; six graduated muted brake drums.
> Player 2 Two sistrums; six graduated sleigh bells; six brake drums; thundersheet.
> Player 3 Three graduated Japanese temple gongs; tamtam; six graduated cowbells.
> Player 4 Six muted Chinese gongs; tamtam; water gong.

But the sense of collaboration is extended further by the following *caveat* in the score: 'Substitutions of the above [instruments], if necessary, may be chosen by keeping the S–A–T–B relation of the parts clear.' This seems to invite others to take part in the creative process. There is also a note regarding the dynamics, which

are scarcely indicated. The first note of each group of 8th notes may be given a slight accent. The piece does not progress from soft to loud but is continuously festive in intention, the changes in amount and nature of activity producing changes in amplitude.

This suggests that they were not decided in advance; indeed, the implication is that they came about by accident.

There must, obviously, have been some prior agreement between the composers regarding the tempo (*Allegro moderato*), metre ($\frac{4}{4}$) and overall length of the piece (200 bars). But it is in the different ways chosen to subdivide this overall length that the freedom offered by Cage's system of durational structuring, and the duality suggested by the title, become clear. Cage's two parts appear to be written within a broad framework of $14^2 + 4$ $\frac{4}{4}$ bars. As with the *Third Construction* there is some flexibility in the way this is handled, the music for part 1 being written particularly freely. Its apparent macrocosmic proportions (defined primarily by changes in instrumentation) of 2:5:7 are unused at the microcosmic level. Rather, the rhythmic motifs seem to be freely composed, combined and varied. Part 3, written more systematically, has a macro-structure of 7:1:1:5 (again defined primarily by changes in instrumentation) which is reflected fairly consistently at the microcosmic level as 7:2:5. However, the micro-structure effectively disappears during the macro-5 section. Once again, the motivic patterns appear to be freely composed.

Harrison, as an outsider, obviously feels less responsibility towards the system than does Cage. Consequently, he treats it with a greater degree of freedom: parts 2 and 4 are both constructed as 21 × 19-minim (i.e. $9\frac{1}{2}$-bar) units, with one minim ($\frac{1}{2}$ bar) remaining at the end. Harrison articulates the 21 macro-units, in both parts, by filling them with either sound or silence. If the former applies, then he uses only one kind of instrument per unit. Each of these 19-minim macro-units is then normally subdivided in the micro-proportions $12\frac{1}{2}:4\frac{1}{2}:2$. (Note that as Harrison's subdivision of the total of 200 bars is not based on a square-root formula – c.f. Cage's 14^2 (+ 4) bars – his micro-structure cannot be replicated at the macrocosmic level.) The rhythmic material Harrison invents articulates both the macro-structure (both parts having an overall A–B–C–B–A shape in terms of the groups of motifs used) and the micro-structure (example 5.28).

The combination of the two composers' ideas produces music of irresistible rhythmic vitality (example 5.29).

Example 5.28. Cage and Harrison: *Double Music*; part 2, bars 1–10

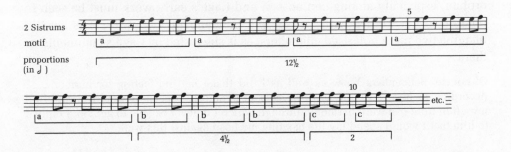

Example 5.29. Cage and Harrison: *Double Music*; bars 1–15
Parts 1+3 © 1961 by Henmar Press, New York, USA.
Parts 2+4 © 1961 by C.F. Peters Corporation, New York, USA.
Reproduced by permission of Peters Edition Limited, London.

Double Music is undoubtedly one of the more successful of Cage's works from this period, this success stemming from its combination of stricture and freedom. The lessons learnt from this piece – and from others in the period after 1938 – were to serve Cage well for almost a decade. However, no one is born an orphan, especially among composers, and Cage's early work must be seen in relation to his studies with Cowell and Schoenberg. Certainly, it is hard to imagine two more polarised characters, as is suggested by Cage's comments on them:

Of course, Schoenberg knew as well as I did that I had no feeling for harmony. . . According to him, I would never be able to compose, because I would always find myself in front of a wall, harmony, through which I'd never be able to get. So, I replied to him that I would spend my life banging my head against this wall.[33]

[Cowell]. . .was not attached (as Varèse also was not attached) to what seemed to so many to be the important question: Whether to follow Schoenberg or Stravinsky. His early works for piano. . .by their tone clusters and use of the piano strings, pointed towards noise and a continuum of timbre.[34]

Given his inborn talent for musical methodology, it was natural that Cage should have studied with Schoenberg. As has been shown, he utilised quasi-serial systems of pitch organisation before, during and after the period of study in the universities of Southern California and Los Angeles. What Schoenberg taught Cage was that structure is a fundamental necessity of musical composition. The difficulty lay in Schoenberg's insistence on that structure being based on harmonic considerations.

What Cage learnt from Cowell – both from the lectures and classes he attended in New York, and from the music he must have seen and heard there and elsewhere – was that all sounds were potentially musical, and that they could be freely brought together in a musical composition.

This duality of stricture and freedom is what animates Cage's music during this period. In an attempt to reconcile the influence of Schoenberg with the increasing influence of Cowell and his own natural instincts, Cage found it necessary to devise a philosophy of experimentation, a personal credo of musical intention. The combination of this philosophy with the development of a 'Schoenbergian' musical structure – paradoxically based on ideas found in works by Cowell, and in non-Western musics – enabled Cage in pieces such as the *First Construction (in Metal)* to encompass Cowell's all-sound universe. Let us remember that it was of the works discussed here – which he knew – and of the procedures they employ that the Teutonic traditionalist Schoenberg was thinking when he wrote of Cage: 'Not a composer, but an inventor. Of genius.'[35]

6   Conclusion: Unity through diversity

There can be nothing 'exclusive' about a substantial art.
Charles Ives

There is a commonly held view, particularly among those concerned primarily with European musical traditions, that the American experimental movement developed accidentally, in isolation, and in a naïve and undisciplined way. It further considers the composers associated with experimentalism as amiable eccentrics, whose works are far less interesting than the anecdotes about them. This view is clearly wrong. The composers discussed here, as representatives of experimentalism's first half-century, had a clear sense of direction both individually and collectively. Their music and ideas are rigorous and highly disciplined, and, at a purely technical level, revolve around a number of recurring preoccupations. Among these are:

1 extreme chromaticism of both melody and harmony;
2 tone-clusters and noise;
3 the use of new or unconventional instruments (both electronic and acoustic) and/or of conventional instruments in an unusual way;
4 rhythmic complexity, both simultaneous and successive;
5 implied or actual polytempo and/or polymetre;
6 implied or actual spatial separation of groups of instruments;
7 independent organisation of the various parameters of a musical line or idea;
8 large-scale and/or small-scale structuring of form, using extra-musical devices and processes, including numeration;
9 graphic notation and/or semi-improvised music;
10 works which are indeterminate of their performance.

What should be clear is that these preoccupations have been shared in common not just among the composers discussed here, but also among their contemporaries and successors in the American experimental tradition (though, of course, not every composer has employed all of these traits, and other preoccupations – including those which have led to so-called minimalist music – have subsequently grown out of this initial list). In evidence, one might point to the range of instrumental resources, both extant and newly invented, employed by Lou Harrison or Harry Partch, and the vocal innovations of Meredith Monk and others; the developments in electronic instruments and music, pioneered by Varèse and to a lesser extent Cowell, and taken up by Cage, Otto Leuning,

Vladimir Ussachevsky, Jacob Druckman, Morton Subotnick, Lejaren Hiller, Robert Ashley, and others; the extreme rhythmic complexity of Conlon Nancarrow's works for player piano and of Frank Zappa's music for rock instruments or orchestra; the graphic notations of Cage, Morton Feldman and Earle Brown; the partial or complete indeterminacy of some works of Cowell, Cage, Christian Wolff and La Monte Young, together with the earlier phase works of Steve Reich; the implied polymetre of much minimalist music; and the spatial separation of groups of instruments by Ives, Cage, Henry Brant, Ralph Shapey and Roger Reynolds.

Beyond merely technical criteria, however, there exists a more fundamental link between experimental composers, one which sets them quintessentially apart from the mainstream of Western art music. In chapter 2 it was suggested that Ives' experimentalism lay not only in his creation of overtly experimental pieces, employing new compositional techniques, but also in his adoption of an unprecedentedly wide variety of supposedly exclusive musical styles, both from work to work, and within individual works. The same observation might be made of Cowell, for whom there were no distinctions between folk and art, European and American, Irish and Japanese. This is shown during the pre-war period by the synthesis of works like *Rhythmicana* (557) (1938) and the *United Quartet* (522) (1936), and in the apparent exclusivity of such pieces as the highly-dissonant *It Isn't It* (355) (1922) and the disarmingly simple *The Aeolian Harp* (370) (?1923).

'The whole spectrum of complex-to-simple'[1] is also displayed in the pre- and post-war musics of Cage and Partch. Partch, like Cowell, was essentially self-taught musically, and cited an equally wide list of influences on his thought and work: 'Christian hymns, Chinese lullabyes, Yaqui Indian ritual, Congo puberty ritual, Cantonese music hall, and Okies in Californian vineyards, among others'.[2]

Cage's openness of mind and inclusivity of philosophy have led in the period since the Second World War to the post-Ivesian collage of such works as *Variations IV* (1963), *Musicircus* (1967), *HPSCHD* (1967–69) and *Roaratorio* (1979).

At a superficial level, the music and aims of composers such as Ives, Cowell and Cage seem utterly different to those implied by the discipline of Seeger's totally dissonant composition. Yet the ultimate goal of dissonant counterpoint was

. . .a new polyphony, 'heterophony'. And since this means real independence of parts, it follows that the parts must be so different in themselves and the relation between them (which makes their simultaneous sounding agreeable) must perforce be such that their difference rather than their likeness is emphasised.[3]

Taken to its logical conclusion, this train of thought suggested

. . .*complete* heterophony. . .a polyphony in which there is no relation between the parts except mere proximity in time-space, beginning and ending, within hearing of each other, at more or less the same time: each should have its own tonal and rhythmic system and these should be mutually exclusive, while the forms should be utterly diverse. Heterophony may be accidental, as, for instance, a radio reception of Beethoven's 'Eroica' intruded upon by a phonograph record of a Javanese gamelan. But from an artistic point of view, a high degree of organization is necessary (1) to assure perfect non-coincidence and (2) to make the undertaking as a whole worth while.[4]

The implication of these statements is that, for Seeger, unity in a totally dissonant composition should be achieved through the diversity of its constituent parts. Clearly, in neither his work nor in that of Ruth Crawford do we find the extremes of stylistic diversity, either simultaneous or successive, employed by Ives, Cowell and Cage. But Seeger's (and Crawford's) theoretical aims are fundamentally the same as those of the other composers discussed here. Indeed, in his accidental heterophony of 'Beethoven's "Eroica" intruded upon by. . . Javanese gamelan' Seeger has described both an extreme conception of stylistic plurality and synthesis (Cowell, Harrison, Partch and – less globally – Ives) and a practical model of it, as might be found in Cage's *Imaginary Landscape No. 5* (1952) for any 42 recordings.

Thus the American experimental tradition is rooted not just in a desire to explore new compositional horizons, but also in a (conscious or subconscious) realisation that musical unity can – and should – be created through stylistic diversity, both individually and collectively, within a work or between works. Experimentalism can therefore take many different forms, and be presented in many different ways, for in Ives' and Schoenberg's terms, substance – or idea – is more important than manner – or style. The concept of plurality is as applicable to the methods of organising materials as to the materials themselves, an attitude which sets experimentalists fundamentally apart from those concerned merely with one tradition or language.

How, then, do we explain the birth of this experimental movement in America during the fifty years preceding the Second World War? It has sometimes been pointed out that a number of experimental composers (Cowell, Partch, Cage, Harrison, Terry Riley) hail from the West Coast, which is 'culturally as well as geographically, farther from Europe than is New York, and closer to Asia. . .[the] West Coast, with more tenuous European ties and a greater variety of influences, has been more open to choices'.[5] Yet while this creates the possibility of influence from non-Western art forms, it does little to explain the 'East Coast' diversity of Ives, Crawford, Reich or Glass. And even if the idea is broadened out, so as to suggest that plurality might be a result of exposure to a wide range of (unspecified) musical styles, it is still unhelpful. For Crawford's formative years exposed her to little other than Western art music, and Seeger was trained at Harvard and in Europe. Nor can simple musical naïvety, or the lack of an academic musical education, be cited as causes.

Perhaps, then, we should look beyond the details of the composers' lives, ideas and musics for an explanation of the American experimental tradition. For this tradition is not limited simply to music, but extends to literature (Gertrude Stein, E.E. Cummings, William Burroughs, Thomas Pynchon, Cage, Kathy Acker), the visual arts (Man Ray, Robert Rauschenberg, Jasper Johns,

Andy Warhol), dance (Martha Graham, Merce Cunningham) and theatre/performance art (Cage, Robert Wilson, Laurie Anderson).

Culture is ultimately a product of its conditioning environment as much as of individuals; and the conditioning environment that was – and is – the United States of America is unique. Walt Whitman rightly called it a nation of nations,[6] for ever since its discovery by Europeans in the late fifteenth century, the country has been besieged by successive waves of immigrants:

The transfer of peoples and cultures to America is one of the great themes of American history and, indeed, of the history of man. Migrations take place everywhere, but there has never been anything like the movement that produced the United States of America and generated continuing complexes of change.[7]

Each new wave of immigrants brought with it its own culture, which was then added to the existing *pot-pourri* until, eventually, the inevitable result, as much in art as in society, was 'a nation unintentionally based upon the tensions of pluralism'.[8] As we have seen, this pluralism is subconsciously acknowledged in the music and ideas of Seeger, Crawford, Cowell and Cage, and was consciously cited in the philosophical arguments developed by Ives in his *Essays before a Sonata*. It also motivated Whitman and, possibly (though again subconsciously), the spirit of Transcendentalism which moved through New England in the mid-nineteenth century, and which later became such an influence on Ives.

Thus, as was intuitively recognised by Cowell in 1931,[9] the musics and ideas of Ives, Seeger, Crawford, Cage and Cowell himself – together with a host of other American experimental composers and artists of the twentieth century – reflect, in their underlying allegiance to the principle of unity being created through diversity, a fundamental characteristic of American society.

Notes

1 Introduction: The new and the experimental

1 For details of American musical life during the nineteenth and early twentieth centuries, see Hitchcock, *Music in the United States*, chapters 6, 8, 9; Kingman, *American Music: A Panorama*, chapters 13–16.

2 Letter from Ruth Crawford to Alice, quoted in Gaume, 'Ruth Crawford: A Promising Young Composer in New York', p. 79.

3 For further details of these various associations, see chapters 2 to 5, plus Kirkpatrick, 'The Evolution of Carl Ruggles', p. 153; Mead, *Henry Cowell's New Music*, p. 24; Tomkins, *The Bride and the Bachelors*, pp. 81–85; Tusler and Briegleb, [Interview with Charles Seeger], pp. 94–104, 166–169.

4 For further details on the Composers' Collective, etc., see Copland and Perlis, *Copland, 1900 through 1942*, pp. 222–230; Dunaway, 'Charles Seeger and Carl Sands: The Composers' Collective Years'; Gaume, *Ruth Crawford Seeger: Memoirs, Memories, Music*, pp. 94–103.

5 For further details, see Burkholder, *Charles Ives: The Ideas behind the Music*, pp. 1–7.

6 For details of Ives' sponsorship of Cowell's activities, see Rossiter, *Charles Ives and His America*, pp. 215–271.

7 See Varèse, *A Looking-Glass Diary*, p. 254; Rossiter, *Charles Ives and His America*, p. 225.

8 See Cowell, 'Trends in American Music', pp. 3–4.

9 See Bernard, *The Music of Edgard Varèse*; Cox, 'Edgard Varèse'; Wen-chung, 'Ionisation'.

10 Cowell, quoted in Rossiter, *Charles Ives and His America*, p. 222.

11 Cowell, 'Trends in American Music', p. 12.

12 Quoted in Rossiter, *Charles Ives and His America*, p. 222.

2 *In Re Con Moto Et Al*: Charles Ives

1 For further details of Ives' life, etc., see Kirkpatrick, 'Ives', in *The New Grove*, vol. 9, pp. 414–429/ *Amerigrove*, vol. 2, pp. 503–520; Rossiter, *Charles Ives and His America*.

2 Ives, *Memos*, p. 45.

3 Kirkpatrick, 'Ives', in *The New Grove*, vol. 9, p. 420/*Amerigrove*, vol. 2, p. 509.

4 See Burkholder, *Charles Ives: The Ideas behind the Music*, particularly pp. 58–66, for an amplification of these remarks.

5 See Kirkpatrick, 'Ives', in *The New Grove*, vol. 9, pp. 416–417/*Amerigrove*, vol. 2, p. 505; Burkholder, *Charles Ives: The Ideas behind the Music*, pp. 93–104.

6 Many of Ives' works are at present either unavailable or available only in inaccurate, incomplete or otherwise unsatisfactory editions; and it would be quite beyond the scope or intention of this survey to attempt to use Ives' manuscripts as a basic source material. Wherever possible, therefore, the following discussion refers to those editions of works approved by the Charles Ives Society; in the list of editions in the appendix these are indicated by an asterisk.

7 Relevant reminiscences are found in Ives, *Memos*, pp. 42–43, 45–49, 53, 114–116, 124, 132–133, 140, 142. See also Ives, *Memos*, pp. 236–237, 245–249; and the Conductor's Note to the second movement of his Fourth Symphony (V39), pp. 12–14 of the published score.

8 Ives, *Memos*, p. 133, note 5.

9 Ives, *Memos*, p. 47.

10 *Ibid.*, p. 46. On *Psalm 150*'s fugue, see also Hitchcock, *Ives*, p. 29.

11 Ives, *Memos*, p. 49.

12 For Ives' comments on these bitonal chords, see Kirkpatrick, *A Temporary Mimeographed Catalogue*, p. 136.

13 From the Conductor's Note to the Fourth Symphony, second movement; pp. 12–14 of the published score.

14 Hitchcock, *Ives*, p. 40.

15 Ives, *Memos*, pp. 132–133.

16 *Ibid.*, p. 56. Ives' words actually relate to his discussion of 'In the Cage' (V22,i).

17 The score specifies only one trumpet, but on a number of occasions seems to call for two.

18 Dissonant rhythm will be discussed in chapter 3.

19 Ives' quotation and use of existing material is well documented. For details, see the bibliography in Kirkpatrick's *New Grove/Amerigrove* articles.

20 Ives, *Memos*, p. 42.

21 *Ibid.*, p. 104. Though describing *The Fourth of July* (V34) (1911–13) Ives seems to refer here to the part of that work borrowed from *Overture, 1776*. See also p. 83 of *Memos*.

22 Note in manuscript: see published score, p. 34, note to bars 70–71.

23 See particularly *Hawthorne*, bottom of p. 28 to top of p. 29 of the published score; and Fourth Symphony, ii, at figure 27 of the published score. This music also appears in *Over the Pavements* (V20) (1906–13) at bars 29–30, and the song *1, 2, 3* (Z135) (1921) at bars 28–30.

24 Hitchcock, *Ives*, p. 68.

25 See, for instance, comments in Morgan, 'Spatial Form in Ives', in Hitchcock and Perlis, *An Ives Celebration*, p. 153.

26 Ives, *Memos*, p. 191.

27 *Ibid.*, p. 56.

28 *Ibid.*, pp. 57–58.

29 *Ibid.*, p. 191. The quotation refers specifically to the performance of *Hawthorne*.

30 Note in score: see bells, bars 15–16.

31 Ives, *Memos*, p. 59.

32 See Marshall, 'Charles Ives' Quotations: Manner or Substance?'.

33 See Brooks, 'Unity and Diversity in Charles Ives' Fourth Symphony', for a brilliant exposition of this approach, and of its application to the Fourth Symphony's first movement.

34 Ives, *Memos*, p. 91.

35 See Kirkpatrick, *A Temporary Mimeographed Catalogue*, p. 65.

36 Ives, *Memos*, pp. 62–63.

37 *Ibid.*, p. 63.

38 Bar numbers refer to the music for strings and trumpet.

39 From the Foreword to the published score.

40 From a note in the published score; subsequent quotations are taken from the same source. The period referred to would appear to be that of the work's composition.

41 See the Comparison of Sources in the published score; subsequent characterisations are taken from the same source.

42 In music of this kind, Ives comes very close to Charles Seeger's concept of dissonant counterpoint (see chapter 3).

43 Ives, *Memos*, p. 63. Note that, as is the case with the earlier *Largo Risoluto* pieces, the second *Tone Road* is lost.

44 *Ibid.*, p. 64. 'Rondo Rapid Transit' appears as a subtitle over the whole work rather than this portion of it.

45 Ives, *Memos*, p. 101.

46 From the Editors' Notes to the published score.

47 The attribution here of the characteristic 'Rejoicing in Beauty and Work' to the bells in bars 4–5 disagrees with that in the published score (where it appears over the organ part in bar 4). This is because the music of *Psalm 90* makes it quite obvious that the organ's chord progression in bars 3–5 is one distinct musical type, and the bells' music of bars 4–5 is another. The two types never appear together. The text of verses 14–17 makes clear the link between 'Rejoicing in Beauty and Work' and the bell music played underneath, while the music for organ and voices in verses 14–17 most closely resembles that of types 1 and 2.

48 See Kirkpatrick, *A Temporary Mimeographed Catalogue*, p. 126.

49 For details of the *Universe Symphony*, see Kirkpatrick, *A Temporary Mimeographed Catalogue*, pp. 26–28; Ives, *Memos*, pp. 106–108 and 125.

50 See Kirkpatrick, *A Temporary Mimeographed Catalogue*, pp. 126–127.

51 Ives, *Memos*, p. 64.

52 *Ibid.*, p. 61.

3 'On Dissonant Counterpoint': Charles Seeger, Carl Ruggles and Ruth Crawford

1 For further details of Seeger's life, see Pescatello, 'Charles Seeger'; Perlis, 'Interview with Charles Seeger'; Tusler and Briegleb, [Interview with Charles Seeger].

2 Cowell, 'Charles Seeger', p. 119.

3 Seeger's influence on Cowell, and in particular on the development and disciplining of the latter's innate experimental leanings, will be discussed in chapter 4.

4 Seeger's long book – 'Tradition and Experiment in Twentieth Century Music' – was never completed. See Gaume, *Ruth Crawford Seeger: Memoirs, Memories, Music*, pp. 71, 86, 96, 127, 152; Tusler and Briegleb, [Interview with Charles Seeger], p. 174. It is possible that 'On Dissonant Counterpoint' was drawn from the unfinished work.

5 See Seeger, 'On Dissonant Counterpoint', p. 25; Tusler and Briegleb, [Interview with Charles Seeger], p. 106.

6 This, and the following quotations, are taken from Seeger, 'On Dissonant Counterpoint', pp. 25–26.

7 Wherever possible, abstract examples of dissonant counterpoint are based on Seeger's own descriptions: see Seeger, 'On Dissonant Counterpoint'; Tusler and Briegleb, [Interview with Charles Seeger], pp. 106–107.

8 See Seeger, 'On Dissonant Counterpoint', pp. 28–30, for details; Nicholls, 'New and Experimental Compositional Techniques', vol. 1, pp. 123–124, for a brief discussion.

9 Cowell, 'Charles Seeger', p. 119.

10 *New Music*, vol. 26, no. 3 (Apr. 1953, but actually delayed until the following year).

11 Seeger, 'Carl Ruggles', p. 24.

12 Seeger, 'On Dissonant Counterpoint', p. 31. See also Seeger, 'Carl Ruggles', pp. 25–27 for an expression of similar sentiments.

13 See also the discussions of Crawford's *Diaphonic Suite No. 1* (chapter 3, below) and of the third movement of Cowell's String Quartet No. 1 (1917) (chapter 4).

14 Seeger, 'On Dissonant Counterpoint', p. 29.

15 Cowell, 'Charles Seeger', p. 119. Cowell develops this statement at some length in the following paragraph.

16 For Cage's possible study, with Cowell, of dissonant counterpoint, see chapter 5.

17 For further biographical details, see Gillespie, 'John J. Becker' and 'John Becker, Musical Crusader of Saint Paul'.

18 Seeger, 'On Dissonant Counterpoint', pp. 28–29. Seeger presumably intended that minor triads might also be covered by this statement.

19 Seeger, 'On Dissonant Counterpoint', p. 30.

20 Kirkpatrick, 'The Evolution of Carl Ruggles', p. 153. This article should be consulted for further biographical details.

21 It is important to note that in most cases the editions referred to here are those of the original versions of works, rather than Ruggles' subsequent revisions. For details of these editions, see the appendix. However, while the details of different versions of the same work may vary, the musical substance is generally very similar.

22 The second version differs in a number of ways – see Ziffrin, 'Angels – Two Views'.

23 The version discussed here is the revision of 1926–29, published in *New Music* in 1930. This version is essentially the same as that of 1925.

24 Originally *Evocation 4*, but renumbered as 3 in the 1954 edition.

25 See Kirkpatrick's sleeve-note to the recording of *Sun-treader* (CBS 79225).

26 *Evocations 1, 2* and *4* of the 1954 edition.

27 For another approach to the analysis of *Sun-treader*, the *Evocations* and the later *Organum*, see Gilbert, 'Carl Ruggles (1876–1971): An Appreciation'; and 'The "Twelve-Tone System" of Carl Ruggles'.

28 For details of biography, and of Crawford's pre-1930 music, see Gaume, 'Ruth Crawford Seeger: Her Life and Works' and *Ruth Crawford Seeger: Memoirs, Memories, Music*; Neuls-Bates (ed.), *Women in Music*, pp. 303–311; and Nicholls, 'Ruth Crawford Seeger: An Introduction'.

29 The *Diaphonic Suites* are discussed in their order of composition.

30 C.f. Ives' *From the Steeples and the Mountains* (W3).

31 Personal communication from Peggy Seeger. See also Gaume, *Ruth Crawford Seeger: Memoirs, Memories, Music*, pp. 161–162.

32 According to the manuscript the soloist in A and Ai is an alto, and in B a soprano. However, some pencilled additions indicate that the distribution of the solo melody between the two voices should be based less on these formal considerations and more on the actual ranges involved.

33 The bar numbering used in example 3.20 includes the three extra bars added by Crawford at the beginning of her manuscript.

34 This would imply that the incident took place before Crawford's departure for Europe (i.e. New Year 1930), a view seemingly confirmed by Seeger's statement that both the third and fourth movements of the Quartet were originally exercises for Crawford's studies in composition. See Perlis, 'Interview with Charles Seeger', p. 38.

35 One pitch (the e″ which should appear at the end of the second ten-pitch group) is omitted in B. The corresponding pitch (e♯″) is also omitted in C.

36 For the orchestral ostinati being written at Seeger's suggestion, see the sleeve-notes to record New World NW285. In the published score of the Three Songs, the ostinati are written at playing pitch. Their music has been transposed here to sounding pitch.

37 The order of the Three Songs discussed here is that of their composition.

38 Seeger, 'Ruth Crawford', p. 111.

39 Note that in the fifth unit one of the non-unisons appears 'early' and is thus separated from the remaining nine non-unisons.

40 See Seeger, 'On Dissonant Counterpoint', p. 27.

4 *New Musical Resources*: Henry Cowell

1 See Tusler and Briegleb, [Interview with Charles Seeger], pp. 99–100. Note that Seeger remembers incorrectly both the date of the meeting and Cowell's age at the time. 'Opus 108' would be the Minuetto (128) (Nov. 1914), the 108th item in Cowell's own list of Compository Dates (CD).

2 For a fuller account, see Saylor, 'Henry Cowell'; Terman, The Intelligence of Schoolchildren.

3 In the mid-1950s, the idea of serially interrelated tempi was rekindled in such works as Stockhausen's Klavierstück VI.

4 For Seeger's remarks, and other relevant descriptions, see Perlis, 'Interview with Charles Seeger', p. 21; Seeger, 'Henry Cowell'; the introductory note to the published score of the String Quartet No. 1 (197).

5 Whether or not Crawford was aware of this Quartet is not known; but Seeger must have been.

6 Seeger, 'Henry Cowell'; quoted in the introductory note to the published score of the String Quartet No. 1 (197).

7 See Cowell's Preface to the published score of the Quartet Romantic and Quartet Euphometric.

8 See Perlis, 'Interview with Charles Seeger', p. 22.

9 The short second movement of the Quartet Romantic is a dissonantly contrapuntal piece, similar to the first movement of the String Quartet No. 1. Its conventional rhythms supposedly prompted the naming of the whole as Quartet Romantic.

10 See the Composer's Working Notes on the Quartet Romantic, in the score of the Quartet Romantic and Quartet Euphometric.

11 In the reconstruction of harmonic theme 3, it was assumed that its fundamental was C; it might alternatively be G.

12 This and the following remark are taken from Cowell's Preface to the score of the Quartet Romantic and Quartet Euphometric.

13 Undertones are discussed in New Musical Resources between pages 21 and 24. The undertone series, though Cowell believed in its existence, is in reality an acoustical red herring.

14 From the story according to John Varian, given at the head of the published score.

15 From 'History of Experimental Music in the United States', in Cage, Silence, p. 71.

16 Hamm, 'Sound Forms for Piano', p. 4.

17 C.f. the playing of the piano's five lowest strings with a padded gong-stick in Synchrony (464) (1930). Cage's later use of the string piano is discussed in chapter 5. It is quite possible that the metal object in A Composition might be a darning egg: see the article 'How the Piano Came to be Prepared', in Cage, Empty Words, p. 7.

18 In his performance of The Aeolian Harp, on Folkways FM3349, Cowell does not adhere strictly to the published score.

19 An exception is found in bars 15–16, which Cowell plays only three, rather than four, times. There are also a number of rhythmic details in Cowell's performance which differ from the printed version.

20 Cowell, 'Current Chronicle', pp. 100–101. Ironically, the example quoted by Cowell and shown on p. 101 seems to be taken from the spurious K.Anh.C30.01 rather than the authentic K516f.

21 For further detailed analysis, see Hitchcock, 'Henry Cowell's *Ostinato Pianissimo*'; Nicholls, 'New and Experimental Compositional Techniques', vol. 1, pp. 232–234.

22 Statement in published score, reproduced in sleeve-notes to recording CRI SD 173.

23 Hitchcock, 'Henry Cowell's *Ostinato Pianissimo*', pp. 40–41, note 16.

24 For a fuller discussion of square-root form, see chapter 5, particularly in relation to Cage's *First Construction (in Metal)*. Cube-root form would in fact be a more accurate description of the structures used in *Pulse* and the first movement of the *United Quartet*.

25 See Tusler and Briegleb, [Interview with Charles Seeger], pp. 103–104.

26 Seeger, 'Henry Cowell'; quoted in the introductory note to the published score of the String Quartet No. 1 (197).

27 See Perlis, 'Interview with Charles Seeger', p. 65 [i].

28 Cowell, Preface to the published score of the *Quartet Romantic* and *Quartet Euphometric*.

5 'The Future of Music: Credo': John Cage

1 For details of Cage's early life, see Tomkins, *The Bride and the Bachelors*, pp. 75–81. Note that Tomkins' datings are sometimes inaccurate.

2 Extracted from the lecture 'Where Are We Going? And What Are We Doing?', in Cage, *Silence*, pp. 234–235.

3 Tomkins, *The Bride and the Bachelors*, pp. 81–82.

4 See Tomkins, *The Bride and the Bachelors*, p. 83; Mead, *Henry Cowell's New Music*, p. 228.

5 All three voices share the same pitch range, which is g–g″. 'Upper', etc., here refers to their position on the printed page.

6 See Cowell, 'Current Chronicle', p. 94.

7 Cage, *For the Birds*, p. 72.

8 Excepting that any one of the four versions (original, inversion, retrograde, retrograde inversion) of the group of tones can be used, and that individual pitches within the group can be subjected to octave transpositions.

9 Cage, *For the Birds*, p. 74.

10 See, for instance, Cage, *For the Birds*, pp. 71–72.

11 *Ibid.*, pp. 73–74.

12 *Ibid.*, p. 74.

13 *Ibid.*, p. 75.

14 *Ibid.*, p. 71.

15 See Tomkins, *The Bride and the Bachelors*, p. 88.

16 Published in the *New Music Orchestral Series*, no. 18. The *Three Dance Movements* were also released by *New Music Quarterly Recordings* during 1936. Russell's *Fugue for Eight Percussion Instruments* had been published three years earlier, in the *New Music Orchestral Series*, no. 6.

17 Originally published in the brochure accompanying George Avakian's recording of the 25-year retrospective concert at Town Hall, New York. Reprinted in Cage, *Silence*, pp. 3–6. All subsequent references are to this latter edition.

18 See Kostelanetz (ed.), *John Cage*, pp. 138–139.

19 In Apollonio (ed.), *Futurist Manifestos*, pp. 31–34; 37–38.

20 See, for instance, Tomkins, *The Bride and the Bachelors*, p. 91; Cage, *Silence*, footnote on p. 63.

21 Crawford's piece had been published in *New Music* in October 1932. Harrison's would be published, again in *New Music*, only in July 1938, two months after the completion of *Metamorphosis*; but he and Cage were already well acquainted by this time and knew each other's work.

22 It is perhaps significant that three of the writers whose texts Cage set in the 1930s and 1940s – Stein, Joyce and Cummings – were breaking down the old and existing grammatical and syntactic walls of the English language, just as Cage himself was intending to do in music.

23 See Kostelanetz, [Conversation], pp. 216–218.

24 See Cage, *Silence*, pp. 23–25.

25 See Griffiths, *Cage*, p. 11.
26 In Cage, *Empty Words*, pp. 7–8.
27 'The Future of Music: Credo', lines 68–69.
28 Cage, *For the Birds*, p. 38. The mention of Hollywood is interesting, given the following statement in 'The Future of Music: Credo': 'The "frame" or fraction of a second, following established film technique, will probably be the basic unit in the measurement of time' (lines 54–56).
29 Cage, *Empty Words*, p. 8.
30 See Cage, *For the Birds*, p. 74.
31 Although born in Austria, Toch taught at the New School for Social Research from 1934 to 1936, and at the University of Southern California at Los Angeles from 1936.
32 'The Future of Music: Credo', lines 74–75.
33 Cage, *For the Birds*, pp. 71–72.
34 Cage, *Silence*, p. 71.
35 Statement found among Schoenberg's papers after his death.

6 Conclusion: Unity through diversity

1 See Kirkpatrick, 'Ives', in *The New Grove*, vol. 9, p. 420/*Amerigrove*, vol. 2, p. 509.
2 Partch, *Genesis of a Music*, p. viii.
3 Seeger, 'On Dissonant Counterpoint', p. 28.
4 Seeger, 'Ruth Crawford', in *American Composers on American Music*, p. 111.
5 Kingman, *American Music: A Panorama*, p. 489.
6 In Whitman, 'By Blue Ontario's Shore' (verse 5): 'Here is not merely a nation but a teeming Nation of nations.'
7 Hindle, 'Introduction', p. xv.
8 *Ibid*.
9 See chapter 1, concluding paragraph.

Select bibliography

anon. 'The Piano Music of Henry Cowell' (sleeve-notes to Folkways FM3349)

Apollonio, Umbro (ed.) *Futurist Manifestos* (London, 1973)

Bellamann, Henry 'Charles Ives: the Man and his Music', in *The Musical Quarterly*, 19 (1933), pp. 45–48

Bernard, Jonathan W. *The Music of Edgard Varèse* (New Haven and London, 1987)

Boatwright, Howard 'Ives' Quarter-Tone Impressions', in *Perspectives of New Music*, 3 (1965), pp. 22–31

Brooks, William 'A Drummer-boy Looks Back: Percussion in Ives's Fourth Symphony', in *Percussive Notes*, 22 (6) (1984), pp. 4–45

    'Unity and Diversity in Charles Ives's Fourth Symphony', in *Yearbook of the Department of Music, Institute of Latin American Studies* 1974 (University of Texas at Austin), pp. 5–49

Burkholder, J. Peter *Charles Ives: The Ideas behind the Music* (New Haven, 1985)

Cage, John *A Year from Monday* (London, 1968)

    Empty Words (London, 1980)

    For the Birds (London, 1981)

    M (Writings '67–'72) (London, 1973)

    Silence (London, 1968)

    X (Writings '79–'82) (London, 1987)

Chavez, Carlos *Toward a New Music* (New York, 1937/1975)

Copland, Aaron, and Perlis, Vivian *Copland, 1900 through 1942* (London, 1984)

Cowell, Henry 'Charles E. Ives', in Cowell (ed.), *American Composers on American Music* (New York, 1962), pp. 128–145

    'Charles Seeger', in Cowell (ed.), *American Composers on American Music* (New York, 1962), pp. 119–124

    'Current Chronicle', in Kostelanetz (ed.), *John Cage*, pp. 94–105

    New Musical Resources (New York, 1930/1969)

    'Trends in American Music', in Cowell (ed.), *American Composers on American Music* (New York, 1962), pp. 3–13

Cowell, Henry, and Cowell, Sidney *Charles Ives and his Music* (New York, 1969)

Cowell, Henry, *et al.* Preface, etc., to *Quartet Romantic and Quartet Euphometric* (New York, 1974)

Cox, David Harold 'Edgard Varèse' (unpublished dissertation: University of Birmingham, 1977)

Dunaway, David K. 'Charles Seeger and Carl Sands: The Composers' Collective Years', in *Ethnomusicology*, 24 (2) (May 1980), pp. 159–168

Dunn, R. (ed.) *John Cage* (annotated catalogue) (New York, 1962)

Gaume, Matilda 'Ruth Crawford', in *The New Grove* (London, 1980), vol. 5, pp. 25–26/*Amerigrove* (London, 1986), vol. 1, pp. 531–532

    'Ruth Crawford: A Promising Young Composer in New York, 1929–30', in *American Music*, 5 (1) (Spring 1987), pp. 74–84.

    'Ruth Crawford Seeger: Her Life and Works' (unpublished dissertation: University of Indiana, 1973)

    Ruth Crawford Seeger: Memoirs, Memories, Music (Metuchen, New Jersey, 1987)

Gilbert, Steven E. 'Carl Ruggles (1876–1971): An Appreciation', in *Perspectives of New Music*, 11 (1) (1970), pp. 224–232

    'The "Twelve-Tone System" of Carl Ruggles – a Study of the Evocations for Piano', in *The Journal of Music Theory*, 14 (1) (1970), pp. 68–91

Gillespie, Don C. 'John J. Becker', in *The New Grove* (London, 1980), vol. 2, pp. 40–41/*Amerigrove* (London, 1986), vol. 1, pp. 175–177

    'John Becker, Musical Crusader of Saint Paul', in *The Musical Quarterly*, 62 (1976), pp. 195–217

Griffiths, Paul *Cage* (London, 1981)

Griffiths, Paul, and Ziffrin, Marilyn J. 'Carl Ruggles', in *The New Grove* (London, 1980), vol. 16,
    pp. 324–326/*Amerigrove* (London, 1986), vol. 4, pp. 105–107
Hamm, Charles 'John Cage', in *The New Grove* (London, 1980), vol. 3, pp. 597–603/*Amerigrove*
    (London, 1986), vol. 1, pp. 334–341
    'Sound Forms for Piano' (sleeve-notes to New World Records, NW 203)
Harrison, Lou 'Carl Ruggles', in *The Score*, 12 (1955), pp. 15–26
Hindle, Brook 'Introduction', in Peter C. Marzio (ed.), *A Nation of Nations* (New York, 1976),
    pp. xv–xviii
Hitchcock, H. Wiley 'Henry Cowell's Ostinato Pianissimo', in *The Musical Quarterly*, 70 (1) (1984),
    pp. 23–44
    Ives (London, 1977)
    Music in the United States (New Jersey, 1969)
Hitchcock, H. Wiley, and Perlis, Vivian (eds.) *An Ives Celebration* (Urbana, 1977)
Ives, Charles [Conductor's Note to the second movement of the Fourth Symphony] (New York,
    1965), pp. 12–14
    Essays before a Sonata (ed. Boatwright) (New York, 1961/London, 1969)
    Memos (ed. Kirkpatrick) (London, 1973)
    [Postface to *114 Songs*] (Redding, CT, 1922)
Kingman, Daniel *American Music: A Panorama* (New York, 1979)
Kirkpatrick, John *A Temporary Mimeographed Catalogue of the Music Manuscripts. . .of Charles
    Edward Ives* (Yale University, 1960)
    'Charles Ives', in *The New Grove* (London, 1980), vol. 9, pp. 414–429/*Amerigrove* (London,
    1986), vol. 2, pp. 503–520
    'The Complete Music of Carl Ruggles' (sleeve-notes to CBS 79225)
    'The Evolution of Carl Ruggles', in *Perspectives of New Music*, 6 (1968), pp. 146–166
Kostelanetz, Richard [Conversation] 'John Cage and Richard Kostelanetz: A Conversation about
    Radio', in *The Musical Quarterly*, 72 (2) (1986), pp. 216–227
Kostelanetz, Richard (ed.) *John Cage* (London, 1974)
Lichtenwanger, William *The Music of Henry Cowell: A Descriptive Catalog* (New York, 1986)
Mannion, Martha L. *Writings about Henry Cowell* (New York, 1982)
Marshall, Dennis 'Charles Ives' Quotations: Manner or Substance?', in *Perspectives of New Music*,
    6 (1968), pp. 45–56
Mead, Rita H. *Henry Cowell's New Music, 1925–1936* (Ann Arbor, 1981)
Mellers, Wilfred *Music in a New Found Land* (revised 2nd edition, London, 1987)
Miller, Perry (ed.) *The American Transcendentalists* (London, 1981)
Nelson, Mark D. 'In Pursuit of Charles Seeger's Heterophonic Ideal: Three Palindromic Works by
    Ruth Crawford', in *The Musical Quarterly*, 72 (4) (1986), pp. 458–475
Neuls-Bates, C. (ed.) *Women in Music* (New York, 1982), pp. 303–311
Nicholls, David 'New and Experimental Compositional Techniques in American Music, from
    Charles Ives to the Second World War' (2 vols.) (unpublished dissertation: University of
    Cambridge, 1985)
    'Ruth Crawford Seeger: An Introduction', in *The Musical Times*, 124 (July 1983), pp. 421–425
Nyman, Michael 'Cage and Satie', in *The Musical Times*, 114 (Dec. 1973), pp. 1227–1229
    Experimental Music (London, 1974)
Partch, Harry *Genesis of a Music* (2nd edition) (New York, 1974)
Perlis, Vivian 'Interview with Charles Seeger' (Oral History Project, Yale University School of
    Music, Mar. 1970) (unpublished)
    'Interview with John Cage' (Oral History Project, Yale University School of Music, Dec. 1975–
    Aug. 1976) (unpublished)
Perlis, Vivian (ed.) *Charles Ives Remembered* (New York, 1976)
Pescatello, Ann M. 'Charles Seeger', in *The New Grove* (London, 1980), vol. 17, pp. 101–102/
    Amerigrove (London, 1986), vol. 4, p. 181
Rorem, Ned 'Lou Harrison', in *The New Grove* (London, 1980), vol. 8, p. 225
Rorem, Ned, and Davies, Hugh 'Lou Harrison', in *Amerigrove* (London, 1986), vol. 2, pp. 337–340
Rossiter, Frank R. *Charles Ives and His America* (London, 1976)
Russolo, Luigi 'The Art of Noise', in Apollonio (ed.), *Futurist Manifestos*, pp. 74–76, 85–88
Saylor, Bruce 'Henry Cowell', in *The New Grove* (London, 1980), vol. 5, pp. 8–12/*Amerigrove*
    (London, 1986), vol. 1, pp. 520–529

Schoffman, Nachum 'Charles Ives' Song "Vote for Names"', in *Current Musicology*, no. 23 (1977), pp. 56–68
 'Serialism in the works of Charles Ives', in *Tempo*, no. 138 (Sep. 1981), pp. 21–32
Seeger, Charles 'Carl Ruggles', in Cowell (ed.), *American Composers on American Music* (New York, 1962), pp. 14–35
 'Henry Cowell', in *The Magazine of Art*, 33 (5) (May 1940), pp. 288–289, 322–327
 'In Memoriam: Carl Ruggles', in *Perspectives of New Music*, 10 (2) (1972), pp. 171–174
 'On Dissonant Counterpoint', in *Modern Music*, 7 (Jun.–Jul. 1930), pp. 25–31
 'Ruth Crawford', in Cowell (ed.), *American Composers on American Music* (New York, 1962), pp. 110–118
Slonimsky, Nicolas 'Henry Cowell', in Cowell (ed.), *American Composers on American Music* (New York, 1962), pp. 57–63
Stuckenschmidt, H. H. *Arnold Schoenberg – His Life, World and Work* (London, 1977)
Terman, Lewis M. *The Intelligence of Schoolchildren* (London, 1921), pp. 246–251
Tomkins, Calvin *The Bride and the Bachelors* (New York, 1976)
Tusler, Adelaide G., and Briegleb, Ann M. [Interview with Charles Seeger] 'Reminiscences of an American Musicologist' (Oral History Program, University of California at Los Angeles, 1972) (unpublished)
Varèse, Louise *A Looking-Glass Diary* (London, 1973)
Weisgall, Hugo 'The Music of Henry Cowell', in *The Musical Quarterly*, 45 (1959), pp. 484–507
Wen-chung, Chou 'Ionisation: The Function of Timbre in its Formal and Temporal Organisation', in van Solkema (ed.), *The New Worlds of Edgard Varèse* (New York, 1979), pp. 27–74
Wooldridge, David *Charles Ives* (London, 1975)
Ziffrin, Marilyn J. 'Angels – Two Views', in *The Music Review*, 39 (1968), pp. 184–196

Appendix: Musical editions and selected recordings

Works are arranged alphabetically, by composer and then title of work.

The recordings noted here are only of works which receive major discussion in the text. For all other works, and for alternative recordings of those works which are listed, see

    1 Oja, Carol J. (ed.), *American Music Recordings* (New York, 1982);

    2 Warren, Richard, *Charles E. Ives: Discography* (New Haven, 1972);

    3 the current Gramophone and Schwann catalogues.

John Becker

Symphonia Brevis (Symphony No. 3)
  The Louisville Orchestra, conductor Jorge
    Mester

Peters Edition 66430
  Louisville Orchestra First Edition Records
  LS-721

John Cage

Bacchanale
  Jeanne Kirstein, piano

Peters Edition P 6784
  Columbia CM2S-819

Composition for Three Voices

Peters Edition P 6704

Double Music (in collaboration with Lou
    Harrison)
  The New Music Consort

Peters Edition P 6296

New World NW 330

First Construction (in Metal)
  Manhattan Percussion Ensemble

Peters Edition P 6709
  Avakian JC-1/JCS-1

Five Songs
  Meriel Dickinson, mezzo soprano, Peter
    Dickinson, piano

Peters Edition P 6710
  Unicorn RHS 353

Imaginary Landscape No. 1
  John Cage, Xenia Cage, Doris Dennison,
    Margaret Jansen

Peters Edition P 6716
  Avakian JC-1/JCS-1

Living Room Music

Peters Edition P 6786

Metamorphosis
  Jeanne Kirstein, piano

Peters Edition P 6723
  Columbia CM2S-819

Music for Wind Instruments

Peters Edition P 6738b

Quartet

Peters Edition P 6789

Quest

Peters Edition P 66757

Second Construction
  The New Music Consort

Peters Edition P 6791
  New World NW 330

Solo. . .and Six Short Inventions
  An ensemble, conductor John Cage
    (*Inventions* only)

Peters Edition P 6752
  Avakian JC-1/JCS-1

Sonata for Clarinet
  Phillip Renfeldt, clarinet

Peters Edition P 6753
  Advance FGR-4

Sonata for Two Voices   Peters Edition P 6754
Third Construction   Peters Edition P 6794
Three Pieces for Flute Duet   Peters Edition P 6761
Three Stein Songs   manuscript – property of the composer
Trio   Peters Edition P 6763
Two Pieces for Piano   Peters Edition P 6813
   Jeanne Kirstein, Piano   Columbia CM2S–819

Henry Cowell

Codes following titles of works refer to William Lichtenwanger's, *The Music of Henry Cowell*. Following the edition for some piano works, (1) = *The Piano Music of Henry Cowell* (Associated, 1960); (2) = *The Piano Music of Henry Cowell*, vol. 2 (Associated, 1982).

A Composition (406)   Peters Edition – rental only
Advertisement (213/4)   Associated (1) (2)
Amerind Suite (564)   Templeton Publishing Co., 1939
Anger Dance (104/6)   Associated (2)
Antinomy (213/5)   Associated (2)
   Henry Cowell, piano   Folkways FM3349
Dynamic Motion (213/1)   Associated (2)
Ensemble (380)   Breitkopf, 1925
Fabric (307)   Associated (1)
   Henry Cowell, Piano   Folkways FM3349
[Nine] *Ings* (353/1–353/9)   Associated (2)
It Isn't It (355) (publ. as *Scherzo*)   *Transition* magazine, no. 25, fall 1936
Incidental music to *Les Mariés de la Tour Eiffel* *New Music*, vol. 19, no. 1 (Oct. 1945)
   (563)
Maestoso (429)   *New Music*, vol. 14, no. 1 (Oct. 1940)
Manaunaun's Birthing (387)   Curwen, 1926
Mosaic Quartet (518)   Associated, 1965
Movement for String Quartet (450)   Associated, 1962
Ostinato Pianissimo (505)   *New Music*, vol. 26, no. 1 (Oct. 1952)
   New Jersey Percussion Ensemble, conductor   Nonesuch H-71291
    Raymond DesRoches
Piece for Piano with Strings (389/1) (publ. as   Associated (2)
   Piece for Piano)
   Robert Miller, piano   New World NW 203
Polyphonica (458)   Associated, 1965
Pulse (565)   Music for Percussion, 1971
   The New Music Consort, conductor Claire   New World NW 319
    Heldrich
Quartet Euphometric (283)   Peters Edition P 66518
   The Emerson String Quartet   New World NW 218
Quartet Romantic (223)   Peters Edition P 66518
   Members of Speculum Musicae: Paul Dunkel   New World NW 285
    and Susan Palma, flutes, Rolf Schulte,
    violin, John Graham, viola
Rhythmicana (557)   Associated, 1975
Sinister Resonance (462)   Associated (2)
   Henry Cowell, piano   Folkways FM3349
String Quartet No. 1 (197)   Associated, 1965
String Quartet No. 4: *United Quartet* (522)   Peters Edition 6248
   Beaux Arts String Quartet   Composers Recordings CRI SD 173
Synchrony (464)   Peters Edition – rental only
The Aeolian Harp (370)   Associated (1)
   Henry Cowell, piano   Folkways FM3349

The Banshee (405)	Associated (1)
Henry Cowell, piano	Folkways FM3349
The Fairy Bells (447)	Associated (2)
The Hero Sun (354/2)	Associated (2)
The Tides of Manaunaun (219/1)	Associated (1) (2)
Henry Cowell, piano	Folkways FM3349
The Voice of Lir (354/3)	Associated (2)
Tiger (463/2)	Associated (1)
Henry Cowell, piano	Folkways FM3349
Time Table (213/6)	Associated (2)
Two Woofs (451)	*New Music*, vol. 21, no. 1 (Oct. 1947)
Vestiges (305)	Associated (2)
What's This? (213/2)	Associated (2)
Where She Lies (400)	Curwen, 1925

Ruth Crawford

Diaphonic Suite No. 1	*New Music*, vol. 26, no. 3 (Apr. 1953)
James P. Ostryniec, oboe	Composers Recordings CRI S-423
Diaphonic Suite No. 2	Continuo Music Press, 1972
Otto Eifert, bassoon, Roy Christensen, 'cello	Gasparo 108 CX
Diaphonic Suite No. 3	Continuo Music Press, 1972
Diaphonic Suite No. 4	Continuo Music Press, 1972
Piano Study in Mixed Accents	*New Music*, vol. 6, no. 1 (Oct. 1932)
String Quartet	*New Music*, vol. 14, no. 2 (Jan. 1941)
The Composers Quartet	Nonesuch H-71280
Three Chants	manuscript – The Library of Congress
(no. 2 only) Priscilla Magdomo, alto,	Vox SVBX 5353
The Gregg Smith Singers, conductor	
Gregg Smith	
Three Songs	*New Music Orchestra Series*, no. 5 (1933)
Beverly Morgan, mezzo soprano, members	New World NW 285
of Speculum Musicae, conductor Paul	
Dunkel	
Two Ricercari	Merion Music, 1976 (publ. as separate items)

Lou Harrison

Double Music (in collaboration with John Cage)	Peters Edition P 6296
The New Music Consort	New World NW 330
Prelude for Grandpiano	*New Music*, vol. 11, no. 4 (Jul. 1938)
Saraband	*New Music*, vol. 11, no. 4 (Jul. 1938)

Charles Ives

Codes following titles of works refer to John Kirkpatrick's catalogue in *The New Grove* (vol. 9, pp. 421–429) and *Amerigrove* (vol. 2, pp. 509–519). An asterisk following an edition indicates its approval by the Charles Ives Society.

All the Way Around and Back (W14)	Peer, 1971
Orchestra, conductor Gunther Schuller	Columbia Masterworks MS 7318
Central Park in the Dark (V23,ii)	Boelke-Bomart/Mobart, 1973/1978*
Boston Symphony Orchestra, conductor Seiji	Deutsche Grammophon 2530.787
Ozawa	

Fourth Symphony (V39)   Associated, 1965
   London Philharmonic Orchestra, conductor   RCA ARL 1 0589
   José Serebrier

From the Steeples and the Mountains (W3)   Peer, 1965
   The American Brass Quintet   Nonesuch H-71222

Fugue in Four Keys on 'The Shining Shore'   Merion Music, 1975*
   (V9)
   The Yale Theater Orchestra, conductor James   Columbia Masterworks M 32969
   Sinclair

Halloween (W11)   Boelke-Bomart, 1949
   The New York String Quartet, with Gilbert   Columbia M 30230
   Kalish, piano

In Re Con Moto Et Al (W20)   Peer, 1968
   The New York String Quartet, with Gilbert   Columbia M 30230
   Kalish, Piano

Largo Risoluto No. 1 (W12)   Peer, 1961
   The New York String Quartet, with Gilbert   Columbia M 30230
   Kalish, piano

Largo Risoluto No. 3 (W13) (publ. as *Largo*   Peer, 1961
   Risoluto No. 2)
   The New York String Quartet, with Gilbert   Columbia M 30230
   Kalish, piano

Over the Pavements (V20)   Peer, 1954
   Orchestra, conductor Gunther Schuller   Columbia Masterworks MS 7318

Overture, 1776 (V13)   Merion Music, 1976*
   The Yale Theater Orchestra, conductor James   Columbia Masterworks M 32969
   Sinclair

Psalm 24 (Y16)   Mercury, 1955
   The Gregg Smith Singers, Columbia   Columbia MS 6921
   Chamber Orchestra, conductor Gregg
   Smith

Psalm 25 (Y26)   Merion Music, 1979*
   The Gregg Smith Singers, Columbia   Columbia MS 7321
   Chamber Orchestra, conductor Gregg
   Smith

Psalm 54 (Y15)   Merion Music, 1973*
   The Gregg Smith Singers, Columbia Cham-   Columbia MS 7321
   ber Orchestra, conductor Gregg Smith

Psalm 67 (Y14)   Associated, 1939
   The Gregg Smith Singers, conductor Gregg   Columbia MS 6921
   Smith

Psalm 90 (Y40)   Merion Music, 1970*
   Esther Martinez, soprano, Melvin Brown,   Columbia MS 6921
   tenor, The Gregg Smith Singers, Columbia
   Chamber Orchestra, conductor Gregg
   Smith

Psalm 100 (Y24)   Merion Music, 1975*
   The Gregg Smith Singers, Ithaca College   Columbia MS 6921
   Concert Choir, Texas Boys Choir of Fort
   Worth, Columbia Chamber Orchestra,
   conductor Gregg Smith

Psalm 135 (Y27)   Merion Music, 1981*
   The Gregg Smith Singers, Columbia   Columbia MS 7321
   Chamber Orchestra, conductor Gregg
   Smith

Psalm 150 (Y13)	Merion Music, 1972*
The Gregg Smith Singers, Ithaca College Concert Choir, Texas Boys Choir of Fort Worth, Columbia Chamber Orchestra, conductor Gregg Smith	Columbia MS 6921
Scherzo: Holding Your Own (W15,ii)	Peer, 1958
The New York String Quartet	Columbia M 30230
Second Piano Sonata (*Concord Sonata*) (X19)	Associated, 1947
John Kirkpatrick, piano	Columbia Masterworks MS 7192
Set for Theatre or Chamber Orchestra (V22)	New Music, vol. 5, no. 2 (Jan. 1932) (reprinted by Kalmus)
Royal Philharmonic Orchestra, conductor Harold Farberman	Vanguard C-10013
The Unanswered Question (V23,i)	Southern, 1953
New York Philharmonic Orchestra, conductor Leonard Bernstein	Columbia 77424
Three Harvest Home Chorales (Y28)	Mercury, 1949
The Gregg Smith Singers, Columbia Chamber Orchestra, conductor Gregg Smith	Columbia MS 6921
Three-Page Sonata (X14)	Mercury, 1975*
Clive Lythgoe, piano	Philips 9500.096
Tone Roads No. 1 (V38,i)	Peer, 1949
Orchestra, conductor Gunther Schuller	Columbia Masterworks MS 7318
Tone Roads No. 3 (V38,iii)	Peer, 1952
Orchestra, conductor Gunther Schuller	Columbia Masterworks MS 7318
Trio (W9)	Peer, 1955
Paul Zukofsky, violin, Robert Sylvester, 'cello, Gilbert Kalish, piano	Columbia M 30230

Carl Ruggles

Angels	Curwen, 1925
Brass ensemble, leader Gerald Schwarz, conductor Michael Tilson Thomas	Columbia Masterworks 79225
*Evocations 1–3**	New Music, vol. 16, no. 3 (Apr. 1943)
*Evocation 4**	New Music, vol. 18, no. 2 (Jan. 1945)
(* Note that the numbering differs from that of the 1954 revision.)	
John Kirkpatrick, piano	Columbia Masterworks 79225
Portals	New Music, vol. 3, no. 3 (Apr. 1930)
Buffalo Philharmonic, conductor Michael Tilson Thomas	Columbia Masterworks 79225
Sun-treader	Presser, 1934/1981
Buffalo Philharmonic, conductor Michael Tilson Thomas	Columbia Masterworks 79225
Toys	H.W. Gray, 1920
Judith Blegen, soprano, Michael Tilson Thomas, piano	Columbia Masterworks 79225

Charles Seeger

Psalm 137	New Music, vol. 26, no. 3 (Apr. 1953)
The Letter	New Music, vol. 26, no. 3 (Apr. 1953)

Index of names and titles